Human Values in Modern Management

Dr. Swami Parthasarathy, is eminent professor, noted author, orator, educationist, spiritual philosopher and philanthropist, and an eminent personality of management academia in India and abroad. He is the Chancellor cum Chairman, Sri Sharada Institute of Indian Management (SIIM) University and Chairman cum Managing Trustee of Sri SIIM-Research Foundation, New Delhi and Ramakrishna-Vivekanand International Foundation (RKVIF), New Delhi. He is also the Member of Joint Commission of BRICS Countries and the Chairman Asia-Pacific Development Initiative, a Joint Economic Forum of 25 Asia-Pacific Countries. He has also been nominated as Permanent Representing Member of India to UN-ECOC.

Dr. Parthasarathy is an MBA in International Business and Ph.D. from University of Chicago Booth School of Business. He has also been conferred with Seven Honorary D.Litt. from different Universities in India and abroad and is also a Distinguished Fellow of Indian Management Association. He has developed various management training modules, which are widely recognized by the corporate and academic world. An internationally noted writer, he has authored 28 books and 129 research papers. His famous title, "Forget Classroom Learning" carries the Foreword by the Apple Inc. Founder, Steve Jobs. Mr. Barak Obama, US President, referred his book "Transforming Personality" during his election campaign number of times. The book "Transforming Personality" was the best seller in European and North American Market in 2007.

Human Values in Modern Management

Second Edition

DR. SWAMI PARTHASARATHY

ACADEMIC FOUNDATION
NEW DELHI

www.academicfoundation.org

Second edition published in 2017
by

ACADEMIC FOUNDATION
4772-73 / 23 Bharat Ram Road, (23 Ansari Road),
Darya Ganj, New Delhi - 110 002 (India).
Phones : 23245001 / 02 / 03 / 04.
Fax : +91-11-23245005.
E-mail : books@academicfoundation.com
www.academicfoundation.org

Disclaimer:
The findings/views/opinions expressed in this book are solely those of the author and do not necessarily reflect the views of the publisher.

Cataloging in Publication Data--DK
Courtesy: D.K. Agencies (P) Ltd. <docinfo@dkagencies.com>

Parthasarathy, A. (Avula), 1927- **author.**
Human values in modern management / Dr. Swami Parthasarathy. -- Second edition.
pages cm
Includes bibliographical references.
ISBN 9789332703995

1. Management--Social aspects--India. 2. Management--Moral and ethical aspects--India. 3. Business ethics--India. I. Title.

HF5387.5.I5P37 2017 DDC 174.40954 23

Typeset, printed and bound by The Book Mint, New Delhi.
www.thebookmint.in

This new edition is dedicated at the
Holy Lotus Feet of my God & Guiding Spirit
their Holinesses Jagadgurus Sri Sri Bharathi Teerth Mahasannidhanam &
Sri Sri Vidhusekhara Bharathi Sannidhanam

Contents

Message

We are passing through the most revolutionary period of our long history and we can come out successfully out of the fire of the transition and maintain our millennia-long historic continuity into the future if our managers understand the spiritual strength behind our age old culture and the human values that has sustained it. Dr. Swami Parthasarathy, often very rightly referred as Peter Drucker, of Indian Management, in his latest book *Human Values and Management* conveys the truth: about the wholesome impact of human values, not only on administration and management but also on the flowering of managerial culture and character in spiritual realisation and fulfilment. Power will come, glory will come and everything will come when you call upon the sleeping human values and see how it awakes. The only way of salvation for mankind is the Indian way and this is the central theme of Swami ji's latest contribution to humanity.

—Prof. G.C. Agarwal
Former Head & Dean, Faculty of Commerce,
Pro-Vice Chancellor, University of Allahabad,
Director MLN Institute of Business Administration,
Hon. Director, Agro Economic Research Centre (GoI)

Foreword

In this age of globalization, market forces have become paramount in all walks of life. "Compete to survive and grow" has become the ruling philosophy. Countries compete with each other; companies compete among themselves and so do individuals. Competitive forces have the power to ignite the latent energies of people, organizations and nations and propel them towards higher levels of performance. The era of deregulation and liberalization triggered by the enunciation of the Government's New Economic Policy in 1991 has helped India considerably. The tremendous growths of the software and telecommunications industries are examples of the positive impact of competition. China's economy has in the recent past benefited considerably from competitive forces unleashed by its policy of deregulation and liberalization. The increasing focus of nations on material progress seems to be paying off very well. In general, man is experiencing a greater degree of physical comfort and material betterment all over the world. However, there are some negative aspects of the unbridled pursuit of material progress. Recent evidence from several parts of the world reveals many undesirable consequences. Consider, for example, the failures of several cooperative banks in India; the stock market crash and the Harshad Mehta episode in India in the 1990s; the failure of the Barings Bank, the Enron, Worldcom and Arthur Anderson related scams, and the recent recession in global economy and the crisis in the banking sector. Economic disparities between the haves and the have-nots are resulting in social unrest all over the world. We are also witnessing increasing incidence of psychosomatic disorders and mental stress all over the world. Medical professionals today talk about the increasing prevalence of life-style diseases. Perhaps these factors have led to an unprecedented mushrooming in the number of spiritual "gurus" in various parts of the world, especially India.

It is amply clear that a single-minded drive towards the creation of material wealth, greater physical comfort and unbridled consumerism has its obverse side. The problem at hand needs an innovative solution. On one hand, the increasing population and rising demand for goods and services requires greater attention to efficiency and effectiveness, and, on the other, there is an emergent need to curb the negative tendencies that arise as a result. The solution probably lies in reinterpreting the meaning of "effectiveness". There seems to be a problem with our understanding of "effectiveness" in purely "technical" and "material" terms. Perhaps there is a need to look at effectiveness from a larger and holistic perspective. Human life and work requires a philosophy that can provide proper guidance. The *Upanisad* and the *Bhagwat Gita* are repositories of the wisdom discovered by the seers in ancient times which has the potential to positively influence our lives in this age. Dr. Swami Parthasarathy in his book entitled *Human Values and Management*, applies the ancient wisdom of India's sages to the problems of modem organizations. It explores the issues of human values; enhancement of human potential; ethical dimensions of corporate governance and achievement of human excellence in organization among others. This book is a welcome addition to several others which have been published on such issues.

—Prof. Shekhar Chaudhuri
Director,
IIM Calcutta

Preface to the Second Edition

Third edition for the title: "Transforming Personality" and the second edition for "Forget Classroom Learning" and "Human Values in Modern Management" are published to present these three titles together in a new compendium form to the reader in a refurbished work of those titles. I am truly overwhelmed with the responses from the readers like Mr. Barack Obama, Mr. Ban Ki-moon, Prof. Colin Clouson-Thomas, Mr. Ravi Shankar Prasad and more such luminaries and other scholars, researchers and practising corporate managers across the globe. Reading these three books in a sequence shall undoubtedly enrich the human mind towards the culmination of human life.

As the world is graduating more and more from modernity to ultra-modernity, similarly human beings are advancing towards the realms of being superhuman. So the animal instincts of human race are getting more and more manifested into multidimensional face of new faculties of cruelty. The violence for ideology of misnomer religion, caste and colour has replaced the true fragrance and philosophy of religion. On one hand, the world is eradicating one form of slavery, on the other, introducing a new form. There is continual unimaginable erosion of 'values': the fourth faculty of humanity, which differentially identifies human beings from the animal world. There is growing evidence of complex obsession of misogynistic conduct and intolerance towards an individual's legitimate views, rights and choices. So we are at the crucial juncture where the planet is under serious threat from unprecedented humanitarian crisis arisen out of steep fall of human values.

Therefore, our effort of publication of this compendium is a humble prescription of solution to the global humanity towards the fundamental laws of human kind as our Vedic scriptures suggest us "*Atmano Mokshartham Jagadhitayo ca*" (Salvation of the Self and Welfare of the World). I am extremely grateful to Shri Sanu Kapila, and Shri Rituraj Kapila of Academic Foundation for undertaking this upheaval task. May the Almighty bless them with his choicest boons.

— Dr. Swami Parthasarathy,
FIMA, Ph.D. (UChicago), MBA (UChicago)

Preface to the First Edition

The glories of human civilization were not achieved in a day. The silent working of manifold creative forces over the centuries gave shape to the world before us. Such a process can also be identified in the formation of the distinctive culture of a nation. The history of India proves that a nation, which stands true to its cultural traditions, where spirituality based on human values provides the foundation, can never die. These values are the life force of any activity and encompass areas of management and administration concern.

India has the eternal wealth of human values that were taught in the cosmic science of *Bhagwat Gita* and *Upanishads*. One has to instil and develop this human wealth through the proper path of management practices not only for achieving a certain goal but also for the betterment of one's own life. Human Values in Modern Management describes the principle values of human life and its retrospective effect in management practices, its application and inculcation in the field of corporate management practices.

I do hope that this book will be of immense help to students of management and practicing management community at large, and will fulfill the demand for a proper guide of such kind.

I am highly thankful and express my sincere gratitude to the entire team of Macmillan Publishers India Ltd. and other members involved in the publication of this book, for their immense cooperation and help.

I am also thankful to Sri Ravinder Singh, Md Alamgeer, and Pankaj Sharma for transcribing the entire manuscript. My debt of gratitude can never be repaid to Professor G.C. Aggarwal, Pro-Vice Chancellor of Allahabad University for providing me all the resource of inspiration for this book and Mrs. Deepika Singh for her unbound support for handling the manuscript into a new and developed format.

May the Almighty shower His choicest blessings on them and may He inspire and motivate the readers of this book for setting an example in the practice of management.

—Dr. Swami Parthasarathy

1

Human Values

Values and Vedanta

The thirteenth Chapter of the *Bhagavad Gita*, has a few verses which deal with what we may call 'values'. The *Gita* calls these values *jnanam*, which means knowledge. However, *jnanam*, used in this sense as values, is not that knowledge of the Self which is both the means and the end of the teaching of Vedanta. Instead, here, *jnanam* stands for those qualities of the mind in the presence of which (in relative measure) knowledge of the Self can take place, and in the absence of which Self-knowledge does not take place, no matter how adequate the teacher is, or how authentic the teaching is.

Knowledge Requires Three Factors

For knowledge of any kind to take place, three factors are required:

1. the knower,
2. the object of knowledge, and
3. the means of knowledge.

This can be illustrated by looking at everyday experiences. Take, for example, knowledge of a sound—I, the knower, must be there to hear the sound; the sound, the to-be-known, must occur; and my ears, the means, must be capable of hearing.

Of these factors the first two are clear, but the third factor requires some explication. Factor number one presents no problems, it is clear to me that if I am not there (within the range of the sound), I will not hear it. Factor number two also is self-evident, if the sound does not occur, I will not hear it. Factor number three is not that simple. If I am within the range of the sound and if the sound does occur (according to reliable reports from other hearers in the vicinity) nonetheless, I do not hear the sound, I have to inquire into the capability of my means of knowledge for sounds, namely, my ears.

Mind Must Back Sense Organs

When I have failed to hear a given sound, and if acoustical tests show that my ears are capable of hearing that sound, the problem must be elsewhere. Where? Perhaps, I shall say, "my attention wandered". It means that my mind was not attentively backing my ears. I was there; the sound occurred; my ears were there; my ears were capable; but, my mind was not there behind my ears lighting them up for listening. Therefore, I had no adequate means of knowledge. To be adequate for obtaining the knowledge of a given object, not only must the appropriate, capable sense organ for the particular perception (eyes for vision; ears for sound; tongue for taste, etc.) be available, but an attentive, capable mind must also be behind that sense organ. So, for simple perceptual knowledge, the sense organs by themselves are not the *pramana*, the means of knowledge. The sense organs along with the mind are the *pramana*. When all factors, including the mind, are `present' knowledge takes place.

Mind Must be Prepared

When all factors, including an attentive mind, are present, does knowledge always take place? What if I am seeking knowledge of calculus? I find a competent professor of calculus, who is a good teacher—one who has the ability to communicate what he knows. He talks to me about calculus in English, the language I know. I recognize the words. To illustrate his talk, he writes numbers and letters on the blackboard. I know and can identify the numbers and letters. I am physically able to see what he writes on the board. I sincerely wish to learn calculus. I come every day. The professor teaches. I listen and look. My mind is behind my ears and my eyes. Alas! Knowledge of calculus does not come to me. Why? My background of mathematics is shaky. In fact, I am not certain whether 7 plus 4 make 9 or 11! Therefore, I lack the necessary preparation for calculus.

Thus, we need to add something more for understanding an adequate piece of knowledge. It has been seen that the means of knowledge must be appropriate, capable, and backed by an attentive mind. Now another qualification needs to be added. The mind, at least in some instances, must not only be capable and attentive but must also be prepared. In order to be ready for knowledge of calculus, a samskara, a certain discipline in mathematics must be established. Only then can knowledge of calculus be obtained.

Words as a Means of Knowledge

For simple perceptual knowledge, no particular preparation may be necessary other than, perhaps, calling the mind to attention. When the object is there, when the eyes are open, when the mind is behind the eyes, the object is seen and visual knowledge of that object obtains without any special preparation. However, for knowledge such as of calculus, which is gained not from simple perception but from words wielded by a competent teacher unfolding certain reasoning, some preparation is always necessary. For a teacher's words to work as *pramana*, a valid means of knowledge, the words must be properly handled by the teacher, and the mind of the student must be ready.

Vedanta is a *pramana*, a *sabda-pramana*, i.e., a verbal means of knowledge. Vedanta is a *pramana* in the form of words and sentences which, when wielded by a competent teacher, are meant to throw light on the Self. Words can give direct or indirect knowledge, depending on the object involved. If the object is away from one's range of experience, words can give rise only to indirect knowledge. If the object is within one's range of experience, words can bring about direct knowledge. Vedanta is about me, about that which is indicated by the first person singular "I". I am always available to myself.

For the words of any teaching to convey knowledge, they must be understood in the same sense as they are understood by the teacher who wields them, i.e., by the one who is using the words to impart a certain vision of the subject taught. General definitions are not sufficient. They carry, inherent in their generality, subjective interpretations. For words to serve as pramana, their precise, intended meaning must be released and the unintended possible meanings must be negated. How does a teacher accomplish this? He establishes a context in which other possible meanings of the words are ruled out. When a teacher fails to create a context for the words he uses, he cannot convey knowledge by their use. Words, then, only become another form of conditioning. This commonly happens when the subject matter is the Self. Frequently, in teaching that attempts to reveal the Self, words such as 'infinite', 'Brahman' and 'eternal' are used but not explained. Such words, so used, only become a new conditioning, thus adding to confusion and vagueness in the mind of the student. However, even when you have both a qualified teacher of Vedanta, learned in the methodology of teaching, one who knows how to unfold the precise meaning of the words used, and a dedicated student who is seeking knowledge of the Self, the knowledge that is Vedanta cannot take place unless the student's mind is prepared. For one with an unprepared mind, Vedanta is like calculus is for a person still working on his multiplication tables. This does not mean that calculus or Vedanta cannot be understood. It simply means that preparation of the mind is required. The antahkarana, the mind, is the place where knowledge is available to the one who wants knowledge. And if knowledge does not occur there must be some obstacle present which is responsible for it. The only such obstacle is the lack of preparation of the mind.

Jnanam Prepares the Mind for Vedanta

What prepares the mind for the knowledge that is Vedanta? Practice, such as pranayama (breathing exercises) and asanas (postures), may be useful in questioning a restless mind but they do not prepare the mind for Self-knowledge. *Jnanam* according to the *Gita*, prepares the mind for Vedanta. *Jnanam* can be defined as a state of mind, which reflects certain universal values and ethical attitudes. Other practices may bring about a mental quietude in which the necessary values are more readily established, but only discovery and assimilation of the values themselves constitute the preparation of the mind. Values alone prepare the mind, all else is secondary. Therefore, the *Gita* raises the appropriate values to the status of knowledge, terming them *Jnanam*, a word that means knowledge. However, the *Jnanam* of values and the knowledge that is Self-knowledge must not be confused. They are not the same thing. The *Jnanam* of values is preparation for the gaining of Self-knowledge. It is not that when the mind enjoys the appropriate values, knowledge of the Self necessarily occurs. It means that with appropriate values, it is possible to attain; without it, it cannot occur Appropriate values present, Self-knowledge may or may not be present; Appropriate values present, Self-knowledge can be gained; Appropriate values absent, Self-knowledge cannot be gained.

Universal Values: Source and Function

What is a value? 'Value' indicates the regard for a thing, situation, or attitude which for some reason is esteemed or prized by the value-holder. The appropriate values which prepare the mind for Vedanta are certain universal ethical attitudes. In Sanskrit, an ethical value can be defined as dharma. Dharma is a standard or norm of conduct derived from the way in which I wish others to view or treat me. Dharma mandates for behaviour and attitude. Though commonly found in religious scriptures, they in fact, trace their source to pragmatic commonsense ethics which religious ethics confirm. In other words, my norm for what is proper behaviour or a 'good' attitude is based on the way I wish others to treat or view me, on what I expect or want. From others come my standards for dharma, right behaviour. What I do not want others to do is *adharma*, wrong behaviour.

I want others to speak truth to me.
I do not want others to lie to me.
Truth-speaking is *dharma* for me.
Non-truth speaking is *adharma* for me.
Scriptures confirm truth-speaking as good behaviour.
Scriptures condemn non-truth-speaking as bad behaviour.

Other behaviour norms, such as non-injury, humility, charitableness, are all based on the same consideration of how I would like others to treat me. Thus, ethical norms are not just arbitrary, man-made rules but stem from an inherent, common regard for one's own interest and comfort. Ethical standards are natural and universal. There may be some cultural variations in degree or emphasis, but the basic standards have certain universality.

Ethical Values: Universal in Content, Relative in Application

The universality of codes of acceptable conduct, that is, of general ethical standards, does not mean that these standards are absolute. *Dharma* and *adharma* are relatives. What is considered ethical in one situation becomes unethical in another situation, depending upon context. That a standard may be relative does not mean that it is purely subjective. Although sometimes relative in applicability, basic ethical standards have a universal content. There is a similarity in one's reaction to being hurt, cheated, lied to and bullied. Ethical standards are based on a human consensus regarding what is acceptable conduct. This consensus is not negated by the fact that the norms may be subject to interpretation in some situations. Even such a pronounced, clear value as non-injury to myself is modified by circumstances, when I willingly submit to the surgeon's knife. Such a suspension of my value for non-injury to myself is situational, and does not affect my basic value for non-injury to myself or its extensions—my general value for non-injury to all beings.

Although my norms or values for behaviour and attitude, themselves may not be subjective, my interpretation of these values is very likely to be highly subjective. My values are universal in content but relative and situational in my application of them. For example, I am likely to apply a value for truthfulness very consistently and absolutely to the words of others. To my own words my application will be much less consistent and quite relative to the situation.

In general practice, I shall apply values more consistently and more absolutely to others than to myself. After all, the source of my values is found in the way in which I want others to treat me, which becomes my norm for 'good' behaviour. I can be the beneficiary. It seems less easy for me to be consistent in the application of these standards to my own behaviour.

Ethical Values Cannot be Dismissed

Can I safely dismiss a concern for values? No. I cannot escape from values because no one living in this world can escape relationships. This is based upon my concern that I may not be hurt or disturbed. From this comes an accepted canon in the criminal code: do not be an informer. The inescapability of the impact of values can be seen by considering a 'hit man'. A veteran 'hit man'—a merciless killer—does not want to be hit himself. He cannot escape the value for non-injury, he can only defy it, which creates conflict even in an insensitive mind. Values cannot be dismissed, nor can they be defied with impunity. Failure to meet a value puts me in conflict with myself. When I perform an action that is a non-value for me, I create a seed of guilt, which is all that is needed to produce sleeplessness, fear and conflict. Even small lies create problems, like the lies sometimes told regarding one's age. Truth about one's age may seem a simple and trivial detail, but small lies register as conflicts in the mind.

Are Values only Mithya (Apparent)?

To those who have had a little exposure to the teaching of Vedanta, it may occur that norm-breaking behaviour, that is, 'bad' behaviour may be dismissed because it is only *mithya*, apparent, not absolutely real. To such an argument, it can be said: if you can dismiss all good acts and all good things as *mithya*, apparent, then, fine, you certainly may dismiss bad acts and bad things as well. When I can see good and bad equally as *mithya*, values are not a problem for me. In the clear knowledge of what is real and what is apparent, my actions in the relative world cannot but be spontaneously good, because I have nothing to gain, nothing to protect. It is clear that I am seeking knowledge of the Self. To be ready to discover that knowledge, my mind must be prepared with proper values. In a mind filled with conflicts, values are dismissed or defied, nothing will happen even when I listen to the teacher of Vedanta.

Values and Conflict

No one wants a mind in conflict. A mind in conflict is not a desirable mind. Once conflicts are there, problems of the mind are unavoidable. Self-condemnation, regret, guilt, a sense of failure, etc. are products of mental conflict. Conflicts come when I am unable to live up to a particular value which, I consciously accept. Societal norms have a universal content, the influence of which I cannot really escape. My inherent desire to be comfortable and secure compels me to set standards for the behaviour of others, establishing a commonsense ethical code which bounces back on my head. Religion codifies society's ethical consensus into a rigid table of `do's' and 'don'ts'. It makes non-conformity on my part even more difficult. When I cannot live up to my value structure, I am in conflict and suffer guilt.

'Dropping-Out' Does Not Solve Conflict

The 'Drop-out' behaviour of the 'hippie generation' prevalent during the 60's in the West, largely seems to have been an attempt to escape conflicts. During the Viet Nam War period, the clash of unassimilated traditional values with situational personal values was particularly acute for young people. The response of many was to attempt to make 'no values' their basic value. Traditional values were condemned and a life-style based on individuality, 'self-expression' and 'spontaneity' was proclaimed in their stead. This did not work. True, values led to conflict. But, as we saw before, values cannot simply be dropped. The universal content of values can be negated only if I have no concern for how the other person treats me. If I want other people to behave in certain manner, I am stuck with a value system.

How Values Cause Conflict

When I have a value structure, which I follow in the same manner in which I expect others to follow, my values cause me no conflict. However, when I want others to behave in a certain way, but for my own reasons, I am not able or willing to behave in that way, I have a problem. What is it that interferes with my expression of my general values? Individual situational values, linked with some highly desired personal end can interfere with my expression of general values, when these values have not become fully assimilated personal values for me.

The universal value for truth provides a good example of a general standard which is often half assimilated:

Value: Speak Truth!

I want others to speak truth to me (universal source).

Authorities tell me to speak truth (obligatory source)

Parents say speak truth.

Society says speak truth.

Religion says speak truth.

Speaking truth is a part of my value system.

Assimilation:

The value of the truthfulness of others is immediately clear:

I can see that false information given to me can be inconvenient or harmful to me.

My value for the truthfulness of others to me is personal and assimilated.

The value of my truthfulness is not immediately clear:

I do not see what I get out of being truthful.

My value for my being truthful is obligatory.

My truthfulness obliges my parents.

My truthfulness obliges my society.

My truthfulness obliges my religious code.

Result: I have a split value: One-half personal and one-half obligatory.

Value: Cherish Money!

The value for money illustrates the development and assimilation of a powerful, personal situational value.

When I was a three-year-old child, I once picked up a piece of paper. It was green, printed, and very colourful. I began, as I did with every paper, to play with it. Mummy said: "No! That is money." Oh, money? I also said, "Money." But I did not know what this money is. "Money-money-money," I kept repeating. Thereafter, whenever I saw that green paper, I knew it was 'money' which I should not touch, but I did not know what money was.

Then one day, when I was a little older, Mummy took me for shopping with her to the store. I saw lots of chocolates and jellybeans. I stretched out my hand: "Give me jelly-beans". The fellow behind the counter raised his eyebrows and looked at Mummy. I wondered why he did not give me any candy when he had so many. Then Mummy opened her purse and pulled out a piece of green paper named money. When she gave that money to the storekeeper, he smiled and handed a packet of jelly-beans to me. I did not understand what had happened, but I was happy with my jelly-beans. Next time we went to the store, she gave money when I wanted chocolates. Out came the money and the man gave me chocolates. One day when we were shopping, I wanted a balloon. Out came the money and the balloon was mine. Oh, ho! If you give money you can get jellybeans, chocolates, and even balloons. This was a great discovery for a small child. I had learnt that money buys things, all manner of things. Not many people understand the monetary system, but everybody knows that money buys!

Later, as I grew up I came to learn how many things money buys: houses, cars, even gurus and gods. Nothing buys like money.

When I come to know how well money buys, how many things money buys, I come to have a well-understood, well-assimilated personal value for money.

Half-Value: More Irritant than Behaviour Norm

When a universal value is split into two halves—a personal value for what I expect from others and an obligatory value for what I expect from myself—there is always a potential for conflict. A personal value is spontaneously observed for its own sake; an obligatory value is subject to compromise when it obstructs a highly desired individual end. When a general ethical half-value loses the battle to an expedient assimilated value, the half-value does not fold up and go away. It stays there as an irritant. What I call my ethical values, often, in fact, are so many irritants in my heart. This is true and totally insensitive to ethical behaviour standards. No matter what choice is made or how many times it is made, the voice of the half-value, reflecting as it does an inherent universal content, is never entirely silenced.

For example, most of us have a well assimilated personal value for money. But when it comes to speaking truth, our value often is general and half assimilated. When this is the case, what happens if there is a conflict between the money value and the truth value? What if a situation arises in which by telling a lie I can make an extra ₹500? Take a case when someone has offered to pay me the same amount of money for an item as I had originally paid for. I had paid ₹1,000, but I can easily say that I paid ₹1500. For this small lie, I will gain an extra ₹500. I know what that extra ₹500 can do for me, what comforts I can buy with it. On the other hand, it is not very clear to me of what benefit speaking the truth in this situation will be for me. Should I tell the truth or should I lie? Which value will win? Most likely the assimilated value for money will be the victor. But, all the same, something goes on murmuring inside me, "Speak truth, speak truth".

I may lie but I will not be comfortable, because I will not be able to avoid what happens when I tell a lie. What happens? First, there is conflict, and then there is guilt. I can ignore guilt but I cannot avoid it because I cannot escape my half-value for truth. Guilt is a great irritant – greater than chillies! Once I have guilt I cannot have a fully comfortable Self. Fulfilling an immediate end at the expense of a general value may bring some passing comfort, but in the long run adds to the discomfort of myself by increasing my accumulation of guilt, large and small.

The Knower-Doer Split

Does anything else happen when I ignore general ethical standards? Yes. I create a "knower-doer" split in myself. For instance, when I lie, I speak contrary to truth. Therefore, I, the knower, am in one position and I, the doer, in another position. By my falsehood, I create a split, a division between the knower—I and the doer—I. Everyone tells a few lies like this. What is your age? What is your income? What are your qualifications? When I lie to a series of questions like this, I create a split in myself, the knower being one and the doer another. I am not integrated.

I have divided myself into an 'ideal' knower who values one course of action and the 'actual' doer who does something else. I have created a Dr Jekyll and Mr Hyde conflict within myself. Living with Jekyll and Hyde, one cannot get anything out of life. It is impossible. Even in small things, the knower-doer split does harm. The knower decides to get up 30 minutes early and do early morning exercises. The doer turns off the alarm and sleeps 45 minutes longer. The knower goes on a diet; the doer has a second helping. The knower begins condemning me. I tell myself that I am useless, that I cannot do what I want to do, that I am not the person I want to be.

When I am 'split', I cannot fully enjoy anything. Even the enjoyment of food cannot be there unless the mind is set on eating. The relationship between thinker and doer perhaps is more recognized in the Indian cultural tradition than it is in the West. In India, the mother instructs the child; "Eat, don't talk. When you are eating, eat. Talk later." In the West, where talking is mixed with eating, only the first spoonful of food is appreciated. The rest of eating becomes mechanical. One eats and talks and then when it is found that no more food can be eaten, one infers that the meal has been good and that a sufficient amount has been eaten. The thinker was not present when the eating was going on; being too busy thinking what was to be said next. This kind of eating is mechanical and often uncontrolled, whereas eating when the thinker is there, can become a beautiful ritual.

The quality of my life always suffers whenever I become 'split'. To appreciate the beauty of life, to be really available to enjoy its comforts, I need to be 'together.' 'Together' is a good Western expression which shows an intuitive appreciation of the problem of 'split'. When my universal values are only half-values, they will always have the potential of destroying my 'togetherness' producing a 'split' in me as they yield to some immediate situational value.

What is the Source of a Situational Value?

How does an individual, situational value have the power to conquer the obligatory half of a universal value that is producing guilt and splits in me? We have seen that the source of ethical values is the natural desire that people treat me in a certain way—which then is extended to oblige me to treat others in the same way. What is the source of a situational value? Take one's value for money. What in the money has such a value for me that I may be willing to tell a lie to obtain it? In the example given earlier (where by 'stretching' the truth I will obtain ₹500) what is the gain that makes the lie, worthwhile for me? Is the money worth a lie?

I cannot eat money or admire its beauty or talk to it or use it as shelter from the rain—so money itself is not the attraction. The attraction for money seems to be in its buying power. It seems it must be the things which money buys that make it valuable, not just the isolated buying power. Why are the things valuable? The things are valuable to me for the pleasure, security, and comfort that they provide. I value things for my comfort.

What defines 'my comforts'? Is there a difference between the two? There is a difference. Sometimes my stomach may be comfortably full, I am out of the rain, nothing is pinching, the heater is working and my chair is soft—still I may not be comfortable with myself. What I really value is not mere comforts outside but to be comfortable inside. It is always my hope that the extra comforts which more money can buy for me will make me more comfortable with myself. I buy comforts only for my sake, not for the sake of the comforts. I do not buy another chair because the chairs in the room are lonely. I buy a chair because, in one way or another, I think that to have a chair is going to make me feel more comfortable, either my body or pride of possession, or both, will be comforted. All comforts are for my sake alone. I choose comforts for me so that I feel good.

So, when I ignore my obligatory value, my value for truthfulness, and tell a lie instead, through which I am going to gain some money, it is because I have concluded that the money will add to my comfort. And, I do not see, in the given instance, truthfulness doing anything for my comfort. The same is true of my other situational choices.

Anything I choose, anything I value is because I think there is some connection between that thing and myself feeling good. The source of the value of a situational value is that I expect to feel good through exercising a choice based on it.

When is a Value Not Subject to Choice?

When I clearly see that a particular choice will make me suffer, I do not make that choice. While seeking comfort, I see that between two choices one is going to bring discomfort and that choice drops out. My action becomes choiceless. It becomes choiceless like the answer to the question: Do you want happiness or unhappiness? Thus, when I become thoroughly convinced that acting contrary to a general value will result in suffering for me, my compliance with that value becomes choiceless. If speaking truth is a value for me, and I am completely convinced that non-truth brings suffering, there is no choice but to speak truth. Speaking truth becomes natural, spontaneous – my personal, assimilated value.

Any value, when it becomes my personal value, becomes choiceless for me. I do not have to think about it. The conduct mandated by a personal value becomes what I do without reflection. Matters of hygiene are good everyday examples of personal assimilated values: even though I may be quite hungry I do not consider picking up and eating food from a garbage heap. Conforming to these values creates no conflict whatsoever for me.

Seeing the Value of a Value

Any value universal or situational is a value for me only when I see it as valuable for me. Me—the comfortable me—is the source of my values. I fail to follow a universal value only when I do not clearly see its value to me. I make expedient situational choices only when I think such choices will make me feel good.

Returning to the example of the Rs. 500 gained by a small lie, what is the actual worth of that lie to me? That small lie would cost me my life (my comfortable self). The extra comforts that I could buy with Rs. 500 acquired through the lie would not be able to deliver their comfort because of guilt and split. Guilt comes because I have a half-value for truth which, when I ignore it, is sufficient to create a problem for me. Split comes because I know I am obliged to speak the truth, and I am doing something else. Once I have guilt, once I am split, I cannot have a comfortable self.

For comforts to be enjoyed I must be there to enjoy them; when I am split with guilt, I am rarely anywhere but with my anxieties, regrets and guilt. Not recognizing the problem for what it is, I seek more comforts to ease my uncomfortable mind; or I try to find some method for turning off this conflicting mind and its brood of guilt. Thus, what actually happens when I tell a lie is I add to the discomfort of myself, while what I actually wanted to gain by the lie was to add to the comfort of myself. This is true of any choice I make which is in conflict with a universal ethical standard – the sought – for comfort prompting the conflicting choice but which cannot be enjoyed due to guilt and split arising from the conflict. When I clearly see this fact, I will see the value to me of applying universal ethical standards to myself. My half-value for universal values will become full value.

Life Expression Comes from Value Structure

The expression of my life is just the expression of my well assimilated value structure. What I do is but an expression of what is valuable to me. I follow other people's values from time to time when it is convenient; but if these values of others have not been assimilated by me, they are simply obligatory values and do not reflect my value structure. They are more a source of conflict than a norm for behaviour and are always susceptible to compromise. Only assimilated values are my personal values. Assimilated value reflects what is valuable to me. An assimilated personal value requires no choice on my part. When I want certain unassimilated values to become part of my value structure, their observance will become spontaneous for me. For the expression of a value to become spontaneous for me, I must see its value in my personal life.

Paying lip service to obligatory values is no more useful than the chorus of parrots in a tree who were singing out, "be careful of the hunter's net!" A wise old parrot had first seen the hunter coming and had called out the warning. But the silly flock did not. They did not establish a personal content for the words they had heard from the old bird. Instead, they continued to sit happily on the branches of the tree repeating the words which were empty of any real meaning for them: "Be careful of the hunter's net!" Even after the net had descended upon them they wriggled and squirmed, caught in its web, screeching: "Be careful of the hunter's net!"

When I claim as my standards those values in which I fail to see any personal gain to myself, I am in as risky a position for expressing those values, as were the parrots in the tree who mindlessly repeated the warning. Enjoined or obligatory values will become assimilated personal values only when I see their value for me clearly and assimilate these values in terms of knowledge.

For the person with assimilated ethical values, life becomes very simple. No conflicts cloud his mind. For him, the teaching of Vedanta is like the meeting of combustible gas and fire. Knowledge ignites in a flash.

2

Twenty Values of Knowledge—*Jnanam*

What Is Knowledge (*Jnanam*)?

The values necessary to prepare the mind for knowledge are set out in the *Bhagavad Gita* in response to a question by Arjuna. The thirteenth chapter of the Gita begins with this three-part request for instruction as addressed by Arjuna to his teacher, Lord Krisna:

Arjuna uvaca:
Prakrtim purusam caiva ksetram ksetrajnameve ca
Etadvediumicchami jnanam jneyam ca kesava
Arjuna said:

Oh, Lord, I would like to learn about: prakrti (insentiency or matter) and purusa (sentiency or spirit); ksetra (the field, which indicates the body, or insentiency) and ksetrajna (the knower of the field, which indicates that which is conscious of the body); *jnanam* (knowledge) and *jneyam* (that which is to be known).'

In some Gita manuscripts this opening verse is not found. In answer to the third part of this request, Lord Krisna lists twenty qualities of the mind which He terms as *jnanam* or knowledge:

Amanitvamadambhitvamahimsa ksantirarjavam
Acaryopasanam saucam sthairyamatmavinigrahah

(1) *Amanitvam*–absence of self-worshipfulness (2) *Adambhitvam*–absence of pretence (3) *Ahimsa*–non-injury (4) *ksantih*–accommodation (5) *Arjavam*-straightforwardness (6) *Acaryopasanarn*–service to the teacher (7) *Saucam*-cleanliness (8) *Sthairyam*–steadiness (9) *Atmavini-grahah*–mastery over the mind

Indriyarthesu vairagyamanahankara eva ca
Jan mamrtyujaravyadhiduhkhadosanudarsanam

(10) *Indriyarthesu vairagyam*—dispassion towards sense-objects (11) *Anahankarah*—absence of egoism (12) *Janma-mrtyu-jara-vyadhiduhkha-dosanudarsanam*—reflection on the evils of birth, death, old age, sickness and pain

Asaktiranabhisvangah putradaragrhadisu
Nityam ca samacittatvamistanistopapattisu

(13) *Asakti*—absence of sense of ownership (14) *Anabhisvangah putra-darga-grhadisu*—absence of close attachment to son, wife, home, etc. (15) *Nityam samaciltatvam ista-anista-upapattisu*—constant even-mindedness in the occurrence of the desirable and undesirable

Mayi cananyayogena bhaktiravyabhicarini
Viviktadesasevitvamaratirjanasamsadi

(16) *Mayi ananya-yogena bhaktih avyabhicarini*—unswerving devotion to Me characterized by non-separateness from Me (17) *Vivikta-desasevitvam*—resorting to a quiet place (18) *Aratih janasamsadi*—absence of craving for the company of people

Adhyatmajananityatvam tattvajnanarthadarsanam
Etajjnanamiti proktamajnanam yadatonyatha

(19) *Tattva-jnana-arthadarsanm*—perspective on the purpose of the knowledge of Truth. (20) *Adhyatma-jnana-nityatvam*—constant application of the knowledge of the Self. This is declared to be knowledge, and what is opposed to it is ignorance.

As we have seen, knowledge as used here does not mean knowledge of the Self. It stands for those qualities of the mind (values) which must be present before the mind of the seeker is prepared for the knowledge of the Self. (Knowledge of the Self in this verse is indicated by *jneyam*—that which is to be known.) *Jnanam* indicates those qualities of the mind which must be present for *vastu* the Truth (that which is ultimately Real: that which cannot be resolved into anything else) to be known.

We have seen in the previous discussion that for values to be personally valuable, they must be discovered through knowledge (seen as valuable by the value-holder) and not simply impressed from without. Therefore, the term *jnanam* is quite appropriate. The list of values constituting *jnanam* is long, but the qualities are interrelated, defining a harmonious frame of mind in which knowledge can occur.

Each of the terms used by Lord Krisna highlights a certain attitude, the value for which must be discovered personally, in order that attitude becomes a natural aspect of the seeker's frame of mind.

VALUE 1

"*AMANITVAM*": Absence of Self-Worshipfulness

Amanitvam comes from the Sanskrit word '*manah*' which means extending to conceit or haughtiness. Thus, *manah* means an exaggerated opinion about oneself. *Manah* does not imply that one is without qualifications but rather that whatever qualifications one has looms large in one's mind as worthy of respect and regard from others. The one who has *manah* is a *mani*. The addition of *tvam* to *mani* creates the abstract noun *manitvam*, which stands for the essence of the quality, that is, for exaggerated self-respectfulness or self-worshipfulness. The prefix embodies a negative meaning of the word; so, *amanitvam* indicates the absence of self-worshipfulness.

A simple, factual self-respectfulness is not a harmful quality of the mind. In fact, it is a good quality. The problem arises only when self-respectfulness is exaggerated into self-worshipfulness. When self-respect becomes self-conceit and exaggerated, it undesirably incites others to show me the respect that I feel is my due. When I demand respect, rarely will it be given to me upon my terms. The person upon whom I make such a demand may not respond. Or, he may, suffering from his own *manitvam*, respond with hostility or make a demand upon me for greater respect. The result can be mutual hurt, friction between each other, troubled minds.

What is the Basis of Self-Worshipfulness (*Manitvom*)?

What is it that causes me to make a demand for respect from others? The cause is not found in my solid respect for my own qualifications, although I may indeed have qualifications in good measure. But the cause is found in a deep, underlying doubt in my mind about my own qualifications. When I am completely certain that

I have in full measure, the qualifications that I claim, I have no need to demand from others respect for those qualifications. No matter how strange or polysyllabic my name is, I don't demand respect from others for my ability to spell my name. In fact, commendation for this skill would be insulting. I take this ability for granted and do not concern myself with it.

Manitvam arises because I am doubtful about my qualifications. I do not seem to accept myself as one who is qualified. The demand upon others for recognition shows that I need some support so that I can feel that I am somebody. This demand comes from an inner sense of emptiness, a lack of readiness to accept myself as I am, because I secretly fear what I am is not good enough at. Although I assert my qualifications, I am really all too conscious of my limitations and am afraid to acknowledge them. I assert not just my qualifications, but my qualification in the glorified light in which I view them.

Demand for Respect Leads to Hurt

People give respect to others for various reasons. Sometimes respect is given solely because the person to whom the expression is made is in a position of power. In such cases, if the position comes to an end, so does the respect. Other times, respect is given because there is some genuine appreciation of qualities in the other person. However, respect when given voluntarily is subject to the whim of the giver. What he finds convenient to give one day, may be too much the next. Also, the giver may cease his respectfulness if it is not returned to him in kind. If he too has an ego that requires extravagant support, he may find it deflating to extend support to another without return in kind so he stops. A relationship in which there is such a mutual demand for respect is likely to become a continuous tug-of-war. 'Hurt' is the usual end result of the demand for respect.

'Hurt' Based on 'Bloated Ego'

Hurt is possible only when there is a 'bloated ego' or pride. Any form of hurt, if analyzed, is found to be only pride or inflated ego. Inflated ego is disproportionate with excessive significance attached to what I know, what I feel, what I possess, what I do and how I look.

With this over emphasis on a 'knower-doer-I' comes the expectation of a certain response from others recognizing my importance; seeing me as I want to be seen. When that response does not come, then comes hurt. A hurt, deflated ego tends to spend a lot of time planning how to teach a lesson to the one who brought about the hurt. And, since a prideful ego picks up a lot of hurts, the list of those who have to be taught a lesson is likely to be long. For such a person, sitting quietly in meditation is not possible. In the firmament of the mind of one with a hurt ego, the luminaries ace all the people who caused the hurt; it is upon them that he dwells in meditation!

'Hurt is Always a Monkey's Wound'

There is a proverb which says "a wounded heart is like a monkey's wound; it does not heal but only gets reopened". A hurt mind may seem to be healed and then a sudden shadow crosses the face as the hurt is called back to memory and the hurt reopens. Like clouds before the sun, gloom closes in. There is no time for Vedanta in the mind of a person who is always nursing hurts; and one who demands respect accumulates many hurts to nurse.

Qualifications should Speak for Themselves

It is fine to have abilities and to use them; but abilities should be allowed to speak for themselves. My attitude towards my accomplishments should be like that of a flowering bush towards its blossoms. In the city or in the wilderness, seen or unseen, praised or decried, the bush spouts forth its blooms. No publicity circulars are sent out to announce the blooming. Whether it is appreciated by someone or not, it blooms because it is meant to bloom. It asks for no respect and claims no glory. It blooms because it must bloom. And this is the way I should be about my gifts and skills. These abilities seem to have come with me and I do not know why. I should simply use them as best as I can because that seems to be what I am supposed to do. People who have a value for these particular abilities may give me some respect for them if circumstances are right for them to do so. People who have no value for these particular abilities, no doubt will ignore them. Neither attitude should make any difference to me. I should let my actions themselves command respect from those who are able and willing to extend it, but I should never demand the respect.

Self-Worshipfulness is Displaced when its Foolishness is Realised

How can I obtain the attitude of *amanitvam* or absence of *manitvam*, i.e., absence of the demand for inordinate respect from others? *Amanitvam* is obtained by losing *manitvam*. I do not have *amanitvam* because *manitvam* has become a value for me, although, no doubt, I would not work up to this. *Manitvam* is a value for me because I think that by receiving from others large amounts of respect I will feel good about myself. *Manitvam* will cease to be a value for me when I clearly see for myself that the basis is false, and moreover, that it does not work.

We have already seen some of the reasons why a demand for respect does not work. Namely, not everyone will have a value for my particular qualification; not everyone will be able to show respect to me (even if there is a value for my qualifications) because of their own ego-needs. The showing of respect will be subject to the convenience, mood and whim of the one making the expression. In this regard, one more observation can be made. It is often not easy to decode another person's attitude from his manner. If I am obsessed with the amount of respect I am receiving from another, I may still not know what his real attitude towards me is. A curt manner may conceal a real value for the other person's qualification. A rejecting manner may mask a real attitude of respect; it may also be clouded by jealousy or competitiveness. Thus, my concern with the respectful attitudes of others is a tremendous squandering of my mind's time. In as much as so many factors having no bearing on the true value of my qualifications may affect the attitude of others, and, in any event, I may be unable to read truly the attitude of others from their manner or words.

Therefore, if I take time to analyse the factors involved, I will clearly see that demanding respect from others cannot possibly bring me much comfort or satisfaction, in spite of the reality of my qualifications. In addition to this insight, a further understanding of the absurdity of demanding respect from others will come if I examine the basis of the qualifications for which I want respect.

Self-Worshipfulness is Never Justified by Accomplishments

Manitvam is born because I do not understand the nature of accomplishment. I claim the honour for my accomplishments because I consider myself the author of the acts, the producer of the skills or gifts. It does not take much analysis to smash this illusion. The analysis can begin with my physical body. For any skill or gift there must be a body to wield it. I did not author the body that houses me. It came to me with a certain inherent potential or predisposition. Even if I subscribe to a belief in reincarnation and consider this body as a vehicle shaped by my karmas, I can claim neither authorship nor knowledge of the particular laws that ordained this body. I do not know whether this particular body reflects my overt actions in past lives or my parents' subtle actions (prayers for a healthy, intelligent child) at the inception of this life. Moreover, I cannot trace this body back to some first or originating body in a *karma*-sustained cause and effect chain of bodies. My *jivatva* (apparent separate individuality) housed for the moment in this particular *upadhi* (body) is *anadi* (beginningless) like creation itself, of which it is a part. I am not the author of creation, nor am I the author of my body. Therefore, whatever possibilities I have, appear to have been provided to me. I can exploit these abilities but I did not create them.

Even in the exploitation of my skills, sheer ability is often not the determinant of success or failure. When I look at any achievement I find that it is there because of certain opportunities I had, as well as because of my personal effort. I cannot claim to have created or commanded the opportunities. They were given to me. I happened to find myself in the right circumstances, so I could grow and learn what I needed to learn. I met the right person; happened to read the right book; I enjoyed the right company; someone came forward with the right guidance at the right time. There are so many factors behind an achievement. I cannot really say I created any of them. When I look at the facts, I must see that any achievement that I claim as mine is not due to my will or skill alone but is due to certain things that were provided to me and certain opportunities I had. Therefore, there is no place for *manitvam* when I see the nature of accomplishment for what it is. I should be grateful for whatever abilities I seem to have. My demand for respect from others will go away when I realise its foolishness.

How Can I Help Myself See the Foolishness of Self-Worshipfulness?

If I assume the position of dispassionate analyst, ready to spot and analyse *manitvam* every time it pops up, *manitvam* will soon disappear from my mind. I should recognize it for what it is when it appears and examine it carefully until I understand its foolishness under the particular circumstances. After a few such inspections it will lose its value for me. When its foolishness is seen in true light, I shall no longer feel that it serves any purpose for me and it will go off.

To be effective, I must conduct my analysis of *manitvam* without self-condemnation or regret and try to see things just matter-of-factly as they are. When someone fails to respond to me in the way I would have them respond, I should review my own actions without further reaction. From the position of observer I can see the senselessness of my expectations in all their absurdity. In addition I see that what I really want is not an expression of respect from others for its own sake, but because I hope such an expression will make me feel more comfortable about myself. I see that my real problem is my basic feeling of inadequacy and self-doubt which is made worse, not better, by harbouring *manitvam*.

Self-Worshipfulness (*Manitvam*): The Apparent of Apparents (*Mithya*'s *Mithya*)

There are a lot of things which are *mithya*. In fact, all perceivable things are *mithya*. *Mithya* is that which has a dependent rather than an absolute reality. This dependent reality which characterises creation is usually translated in English as 'apparent', which is meant to indicate that the reality is not absolute but is subject to negation.

All objectifiable things in creation are *mithya*. They begin and end, and they can be resolved (in ever finer, progressive resolutions) into constituents. However, 'apparent' things, although subject to negation, still enjoy a certain level of reality.

Manitvam, or on the other hand the ego, which manifests as *manitvam* or pride, does not enjoy even apparent reality. Ego is not even *mithya*! When I search for my ego, it is not there. It disappears. It just goes away. I find there is no such thing as ego. It does not require Self-knowledge to discover that there is no such thing as ego. Just a careful, dispassionate analysis of the source of my skills and abilities and of the history of any achievements that I claim, will erase the ego. It will knock off the proud claim that I am entitled to credit for some achievement.

Manitvam, ego, pride, is *mithya*'s *mithya*. When I see this, when I see that ego cannot even be justified as blessed with a dependent reality, when I see that *manitvam* is as myth, it will just disappear. When *manitvam* goes away, what remains is *amanitvam*. *Amanitvam* is not developed. It is very natural. When I enjoy *amanitvam* I become a simple person, a person who doesn't have any complexities.

Manitvam/pride/bloated ego simply disappears when its foolishness is seen. It is not practical advice to be told to give up pride or ego. Irrational as it may be, a prideful ego is very common. Especially in Western society where individualism has come to be so highly prized, ego is a problem.

Emphasis on individualism makes a person more proud and more subject to the hurts that go with pride. However, ego will not be banished until it can be replaced with knowledge. In the light of knowledge, ego, pride, or *manitvam*, seems silly. Ego is not given up. Ego goes. Ego goes in the light of a certain understanding. It does not require Self-knowledge to see the foolishness of ego. When I realise that foolishness, I will be able to keep ego to the minimum useful level necessary to conduct my affairs. I also will enjoy *amanitvam*—a quality of mind conducive to discovery of the Self.

VALUE 2

"*ADAMBHITVAM*": Absence of Self-Glorification

Adambhitvam is the mental state in which *dambha* is absent. *Damhba* is a mental attitude which results in an expression quite similar to the expression of *manitvam*, namely, manifestation of self-glorification. However, between the two, the foundation of the expression differs. *Manitvam*'s conceit is an expression based on real achievements and abilities; whereas, the claim to fame caused by *dambha* stems from pretended or fabricated accomplishment and abilities. *Dambha* means pretence or feigning. A *dambhi* is one who claims achievements that are not his or pretends to possess abilities which he does not have:

It is called *dambha* when I trumpet my glory for what is not there, when by design I give the impression that I am something, which I know I am not. When I dress as if I were a wealthy person while in fact my bank account is overdrawn and I am dodging bill collectors, it is an expression of *dambha* by *vesa*, by dress. When I claim recognition as a scholar alluding to papers or books which have been published or are about to be published, when in fact all I have ever written are letters to relatives asking for loans, that is an expression of *dambha* by *bhasa*, by words.

What Causes Self-Glorification (Dombhitvam)?

When I give expression to *dambhitvam* it is because I think that through my pretences I will impress others who will then respond to me in a way that will make me feel good. *Dambhitvam* arises because I do not feel good about myself I do not accept myself as I am. I want to be different. I find myself unacceptable. So, in order that others too will not find me unacceptable, I present myself as I think I would like to be or in a way which I think will impress others. I do this whether I like to be that way or not.

Self-Glorification Requires a Long Memory

We have seen the reasons why *manitvam*, a self-conceited demand for respect from others, is a foolish attitude. These reasons apply to *dambhitvam* too. There is no way to compel others to respond favourably to my accomplishment, whether they are real or fancied. In the case of *dambhitvam*, there is no problem in seeing that I cannot claim authorship of the accomplishment which I am publicizing, in as much as they are pretence, not fact. In addition, *dambhitvam* is particularly absurd because it brings even less comfort than *manitvam* to the mind which harbours it. It instead brings a big load of tension. It brings tension because the *dambhi* must always be on guard against being 'found out'. Here's an example:

Friend: Where have you been? I haven't seen you around for several days.

Dambhi: I've been at the capital. The PM wanted some regional input on the tax reform proposal.

When *dambhi*'s wife appears, he must hastily end the conversation before she reveals that he had simply been out of town helping his brother-in-law move. *Dambhitvam* brings with it the need to be ever alert and to have a long memory. Truth does not require special remembering.

Self-Glorificationis a Big Problem for the Mind

The mind being what it is, there is always a tendency for *dambhitvam* in small measure. I always tend to present myself somewhat better than what I am. This attitude is not conducive to the frame of mind which is receptive to the teaching of *Vedanta*. Any *dambhitvam* is a commitment to falsehood. A mind which expresses *dambhitvam* is not receptive to the teaching of *Vedanta*. When I suffer from *dambhitvam*, I do not accept myself, but instead commit myself to an image I know is false. Whereas, the whole teaching of *Vedanta* is owning up and seeing myself as I am. The end of Vedanta is knowledge of the truth of myself. If I reject myself forthwith as an attitude of *dambhitvam* indicates, I will have a very difficult time accepting and assimilating the knowledge of the truth of myself. The truth of the Self that *Vedanta* reveals to me is that I lack nothing. *Vedanta* shows me that the multiplicity of creation is but apparent *mithya* and that the non-dual reality of myself is limitless. However, to be ready for this teaching which will reveal to me my limitlessness,

I must enjoy a mind which grants acceptance to me as it thinks I am, right now, with all my apparent limitations.

Self-Acceptance Prepares the Mind for Vedanta Study

To be ready for the study of *Vedanta*, I should be able to accept myself just as I think I am and be willing to present myself to myself as I am. I should like myself as I am but at the same time limitations bind me. I should be free of self-condemnation. I should simply like myself but, knowing that I seem to be bound, I long to be free. When I suffer from *dambhitvam*, it is scarcely possible for me to have a true desire to be free. My commitment to falsity and outright rejection of my relative self falsify even a desire for freedom.

When *dambhitvam* goes, the mind will enjoy the state of *adambhitvam*, the absence of phoniness, the absence of hypocrisy and pretence. With such a mind I become a real person. A real person is a simple person. The complex person is a false person. A simple person may not be without problems. He may get angry. He may make mistakes. But, in his simplicity and straightforwardness he is able to get rid of his anger, to learn from his reactions. For the false person committed to pretence, there is no learning, only hiding and tension.

When I truly see the futility and absurdity of both the attitude of *manitvam* and *dambhitvam*, these negative values will drop off, leaving me with a mind reflecting *amanitvam* and *adamibhitvam*, the absence of pride and the absence of pretence. No scripture or any master can help a person with a mind ruled by pride and pretence. A mind which is simple and factual is the kind of mind which is ready to discover the truth of the Self.

VALUE 3

"AHIMSA": Non-Harmfulness

Ahimsa comes from the Sanskrit verb hims which means 'to hurt, injure, or cause harm.' Ahimsa, which means "non-injury or non-harmfulness,' reflects one's inherent desire to live free of hurt or pain or threat of any sort. Even thoughts can cause pain. If I know that someone holds hurtful thoughts about me, even if these thoughts are not expressed in deeds or words, I am hurt. Ahimsa means not causing harm by any means: by deeds, *kayena*; by words, *vaca*; or by thought, *manasa*.

Why should I not hurt other beings? Because I do not want myself to be hurt. Commonsense ethics dictates that I cannot do unto another what I do not want to be done to me. So ahimsa, non-injury, becomes a value for me. Ahimsa is simple commonsense dharma, confirmed by the Vedas and by all scriptures but subject to interpretation. If an act which is literally injurious is otherwise meant for the benefit of another, such as the cut of the surgeon's knife, it is not himsa. In a relative world absolute ahimsa is not possible.

Vegetarianism: Expression of *Minna*

Vegetarianism is an example of the application of the value of ahimsa. Many arguments in favour of a vegetarian diet can be made, but the basic argument supporting no flesh eating is simply ahimsa. In India, where there are more vegetarians than anywhere else in the world, vegetarianism is squarely based on the Vedic mandate:

Himsam na kuryat: Do not do harm!

Why is more himsa involved in eating an egg than an egg-plant or a steak than a pumpkin? Every life form requires food of some kind. One life-form feeds upon another. A cat may kill a canary for its food. What is tragedy to the bird is dinner to the cat. Because human being is not in the same choiceless category as the canary-eating cat, he cannot use the cat's example for his justification. For the cat and other non-human life forms, choosing what to have for dinner is no problem. They select their food by instinct. They come pre-programmed knowing their proper menu; they need only locate it. This is not so with man whose self-consciousness brings into play a will that is free to choose many means to meet life's ends, including the basic need, food. Being not pre-programmed, man must choose the kind of food he eats.

Several arguments other than ahimsa are offered to support the position that vegetarianism is a better diet plan than meat eating. There is evidence that human dental and digestive systems are more suitable for a fruit-grain-vegetable diet than for meat. Vegetarians have fewer degenerative diseases and live longer, and enjoy a more vigorous old age than meat eating people. However, persuasive these arguments may be, the value of ahimsa is still the fundamental argument in favour of vegetarianism.

All Creatures Seek to Live Harm-Free

It is plain to see that all living beings have a value for life, Anything alive tries to stay alive, including plants and very simple life forms. However, it is also plain that all beings do not seem to have the same relative level of awareness of life, the same conscious ability to perceive threats to life or to struggle to preserve life. Creatures in the animal kingdom are closer to man than plants in their response to threats to life and in their struggle to stay alive. Animals, birds, fish—all mobile creatures—run away when they know I am trying to catch them for the stew pot. When I do catch them, they struggle and cry. Therefore, it is evident to me that they do not want to be hurt, that they want to live. No mobile creature wants to be my dinner.

Since I have been given free will to choose the food which I eat to sustain my life, I must find some norm to guide me in choosing that food. The gift of free will carries with it a responsibility to follow an ethical norm in the exercise of that will. What is the commonsense food? The Veda tells me: *Himsam na kuryat*. My commonsense dharmic norm for choice of food tells me that I should not make 'somebody' my dinner since I do not want to be somebody's dinner. What is a 'somebody'? Those who cry in protest or struggle against me are more a 'somebody' than plants rooted in one place, which quietly give up their fruits for my food, normally without even surrendering their lives.

Plant Food: The Rational/Ethical Choice for Human Diet

In view of research indicating that a blanket vegetarian diet is complete and healthful, the use of meat in my diet cannot be justified on the basis of nutritional need. If I choose to eat meat, that choice must be put as simply a preference on my part. To fulfil a preference is fine if there is no overriding ethical reason for not fulfilling it. In the case of meat eating there is a strong commonsense ethical reason for not fulfilling such a preference, if it exists.

Since I do not want to be an animal's dinner, I should not make an animal my dinner. Plant food, rather than meat, is the choice because: (1) many plants seem designed to give up their produce as food for other life-forms without surrendering their own lives, and (2) even when the usage does destroy the plant, the plant would appear to have less conscious appreciation of the threat or the fact of harm to it, than animals would.

If I insist upon including meat in my diet, to raise such a decision to ethical status, I would have to put myself on the same basis as other carnivorous animals. To be on the same basis I shall be required to kill my prey bare handed without the assistance of weapons, thus, exposing myself to the possibility of being 'someone's' dinner while seeking other creatures for my dinner. If I am not willing to do this, use of animals for food will be unethical, conflicting with my half-value for non-injury. That I have such a half-value is revealed by my failure to risk the possibility of suffering the same result.

Non-Harmfulness Requires Sensitivity and Alertness

The value for ahimsa requires daily alertness and sensitivity in all areas of life. It is a value that finds expression in my attitude towards plants also besides toward human beings and animals. Wanton destruction of plant life indicates a lack of sensitivity for the value of ahimsa. Ahimsa is a value for, not destroying or damaging any part of creation. A creation of which I too am a part. As for plants, I do not causally crush, strip, uproot or cut them down. With regard to my fellow human beings, I watch out for those words or acts or even thoughts which may be hurtful. I develop a finer appreciation of the feelings of others. I come to see beyond my own needs, to the needs of those around me. I treat all things and beings with sensitivity and appreciation of their common existence with me.

With such an attitude I become an alert, observant person with a sensitive saintly mind which is ready to hear and appreciate the truth of Vedanta. Ahimsa is an important value among the values that constitute the *jnanam* for gaining Self-knowledge.

VALUE 4

"*Ksanti*": Attitude of Accommodation

The Sanskrit word *ksanti* often is translated as 'forbearance' or 'endurance'. But these two English words carry a negative flavour of 'resigned sufferance' whereas *ksanti* is a positive attitude and not painful resignation. A better translation is 'accommodation'. The attitude of *ksanti* means that I cheerfully, calmly accept the extraction or demand that another person (or situation) should make, in order to conform to what I think would be pleasing to me. I accommodate situations and people happily.

All Relationships Require Accommodation

This value must be built upon an understanding of the nature of people and relationships between them. I will never find in one person all qualities which I like, or all qualities which I dislike. Any given person is going to have a mixture of things which I find appealing and others which I find non-appealing. Similarly, I am also both appealing and non-appealing. I am going to have the same impact on others. No one is going to find me totally likeable. When I recognize these facts, I will see that every relationship is going to require some accommodation from me. I am not willing or, perhaps, be able to change and meet all expectations other people have of me, nor are they for themselves. I will never find a relationship which does not require accommodation.

In particular, relationships wherein there are things which I strongly dislike require accommodation from me. If I can change the person or can put distance between him/her and me without avoiding duty, it is fine. But if I cannot, I simply must accommodate happily. That is, I must take the person as he/she is. I can expect neither the world nor the people to change in order that I may be happy. It is just not possible to compel people to change to meet my image of what they should be like. Sometimes some may change a little for me or may try to change, but I cannot count on this. More often than not, when I want change from others, they will just as strongly want change from me. It will be often an avoidable stand-off.

Lessen Expectations for Attitude of Accommodation

When I examine my mental processes I will probably find that to my surprise, I extend *ksanti* more readily to an insufferable fool than to my best friend. This is because I do not expect anything wise or intelligent from a fool; whereas I expect my friend to live up to certain standards which I consider appropriate. A hopeless fool can never disappoint me, but everyone else, for one reason or the other, at some time, can. This should not be so. As far as my expectations are concerned, I should place everyone in the same category as the hopeless fool. No one should ever be able to disappoint me but should only be able to surprise me. And, my attitude should be that I am prepared to accommodate all surprises!

Thus, I should accommodate people the same way as I accommodate inert objects. That is, I should take them as they are. I do not like to be over-baked by the summer sun but I do not ask the sun to quit shining. I appreciate the mixed blessing of a hot shining sun. Nor do I hate honey bees if I get in the way of one and receive a sting; I still appreciate the honey bee and enjoy honey.

However, this attitude I have towards insects or inert objects, I find much harder to have towards people. I am able to relate myself properly to an inert thing or to a wild creature because I do not expect any change from it. But I expect people to be able to change to become more pleasant to me. I keep my mind troubled with continuous demands for change so that others in my life will be more to my liking. Actually, the humans may also not be able to change. Often, humans cannot change either for want of will or for want of willingness. When a person does not change, even though willing to change, he/she has no strength of will. There is nothing you can do but accommodate such a person. When the other person does not change because he or she is not willing to try to change, you can try to convince the person of the desirability to change. If you cannot so convince the person, well, then you must accommodate. What else can you do? Anyway the world is large. Variety makes it more interesting. There is room enough to accommodate all.

Respond to the Person, Not to the Action

In order to discover within myself a value for accommodation, I should look at the person behind the act. Usually it is when I am responding to the behaviour of the person, responding to his action, that I find it difficult to be accommodative. But when I try to understand the cause behind the action, when I try to understand what is behind the fit of anger or outburst of jealousy or domineering manner, and then respond to the person, not to the actions, I find it easy to be accommodative. If I cannot see what is behind the actions, I nonetheless keep in mind the fact that many reasons unknown to me set the state for any action on the part of the other person. With this frame of mind I will find it natural to be accommodative.

Mechanic Reactions Block Accommodation

To be free to respond to a person I must be free of mechanical reactions. I must choose my actions deliberately. A reaction is a mechanical non-deliberate behaviour on my part. It is a conditioned response borrowed from previous experiences, one not given prior sanction by my will. It is a response which I do not measure against the value structure which I am trying to assimilate but which I just allow to happen. Sometimes my reaction may be an action or attitude which I would make after reflection. Some other times my reaction may be completely contrary to the attitude and actions I would choose to hold or do. Reactions can go against all my wisdom and learning and prior experiences. These factors just get relegated into the background and the reaction comes; what I have previously learnt is worthless to me. I may have read all the scriptures of the world; I may be a great student of ethical systems; I may be a qualified professional counsellor to others, but when it comes to a reaction, mine will be just as mechanical as that of anyone else. Wisdom, learning, experience, won't count at all. Therefore, until my ethical values become thoroughly assimilated and comprise a ground out of which right attitudes and actions spontaneously arise, I must, through alertness, avoid reactions and, instead, deliberately, reflectively choose my attitudes and actions. When I avoid reactions, I am free to choose my actions and attitudes—I can choose to be accommodative in my thoughts, words and deeds. Attitude of Accommodation—Non-Harmfulness: Qualities of a Saint

Accommodation is a beautiful and saintly quality. Among all the qualities, ahimsa and *ksanti* constitute the qualities of a saint. The minimum qualifications for a saint are these two qualities. One need not have wisdom, one need not have scriptural learning to be a saint, but one must have these two values. A saint is a person who never consciously hurts another person by action, word or thought and who accepts people—good or bad just as they are. He is one who has an endless capacity to be accommodative, forgiving and merciful. These qualities—accommodation, forgiveness, mercifulness—are included in the quality called *ksanti*. A saint always has *ksanti* which is an infinite capacity for mercy. He responds to the person, not to the action. He sees wrong action as a mistake born of inner conflict and is humane to the person who commits it. An attitude of *ksanti* or accommodation, expands one's heart. The heart becomes so commodious, it accommodates all people and circumstances just as they are without desire, nor demand that they be different. This is *ksanti*.

VALUE 5

"*ARJAVAM*": Straight Forwardness

Arjavam means 'straightness'. When used as a value, 'straightness' or *arjavam* is like the English word rectitude (from the Latin rectus, straight) which means 'conduct in accordance with one's thought and words'. When there is *rjubhava* (arrow-like straightness) between a physical action and the word, or between the word and the thought, the alignment is called *arjavam*.

What is non-alignment of thought, word and act? When I think of one thing and say another, or when I say one thing and do another, or when I think about one thing and do yet another third thing, all of these constitute a non-alignment of thought, words and deeds on my part. Avoidance of this gap, this division between word and action, word and thought, and action and thought, is *arjavam*. *Arjavam* can be considered to be an extension of *satya vacanam*, truthful speech.

Arjavam covers more ground; it includes not just *vacanam* or speech but thoughts and actions. For *arjavam*, my actions must be true to my words and my words true to my thoughts.

Non-Alignment Results in a Splintered Person

What is the importance of alignment between thought, word and deed? By non-alignment I become disintegrated. I am no longer a whole person. When there is conflict between my values and myself I become splintered. I am not 'together'. If there is a gulf between me the thinker, and me the speaker or actor, the result will be a restless mind troubled by guilt and conflict. For such a mind, self-knowledge is a far cry. To be prepared to listen to the teaching of Vedanta, one needs to be 'together', not split. Therefore, *arjavam*, the alignment of thought, word and deed is included as one of the values of *jnanam*.

VALUE 6

"*Acaryopasanam*": Service to the Teacher

Acaryopasanam primarily means 'service to the teacher'. This value is one which is deeply embedded in Hindu culture. Its intensity and universality within the culture show the high regard for knowledge and for the teacher who imparts it.

Acaryopasanam is also used to indicate specific aspects of the student-teacher relationship. Gurukula vasa, living with the teacher for a length of time in gurukula and learning from him, is one meaning of *acaryopasanam*. 'Meditation upon the teacher' is another. Together these words form the Sanskrit compound *acaryopasanam*. Meditation upon the teacher means meditation upon the teachings by keeping the *acarya*, the teacher (who stands for the vision of the teaching) always in one's heart.

'Service and surrender', however, is the general meaning of *acaryopasanam*. This is the sense in which Lord Krisna uses the term when talking to Arjuna. In this sense, *acaryopasanam* requires certain discrimination in its exercise. Care must be taken in choosing, as it can lead to exploitation of the value holder if the teacher is not a responsible person.

Service to the teacher implies a whole frame of mind towards the teacher—a frame of mind characterized by surrender of personal ego, subordination of personal likes and dislikes, willingness to give without demanding any return, and general attitude of respect and devotion. Thus, *acaryopasanam* means a great personal surrender. This kind of surrender to another person should be made only when the person to whom you are surrendering has no need for the surrender, no need for the service, no need of any kind to be the beneficiary of the attitude of *acaryopasanam*. Only a person who has clear steady knowledge of the truth of the Self is without needs. Such a person is one who can be a real teacher, a teacher who can unfold the knowledge of the Self that is the ground of all knowledge. So, when Lord Krisna tells Arjuna that *acaryopasanam* is one of the values constituting *jnanam*, it is understood that the teacher at whose feet the student surrenders must be a teacher of such integrity and freedom from need for service, that only the student, not the teacher, will be beneficiary of the surrender.

In *acaryopasanam* willingness to serve is the most significant, rather than the particular act of service done. Willingness to serve means an inner stance of readiness to serve whether or not one is called upon to serve. It means a happy acceptance of any way in which I am asked to serve, an attitude in which nothing asked of me is considered too small or too large a service. In service, large is small and small is large. I am simply ready to do any action I can do. In this guru-disciple relationship there is no give and take as there is in other relationship. There is only giving on the part of the student. Through such an attitude of unquestioning, complete service the student becomes blessed. The teacher becomes an altar at which he can surrender.

Earlier, Lord Krisna had told Arjuna:

Tadviddhi pranipatena pariprasnena sevaya
Upadeksyanti the jananam janainastattvadarsinah

"Know that by prostrating thyself, by inquiry and by service, the wise who know the truth will teach thee that knowledge".

(*Bhagavad Gita*, Chapter IV, Verse 34)

It is this description of 'discipleship' that is embraced by the term *acaryopasanam*. When the teacher is true to his name and the nature of service is understood, the surrender of *acaryopasanam* is a beautiful thing, blessing the student and making his mind receptive to the knowledge to be unfolded. In gaining any discipline of knowledge, respect for the teacher is an essential element.

VALUE 7

"*Saucam*": Internal and External Cleanliness

Saucam is cleanliness in a two-fold sense: *Bahya*, outer cleanliness; and *antara*, inner cleanliness, *Bahya saucam*, external cleanliness, is a well understood universal value. It is easy to see the benefit that comes to me and to others from external cleanliness. Clean body, clean clothes, and clean dwelling place make life more pleasant. In addition, the daily discipline of maintaining cleanliness brings about a certain attentiveness and alertness of mind.

Antara saucam, internal cleanliness, is less easily recognized. *Antara saucam* means cleanliness of the *antahkarana*, of the mind. What is *asaucam* of the mind? What makes a mind unclean? Jealousy, anger, hatred, fear, selfishness, self-condemnation, guilt, pride, possessiveness, all these negative reactions and the climate of despair and resentment which comes in their wake, are the unseemliness, the *asaucam*, of the mind. While I go about my business, a little dust settles on my skin; some dirt smudges my clothes; my desk becomes littered—so my body gathers daily *asaucam* in my transactions with people and circumstances. Similarly, linked to my ragas and divests likes and dislikes which produce desires and aversions smudges of envy settle, a spot of exasperation lands, streaks of possessiveness appear; and overall, the fine dust of self-criticism, guilt and self-condemnation spreads.

Each day I wash my body, launder my clothes, and clear my desk. It is a day-to-day affair, *amaranam*, until death. Until my body goes, I must do this. So, too, with my mind. Each day my mind must be cleaned until my false identification with the mind goes, in the knowledge of the Self. When there is no daily cleaning outside or inside, the accumulation makes the task much more difficult.

Pratipaksa Shawn: Mind Cleanser

How do you clean the mind? What is the detergent for the mind? There is one—*pratipaksa bhavana*. *Prati*, means 'opposite'; *paksa* stands for position or 'point of view', *bhavana* indicates thinking or 'state of thought.' Thus, *pratipaksa bhavana* means the 'opposite point of view'. The proactive of *pratipaksa bhavana* is to deliberately take the opposite point of view and to willingly think the opposite of the unclean thought.

This 'opposite thing' is to be undertaken even though my negative attitude seems justified to me. Someone may do an improper action which insults or injures me. Resentment settles in my mind. The action may have been inarguably improper, but the resentment nonetheless is mine, it is my *asaucam* of the mind. Allowed to remain, this resentment can build up to hatred, a painful, disturbing mental state. Seeing, therefore, the personal consequence of allowing *asaucam* to remain, when the object of resentment comes to my attention, I summon the wilt to think thoughts opposite to the negative thoughts that first came to mind.

Banish Resentment by Seeing the Saint

By analysis I see that a person I resent or dislike is not disliked by everyone. Deliberately I search for the reasons why others like him. I think of the positive facts that I know concerning him—he is kind to his children, he cares for his parents, he gives charity. I call to mind whatever good things I know of him.

When I look into any person I will find love. I am capable of loving. Any person is capable of loving. Even a rank criminal has within him the elements of love and sympathy. It may be that the criminal's capacity for love is so obscured that it hardly shows; but it is there to be discovered. Manifest or not, everyone has the qualities which make a person a saint—compassion, mercy, love, harmlessness. Therefore, to clean the mind of resentment and dislikes which solidify into hatred, it is essential for a deliberate search for those things in another person which indicate ha humaneness, his saintliness. They are there in everyone.

When you draw your attention to glimpses of saintliness in another person, all other things you have observed in him are attributed simply to error, mistake, habit, wrong thinking, wrong environment or wrong upbringing. Take it as your blessing that you are not in the same position that he is in. With the same parentage, the same environment, you too could be performing the acts that you find objectionable in him. See behind the acts of the person possessed of all the saintly qualities, because innately these qualities are the human qualities. Saintly qualities are the qualities of the Self, the qualities which really constitute human nature. Negative qualities are incidental; they come and go.

So, when resentment, dislike or hatred towards someone arises, introduce thoughts which are their opposite. See the person behind the action from an opposite viewpoint, and you will discover an attitude of *ksanti*, accommodation towards him. In this manner, any resentment, any hatred that appears is erased, cleaned away on a daily basis.

Non-Cleanliness (*Asaucam*): Selfishness

Selfishness provides a good example of *asaucam* which yields to *pratipaksa bhavana*. In the case of selfishness, the *pratipaksa bhavana* thoughts can often be reinforced by action as well. When I see in myself non-consideration for the wants, needs, happiness of others, I can deliberately programme myself to overdo in the opposite direction. Making myself alert to the needs and happiness of those around me, I can find ways to be considerate. Whenever I do an act which compensates some selfish omission or frees my mind from that account, it also underlines by deliberate decision the change of an attitude; it is well expressed physically, that is, confirmed by action. It is hard for the negative opposite attitude to become lodged again.

Non-Cleanliness: Self-Condemnation

Universal ethical values, consciously or unconsciously remain as a matrix for self-judgment for any thoughts or actions which transgress their standards. Whenever I fail to abide by a general value, some conflict usually registers in my mind. Conflict becomes guilt and guilt turns into an underground chorus of self-condemnation which becomes a subtle *asaucam* pervading my mind.

Self-condemnation can be called subtle *asaucam* because to many it is not at all apparent that self-condemnation is *antara asaucam* of the Self. We may regard self-condemnation as a useful goad to make one to 'change one's nature'. This is not a correct or useful damnation of oneself. It can no more be justified than condemnation of others. Both rest upon the faulty understanding of the Self. Both produce turmoil in the mind.

Self-condemnation can be controlled by *pratipaksa bhavana*, i.e., by refusing to condemn myself while at the same time deliberately thinking non-selfcondemning thought. Analysis of the nature of self-condemnation will help me exercise *pratipaksa bhavana*. Upon analysis I will always find that in this body-mind package which I term 'I', the body which carries out the act cannot be condemned. The hands, the legs, the feet, the tongue, all parts of the body, are *jada*, inert. The body itself lacks self-consciousness or independent conscious processes. Performing its jobs indiscriminately, either automatically or upon direction from the mind, it cannot be held culpable. No more can the mind be labelled the culprit. The mind is not a simple, definable entity, but an ever-changing aggregate of thoughts in motion: some beautiful, some not beautiful; some useful, some inconsequential. Mind is an aggregate of available thoughts at a given point of time, in an ongoing process characterized by constant change. Mind is only a process that performs as a useful instrument. Mind cannot be condemned. Then what is it that can be condemned? Can alma be condemned? From *Sruti* (scripture) I know that *atma* illuminates the mind. But *atma* (the name for first person singular, I) is *satcitananda*: boundless, timeless, full of awareness, form-free, action free. Neither *karta* (doer) nor *bhakta* (enjoyer), *atma* cannot be blamed.

Therefore, what can I condemn? Not my body. Not my mind. Not alma. If there is anything that can be justifiably condemned, it is but a given thought born of ignorance and error; a thought that ordered an improper action.

Thus, if self-condemnation is analyzed properly and an inquiry is made into what it does, the result will show no condemnation of self. It will instead be condemnation, if any, of an act simply for what the act is, and of the particular error born of the thought behind that act. Clearing away self-condemnation leaves the mind free to discover, as a personal value, the ethical norm which has been transgressed. The *asaucam* of regret is removed. If 'I' have done the act, there is regret. I can address myself to understand what gave rise to the thought.

In India we used to traditionally repeat the following Vedic mantra 1,008 times as small boys, each year on a special day:

Kamo karsinnamo namah
Kama karsit kamah karoti nahankaromi
Kamah karta nahankarta
Kamah karayita nahankarayita esa to kama kamaya svaha
Manayurakarsinamo namah
Manyurakarsinmanyuh karoti nahankaromi
Manyuh karta nahankarta
Manyuh karayita nahankarayita esa to manyo manyave svaha

'Desire did (it). Salutations (oh, Lord Desire).
Desire did (it). Desire does (it). I do not do.
Desire is the doer. I am not the doer.
Desire causes the act. I do not cause the act.
Salutations to you, desire,
Anger did (it). Salutations (Oh, Lord Anger).
Anger did (it). Anger does (it). I do not do.
Anger is the doer. I am not the doer.
Anger causes the act. I do not cause the act.
Salutations to you, Anger.'

(*Krisna-Yajur-Veda: Taittiriya-Aranyaka*)

Repetition of the *mantra* in this way, even though only once a year, is a wonderful thing, because there is no self-condemnation in it. But at the same time, there is the knowledge that there were some actions which were not appropriate. It is recognized that those actions had a certain basis in desire, or a basis in anger. Recognition of the basis of an action is conducive to an alertness of the mind that can break conditioning and receive the knowledge that dispels ignorance.

Non-Cleanliness: Jealousy

In Sanskrit, jealousy is called *matsarya*.

Matsarya is defined as:

Parotkarsam drstva joyamanah santapah

'The anguish that is born, seeing the rise of another.'

(*Drstva*—having seen, *utkarsam*—the superiority or excellence of someone, *santapah*—a pain, or sadness is born that is *matsarya*—jealousy)

Of all *asaucam*, jealousy is the most illegitimate of attitudes because even by the standards of the relative world it is "unreal". Most of the reactive attitudes, which are considered *asaucam*, are based on either the pursuit of or the threat, real or imagined, to some objective that is capable of being achieved, at least theoretically. Not so with jealousy. Jealousy is a reaction of sorrow over a lack which I conclude exists when I compare myself with some other human being who is seen as superior. This supposed superiority, when examined, will always be found, that is if it exists at all, as partial and incomplete. Upon close examination, the one who is jealous, would never be able to consider the aggregation of parts and functions which constitute the entity, that is the object of jealousy. I will never be jealous of all the aspects of another person. Nor will anyone who is jealous of me ever find me totally superior. Since whatever endowments, skills, graces, possessions inspire my jealousy cannot be separated from the entire entity, and since that entire entity will never totally be an object of my jealousy, there can be no real locus of jealousy for me.

Jealousy has no ground at all, but still, at the level of *upadhi* (that is, at the level of identification of 'I' with a particular assemblage of body-mind aspects), no one except *paramesvara*, the Lord Himself, seems to escape this special pain. (*Paramesvara* whose body/mind complex is the aggregate of all *upadhis*, is all-knowing, all-powerful, all-pervasive. He is the totality of all names and forms. Therefore, at the level of *upadhi*-identification, no other entity or aggregation of entities less than a total aggregation (which is *Paramesvara*, Himself) can equal him. Thus, *Paramesvara* could not be jealous because he knows there is no other person who is His equal. In addition, of course *Paramesvara* could not be jealous because, undeluded by ignorance, knowing both the truth of Himself as well as of the created world, He knows that there is no 'other' at all. No second person, in terms of superior attributes, is available to *Paramesvara* to trigger jealousy and, in fact, He knows there is no second person).

For a *jnani* who knows the truth of himself (who therefore does not identify with *upadhi*, with the body-mind assemblage), there is no jealousy. A*jnani* is not jealous because he knows that no second person exists. Thus, the *jnani*, who knows himself to be non-dual brahman, and *Paramesvara* who as the Lord is not only the totality of the apparent but also knows the truth of Himself, both know no jealousy, and, in fact, cannot be jealous. For others, jealousy exists and operates endlessly. Seeing themselves as separate entities, they see the world as filled with millions of other entities, countless numbers of whom will daily present opportunities, real or fancied, for self-demeaning comparative judgments of excellence, followed by the pain of *matsarya*.

When analyzed, the baselessness of jealousy becomes apparent. At the most elementary level of analysis, I can see that there is no absolute ranking of entities as 'subject to jealousy' or 'causing jealousy'. I am jealous of some; others are jealous of me. I can also see that there is no one who is an object of 'absolute jealousy'. Close scrutiny always shows me things in another person I do not want. Those who are jealous of me also would reject many things associated with me. Within the relative framework, jealousy is an illegitimate protest against the nature of apparent reality itself.

Jealousy, baseless as it is, nonetheless strikes at the heart of my deep dissatisfaction with myself, my desire to be different, to be full, to be complete. The undercurrent that always haunts me, the sense that I am lacking, the need for something to make me complete—all feed the fantasy of jealousy and give it great power to build up in my mind.

When the illegitimacy of jealousy has been seen, it will readily be susceptible to *pratipaksa bhavana*. If the skill or grace or accomplishment of another causes me a stab of *matsarya*, I deliberately think: "I am happy to see someone with such excellence. I am happy to see the happiness of this person. I admire the person. I appreciate the person". By deliberate *pratipaksa bhavana* thoughts, I nip jealousy in the bud.

Pratipaksa Bhavana: A Daily Act

Jealousy, resentment, selfishness and self-condemnation are only a few of the attitudes which can be handled by *pratipaksa bhavana*. Any attitude that settles in my mind which is opposed to peacefulness, accommodation, non-injury, non-pridefulness and similar values, can be neutralised by choosing to entertain the opposite point—'if view'. This should be done daily. *Pratipaksa bhavana* is a daily act for the mind, like bathing for the body. *Pratipaksa bhavana* thoughts at first may seem false but as they are deliberately done, day by day, they will become real and spontaneous. A mind kept clean in this manner will be a quiet and alert mind. A clean, quiet, alert mind is comfortable with itself and ready to learn, to be taught.

VALUE 8

"*STHAIRYAM*": Steadfastness

Sthairyath is *nistha*, 'firmness' or 'steadiness'. Derived from the Sanskrit root 'stha' to 'stand', *sthairyath* indicates constancy or perseverance. *Sthairyath* is:

Karma nistha, svadharma nistha

"Steadfastness in action; steadfastness in one's own duty."

A steady effort on one's part toward whatever goals one has committed oneself to achieve or toward whatever duties one's responsibilities impose upon one, is *sthairyath*.

When it comes to applying effort towards a goal, most of us find ourselves to be *arathbhasurah*, that is, 'heroes at the beginning'. We start any undertaking very bravely; we are lions of resolution at first, but then enthusiasm wanes. The energy of the 'heroic beginner' dwindles when the total effort required becomes clear. Then, some pretext is found to escape completion of the job. Lack of steadiness towards a commitment results in goals not being achieved. This brings a build-up of guilt over failure to complete what was started. *Sthairyam* means there should be steady effort towards whatever you have committed yourself to achieve until it is achieved; a steadiness that neither yields to laziness nor is disturbed by distraction.

In the context here, where Lord Krisna is talking about the values which make the mind ready to discover the truth of myself, the *sthairyath* highlighted is a *nistha* or firmness in seeking Self-knowledge. When my commitment is to achieve knowledge of the truth of myself, *sadhana nistha* steadiness in the means to accomplish this goal, is required. I must apply myself steadily to the secondary qualifications, such as certain attitudes, study of the language of the scriptures, and similar pursuits, which prepare my mind for Self-knowledge.

The knowledge of the Self is not a partial knowledge. It is not like the knowledge of a given discipline, but is something total, the total content of all knowledge. For this goal, in which all other goals resolve, total commitment is involved. In this total commitment, there must be *sthairyath*; steadiness must be there.

VALUE 9

"*Atmavinigraha*": Mastery over the Mind

Atmavinigraha means mastery over the mind, The Sanskrit word atma' basically is the name for whatever is meant by the first person singular 'I'. In this capacity, atma indicates many things which, depending upon the frame of reference, have a sense of 'I'. 'Atma' can be used for the physical body or it can refer to the vital functions of the body. Mind can be called atma or sometimes atma just stands for the 'ego' sense of the mind, the *ahankara*. Atma is also *saccidananda*, the timeless, limitless awareness that is the truth of 'I'. Less clearly but in a similar sense, the English word 'I', when analyzed, refers to various functions and assemblages, as well as to the ultimate content of 'I-ness', depending upon the speaker's context. "I am tired" is a body-I. "I am hungry" is a function-I. "I know this", "I am sad", "I have decided to do this", all are various activities of the mind-I. "I own it", "I did it", "I enjoy it", are all *ahankara*-I, the ego-I. The English 'I' can mean, when the speaker knows the nature of himself, the simple "I am" of *saccidananda*, the fullness that cannot be qualified. Here, in the context of Lord Krisna's instruction to Arjuna, atma simply means the mind or the *antahkarana*. *Vinigraha* means 'restraint' or 'curbing' which, in order to avoid any connotation of coercion or repression, is translated with reference to this value as 'mastery'. What is mastery of the mind? Is it checking or controlling the grey matter, the cells of the brain? No. That which must be mastered is not the brain. What must be mastered is one's ways of thinking. The mind is a colourful kaleidoscope of fanciful thoughts which come and go. Never constant, rarely still, subject to sudden starts and turns, capricious notions, the mind is whimsical by nature. But I, the thinker, need not fulfill the fancies, or yield to the caprices. Fancies and notions are many; that is the mind. But I am the sanctioning authority.

Even in relative terms the mind is not a definable entity but only a changing collection of thoughts shaped by several ways of thinking. In general, these ways of thinking will be of three types: impulsive, in which unexamined thoughts born of instinct hold sway; mechanical, in which prior conditioning is the dictator; and, deliberate, wherein my *buddhi*, the evaluating function of my mind, consciously examines my thoughts, accepting or dismissing them in accordance with my value structure.

There is a fourth way of thinking—spontaneous, in which my thoughts, without deliberation, conform to the highest universal values. Spontaneous thinking of this kind manifests at an absolute level only in one who has Self-knowledge. At a relative level, spontaneous thinking reflects the degree to which universal values have become my personal and assimilated values. In essence, spontaneous thinking is complete *atmavinigraha*. As preparation for Self-knowledge, we are concerned with relative *atmavinigraha*. *Atmavinigraha*, mastery over the ways of thinking, can be relative only because complete mastery requires knowledge of the Self. It is only knowledge of the Self that can completely destroy the hold of the likes and dislikes that compel and condition the ways of thinking. Thus, when Lord Krisna tells Arjuna that *atmavinigraha* is part of the *jnanam* preparatory for Self-knowledge, this qualification must be taken as relative. What is relative mastery? Complete mastery is characterized by spontaneity. If I am impulsive or conditioned, I am not a master. If I am deliberate, I am not a complete master. But through deliberateness I can be a relative master. Relative mastery is characterized by alertness and deliberateness. I have relative mastery over my way of thinking, when I rationally examine my thoughts and either consciously accept them or dismiss them. Relative mastery means both submitting all impulse to rational scrutiny, and breaking any habit of lapsing into the mechanical.

Sama, *dama*, and *samadhana* are Sanskrit terms often used to indicate different aspects of *atmavinigraha*. *Sama* is understood to mean discipline over thinking at the level where the thoughts arise, whereas, *dama* indicates choice exercised over thoughts and actions at the level of sense organ expression. *Samadhana* means *cittaikagrata* which literally indicates single pointedness of the mind, a metaphorical way to describe the capacity of the mind to stay with a given pursuit of thinking, a certain steadiness of thought of the mind. *Cittaikagrata* is the art of applying the mind consistently to a given pursuit for a length of time.

The exercise of choice at the level of *sama* and *dama* establishes an abiding mind capable of *samadhana*. The art of *samadhana*, or *cittaikagrata* can then be learned by beginning to apply the mind with a sharpened awareness for distractions. The whole of *atmavinigraha* is a matter of alertness and awareness. If I am alert and conscious of what my mind is doing, I always have choice over my way of thinking. With choice, I can change. I can conform my behaviour to values. With choice, I can learn from mistakes. With choice, I can hold to commitments in the face of distraction. Choice requires alertness which makes it possible for relative mastery over my way of thinking.

VALUE 10

"*Indriyarthesu vairagyam*": State of Dispassion Towards the Object of Sense Organs

Indriya means 'sense organs' and *artha*, stands for 'object'. *Vairagya* comes from *raga*, 'passion' or 'desire' joined to the negative prefix, *vai*, which turns the meaning into 'dispassion'. Thus *indriyarthesu vairagyam* means a 'state of dispassion towards the objects of sense organs' or 'the absence of a compelling drive for worldly pleasures and possessions'. *Raga* is more than just a fancy or preference; it is a craving for something. One who is free from such cravings is called a *vairagi* and his *bhava*—the state of his mind—is called *vairagyam*, dispassion, toward sense objects. What does dispassion mean? Does it mean putting a barrier between sense objects and me? Should I turn my head away, not look at or listen to when something is there that might fascinate me? No. Dispassion is not a state of inner suppression. It is a serene state of mind characterized by total objectivity towards the things of the world, the objects of the senses.

Dispassion is not suppression of desire. Dispassion and self-suppression are contradictory states of mind; they are mutually exclusive. Self-suppression is overpowering or crushing passion. In dispassion there is nothing that requires suppression. No compelling desires command the mind of the *vairagi*.

How can a mind be freed from compelling desires? How is a dispassionate disposition gained? Dispassion is gained by clearly seeing objects for just what they are; by seeing, without subjective distortion, just how objects relate to me, to my happiness and welfare.

Basically, a human being seems to find himself to be a wanting person. All my compelling desires turn upon this human sense of want. That I want to be a complete person and which, I am not, as I am, is the common human experience. Seeing myself as incomplete unfulfilled, inadequate, insecure, I try to bring completeness to myself by the pursuit of pleasure and the acquisition of things. I devote myself to two of the fundamental human pursuits—the struggle for *kama* and that for *artha*. *Kama* is the Sanskrit word which stands for all forms of sense pleasures. *Kama* indicates not just eating, but gourmet eating; not just drinking, but drinking as a compelling pleasure. *Artha* stands for all the things which I think will bring security in life to me: wealth, power, influence, fame and name.

As a human being, there will be no end to my longing and struggle for *artha* and *kama*, so long as I feel both insecure and incomplete and think that *artha* and *kama* can make me complete and end my insecurity. As long as I think that *artha* and *kama* have this capacity, I will not be able to gain *indriyarthesu vairagyam*, dispassion for sense objects. To become free from the compelling drive that is called raga, the desire for *artha* things, and *kama* pleasures, I must by analysis and discernment recognize that no number of things would ever make me secure nor could any amount of pleasure fill my sense of emptiness. I must discover that my struggle to fulfill my sense of want is endless. No accumulation of wealth is ever enough to silence the inner anxiety, no pleasure sufficient to bring lasting fulfillment.

Gain of any kind of wealth also involves loss. No gain I obtain through effort is ever absolute. Every such gain involves a concomitant loss: a loss through the expenditure of time and effort required; a loss through responsibility assumed; a loss through some other alternative abandoned. Gain involves loss. A lasting sense of security is never achieved through *artha*.

When I analyse pleasure I find the same result. Human struggle for pleasure does not produce lasting contentment. I, like other human beings, live in a private, subjective world where I see objects as desirable, undesirable or neutral (neither desired nor undesired). When I observe reflectively, I find that what I desire is not desired by me at all times and at all places; nor is what I desire necessarily desired by other persons. What I desire, what brings me pleasure, is subject to constant change. Moments of pleasure require the concurrent availability of three factors: availability of the object of pleasure; availability of the appropriate, effective instrument for enjoying the object; presence of the proper frame of mind for enjoying the object. Being dependent on these ever-changing factors, moments of pleasure are occasional and fleeting. Objects and instruments are bound by time. The mind is whimsical, subject to mood-change and finding monotony in what was formerly desirable.

Analysis of pleasure shows that pleasure, like possessions, fails me in my effort to find fullness and completeness. Pleasure proves to be momentary and capricious while possessions no matter how many, do not equate with security. My *raga*, my passionate desire for possessions and pleasure, is based upon my conviction that through the gain of *artha* and *kama*, my sense of want will end. When I clearly see that is not the case, that the best I can hope for in the aggregation of wealth is the exchange of one kind of anxiety for another; the most I can claim from pleasure is a collection of fleeting moments that are impossible to hold or predict. I am ready to discover in myself the state of *vairagya*, not from self-denial but from an understanding which loosens the hold of raga upon me. I see that objects, whether sought for pleasure or security, really cannot give me what I basically seek. For dispassion, this fact must be known by me. Objects are useful, but none of them can give me what I really want. I see that I cannot find complete or lasting security in wealth or power or fame, nor can I find lasting fullness in accumulated moments of pleasure.

When I don't place my security, my fullness, my happiness in these things, they gain an objective disposition for me. They become just objects for me, which I can assess for what they are rather than for what I subjectively expect from them. As simple objects they assume their proper position rather than answers to my most profound needs. I quit giving them an extra capacity which they do not have in reality. I see money as money, not as a guarantee against insecurity. I see a house as a house, not as a source of happiness. I see land as land, not as an extension of myself through possession.

I see these things as they are and do not give them any extra subjective value. When objects are stripped of the subjective values projected upon them by me (which they seem to have when I look at them as a source of happiness), I am objective about them. I am dispassionate. This is the mental state of *vairagya*.

Vairagya is an important value, one which must be understood correctly. Much nonsense is written about *vairagya*, leading to confusion. *Vairagya* is a state of mind brought about by understanding, not a state of mind compelled by a commitment to self-denial or deprivation. *Vairagya* is not born out of fear or teeth-clenched effort of the will but is born of sheer understanding. It is a knowledge produced by observation, inquiry and analysis. I look at what and why I desire and what I achieve through fulfillment of my desires. The understanding born of this analysis reduces the world to an objective fact for me, releases it from the tangle of my own subjectivity, the tangles of my *ragas* and *dvesas*, my likes and dislikes which bind me to situational happiness.

It is my subjective value for things which-makes a simple object into an object of special distinction, an object peculiarly important to me. By such objects I become bound. Why? The reason is I bind myself, not because the object binds me. No house binds me; I am bound to the house because of the subjective value I place on it, a subjective value based upon my failure to understand its inability ever to deliver what I expect from it. Things do not catch and hold me. I catch them. The handle is in myself, my subjective values based upon failure to understand the limitations of things to fulfill me. When I understand, the handle disappears and I see things as they are. That state of seeing is called *indriyarthesu vairdgyam*, dispassion toward sense objects.

VALUE 11

"*ANAHANKARA*": Absence of Self-Egotism

Ahankara is the Sanskrit word which indicates the conception of one's own individuality; that is, the individualized I-sense of 'I do', 'I own', 'I enjoy'. An is a prefix which negates the meaning of the word it precedes. Therefore, *anahankara* means 'absence of the sense of *ahankara*, freedom from an individualized I-identification.

Total nasa or destruction of *ahankara* means Self-knowledge. Only one who knows the truth of the Self is completely free from *ahankara*-identification with an individualized I. This meaning of *anahankara* (total destruction) cannot be intended by Lord Krisna because *anahankara* has been included here as one of the values which prepares the mind for gaining knowledge. Therefore, *anahankara*, absence of I-sense in this context is not being given its primary meaning of Self-knowledge but instead, has a relative meaning in which it is a preparatory means for knowledge.

What is meant by relative absence of *ahankara*? *Ahankara* is ego. How can you bring about relative absence of ego? By understanding what causes the presence of ego. Presence of ego is the result of sheer ignorance. Ego gains its status because I never think of examining its reality. The aggrandizement of ego comes about purely due to lack of thinking on my part. When I clearly, objectively examine the claims made by ego, it cannot but quietly deflate. No claim made by ego will hold. Neither to knowledge nor to ignorance, nor to power, possessions and accomplishments can a claim be established.

In a given lifetime, when the individualized sense of I begins in infancy, its essential characteristic is ignorance. Ignorance is the capital with which I, ego begins life. I maintain that capital and spend it very carefully throughout the years to come! Ignorance is not an ego inflator. Ignorance is not something to which I proudly lay claim. Knowledge, however, is another matter. I gladly claim title to knowledge. This is a spurious claim. Knowledge is not anything created by me, but only discovered in the wake of the loss of ignorance. Knowledge is always there. No one owns or creates knowledge. To be knowledgeable is only a matter of shedding ignorance. I can never be the author of knowledge. Nor can I assign to *ahankara* personal credit for skill or speed in shedding ignorance.

When this individualized sense of I comes to self-consciousness, it is endowed with a certain kind of physical body, born into a particular set of circumstances or environment. Both these preset factors condition the learning opportunities. Parents, teachers, neighbours, schools, various experiences, all contribute to removal of my ignorance. *Ahankara*, ego, does not create the people or circumstances but claims the result.

Ahankara (ego) and *manitvam* (pride) are closely related. These are two almost synonymous effects born of the same cause, that is ignorance of the relationship of the individualized sense of I with the world. We previously saw when *manitvam* was examined, that pride in anything is a logical absurdity. Although, I am graced by free will and have the power to choose my actions, I have no power over the actual result of the action chosen. The result I anticipate can never be more than a probability among possibilities. I do not produce the result. The result of any act of mine occurs both as the product of materials which I have not authored, and as the outcome of many circumstances, past and present, known and unknown, which must operate in concert for the given result to occur.

If my strong skilful arm throws the winning pass in the final seconds of an American football game, the material and circumstantial factors that come together to produce this are too many for the final result to be a matter for personal pride. I am creator neither of football itself nor of my athletic body. Many people and experiences contributed to the development of the skill in the arm that threw the football. I am not responsible for the clearing of the rainstorm so the game did not have to be cancelled, or for the sharp earth tremor that occurred 60 seconds after my pass—a minute earlier, my pass would have been spoiled. Nor can I claim credit for my colleague who caught the pass to convert the possibility into the winning goal.

Pride and ego, when examined, become so silly that humility really cannot be considered a virtue. Humility is simply the understanding of the world, including myself, because I am part of the world, just as it is. When I understand things as they are, I will be neither proud nor will I be self-condemning. Self-condemnation also is an expression of *ahankara* ego.

We have already seen that self-condemnation is *antara asaucam*, an impurity in the mind, to be cleaned by understanding that there is no locus for condemnation other than a particular thought.

In correct understanding of myself and my relationship to the world there is no room for either pride or self-condemnation. I see the world—me included—as it is. The world is filled with wonderful opportunities; therefore, I make use of these opportunities as a source of learning, I make use of this vehicle, the body-mind, etc., to the best of my ability. It is my means of shedding ignorance. I see that personal credit for anything is irrelevant and cannot be substantiated. I simply enjoy the world as a field for the discovery of knowledge, without pride, without egotism. This is the attitude of *anahankara*.

VALUE 12

"*JANMAMRITYUJIMAVyadhiDuhkhaDOSANUDARSANAM*": Repeated Review of Process of Life-Death-Ageing-Ailments-Pain

This long word, *janma-mrityujara-vyadhi-duhkha-dosa-anudarsanam* is a Sanskrit compound noun which stands for a certain rigorously objective attitude toward life. *Anu*, the next to the last word of the compound, means 'repetitively', or 'again and again'. *Anu* is prefixed to *darsanam*, a beautiful word which means 'seeing'. 'Seeing' also indicates ' knowing'; when I see, I know CI see the solution' means 'I know the solution').

What is *anudarsanam*, 'seeing again-and-again' that Lord Krisna is talking about? It is the seeing of the *dosa*, the 'faults' or 'defects', in life itself, from birth to death.

Life begins with birth, *janma*. Along with *janma* comes *mrityu*, death, the inseparable mirror-twin of birth. There is no birth that does not bring death along with it. Everything that begins ends. What is born dies. While you are busy doing things, death is there patiently waiting. 'All right, let him be busy', it says, but when it thinks you have played enough, it comes. *Janma-mrityu*—they are but the opposite sides of a single coin.

In between *janma* and *mrityu* there are other *dosa* to see. What are they? *Jara*, old age. You may still be very young or perhaps strong and vigorous in your middle years but one thing you can count upon; if *mrityu*, death, sufficiently spares you, *jara* will come. The longer you elude *mrityu*, the more certainly a time will come when your hearing will grow dull, your vision will grow dim, your steps will be unsteady, you may be uncomfortable while sitting, you may be uncomfortable while lying down. It is old age, *jara*, and it is always around the corner.

"Well and good," you may say, "so death and old age are *dosa*, limitations that come with birth, *janma*. I will try to remember them once in a while, but both are a long time away for me. I am young and healthy. There is a lot of life to enjoy before *jara* and *mrityu* draw close to me."

Young you may be, but youth is no escape from all the *dosa* of life. Two others, *vyadhi* and *duhkha*, will introduce themselves to you in infancy, perhaps even before birth. *Vyadhi* means disease; *duhkha* means pain. *Vyadhi*, disease, is something that goes with you all the time. Even before birth it is there. Sometimes it shows up, sometimes it does not, but it is always there—a shadow in your life. All may be bright and beautiful today. Three days from now you may be too sick to eat, too weak to move. You may be a champion athlete now only to be a chronic invalid with a lingering illness by this time next year. Disease can come any time, any place. It is not limited to a particular time or age.

Similarly, *duhkha*, pain, is a life-long companion. *Duhkha* means all forms of pain. It can be physical or mental, large or small, from the bite of a mosquito to the grief over loss of a loved one. Pain, like disease, cannot be avoided. Careful as you may be, pain will catch up with you. A truck driving on the wayside of the street may send you to hospital or, in California the earth rumbles beneath your feet, shaking down the house to which you are so attached and giving you a bump on your head, for good measure. This is called *duhkha*, pain. Pain of various kinds comes in a variety of ways.

Pain or troubles coming from the inside are *adhyatmika*, from the outside *adhibhautika*, and from a heavenly source *adhidaivika*. *Adhyatmika duhkha* or internal pain comprises the aches and pains and troubles of my own individualized person. *Adhibhautika duhkha*, which is external pain, is made up of the problems of the world around me like the smoke in the air, the blast of my neighbour's radio, the furnace that fails on a cold day. *Adhidaivika duhkha* is the painful result of an event over which there is no control whatsoever like a tidal wave or an erupting volcano.

Thus, we see *dosa* as the faultiness in life. With birth, certain defects come like death, old age, disease and pain of all kinds. There is no escape from them. Therefore, bear in mind the nature of life. It is uncertain, painful and swiftly moving towards old age and death. Keep your mind on your purpose in life. Don't fritter it away. Remember time, kala, is the devourer of the world: *kalo jagadbhaksakah*.

Thus, Lord Krisna says to Arjuna: *Janma-mrityu jara-vyadhi-duhkha-dosa-anudarsanam*. This is an important value. It is not negative but simply factual. Its purpose is to direct your attention to the need to see life objectively just as it is, so that you will be able to make use of the time that is available in your hands right now. Available time is precious time. Make use of it, consciously, alertly. Use your time consciously for your activities and pursuits—working, playing, sleeping, eating, relaxing, walking. Make use of time consciously and then you won't find one day, that time has passed over you and suddenly you are old. If you make use of time alertly, consciously, you are a Swami of time, a master of time.

VALUE 13

"*ASAKTI*": Non-Attachment

Sakti means clinging attachment to things. This attitude of 'holding fast' to things underlies the notion of ownership. *Asakti* means absence of the attitude of ownership, absence of the attitude that anything particularly belongs to me. Ownership is notional; possession is factual. *Asakti* is reduction of all false relationships involving claims of ownership to factual relationships.

Analysis shows that no claim to ownership can survive close scrutiny. Nothing is really mine. I cannot claim exclusive, permanent title to anything—not to land, to knowledge, to people, to things, or even to my own body-mind unit. When I analyse anything that I think I own, I find that there is nothing to own. Take the house where I live. That I possess the house is a fact. Physically I am present there in my person and use my property. But whether or not I am the 'owner' of the house depends not upon the physical fact of my presence there but upon a consensus of notions about my relationship to the particular property. To see how notional ownership is, consider this situation:

A friend of yours, who owns a nice house with a large compound, decides to go to the United States to expand his career opportunities. He asks you to "house-sit" for him while he is gone. You will live in the house and protect it from vandals. He will not charge you rent, but you are expected to do ordinary maintenance and pay the insurance and taxes while you live there. Since this is a very good deal for such a fine house you quickly accept. Your friend, who does very well in the States, postpones his return home to reclaim his property, from year to year. One day while you are at work you receive an overseas telephone call from your friend. He is jubilant. He has struck it rich in a mining syndicate and is settling abroad permanently. In a magnanimous gesture, he makes a gift of the house to you. You now possess it. He has already instructed his lawyer to prepare and record a deed.

That night when you go home, nothing physical, nothing tangible, would have changed about you and the house. You still live there as you have for the past five years. You intend to continue living there. You have been paying for the maintenance, taxes and insurance. You will continue to do so. You don't intend to sell the house. There has been no material change, but now you are 'owner' of the house, and your whole attitude towards it has changed. You call a real estate broker to see how much it is worth. You decide to put up a fence. You inquire about the zoning laws. You go across the street to get a better perspective and look at the house with a proprietary feeling. No fact has changed. You haven't even received the deed yet. But your attitude has changed. It is now 'your' house. You now consider yourself the 'owner' which gives that property a special hold upon you.

That 'ownership' is purely notional is even more clearly seen in the case of flats or modem condominiums. A few years ago a young friend told me that he had bought a new place in Mumbai, which he invited me to see. When we arrived at his house, I found myself looking at a seven-storey structure. Since this young man has a relatively modest position I was surprised. "You bought this?" I said. "Not all of it," he laughed, "I own a flat on the third floor." So we went to the third floor and he ushered me in, saying, "This is mine. This is the flat I own."

This was the first time I had heard of such an arrangement, so I was still puzzled. "Do you own the land?" I asked. "No" he said, and explained that a co-operative management society owned the land. All he owned was one rather small flat-two rooms and a kitchen. So I asked:

"What is it you own of this flat? Do you own the floor?"

"No. My floor is the ceiling of the fellow downstairs."

"Do you own the ceiling?"

"No, the ceiling is the floor for the family upstairs."

"How about the walls?"

"Well, the inner walls are shared with other flats. The outer wall, of course, belongs to the whole building as part of its structural support."

"So what do you own?"

"Well, Swami, I own the space."

So now you can see the nature of ownership! A claim of ownership is always connected with something over which the most I can assert, actually, is a temporary possession or control. Even my right to sell that which I 'own' is a possessing right, nothing more. I can transfer my possession or control of something to another for which I receive certain money. This is but the transfer of possession. For me to claim an ownership, which factually is more than a temporary possession, I would have to be the sole, absolute author of the owned object. Otherwise many before me as well as those who come after me will also be able to claim rights on the object, thus reducing my factual status to its temporary possessor or controller.

As we have seen before, I cannot claim to be the sole author of anything. The land my house stands on was not created by me. The materials which went into the house were not made by me. Fire and water were needed. The work of many other people went into the house: masons, carpenters, electricians and plumbers. Conformity to certain physical laws, not my creation, made possible the assurance that the walls will stand.

Thus, my house, which is made up of the materials available in an existent creation, as assembled by or in accordance with the knowledge of countless human beings unknown to me (some long dead), is simply an aggregate structure available for my temporary possession and control.

That is well and good, you may say, for a tangible object external to me, like a house. But there is something uniquely and specially mine, for which I certainly can claim factual ownership. That unique thing is my own body. Who else can claim my body?

Many others can make claims over any given body. The mother can say, "I bore this body. It is flesh of my flesh. It is mine, not separate from me!"

"No!" says the father. "I am the *nimitta karana*, the instrumental cause of this body. I was involved in its creation. Not only did I provide all the food necessary for this body to grow but the clothes and shelter also to protect it!"

Society can say that the community has a claim to the body. Collectively the efforts of many have made available the things necessary for this body to be nurtured and have provided a society in which it can live. A spouse can say, "This body belongs to me, a partner in marriage. We are two halves of a single marriage unit. I too have a claim." A child born to the marriage also will assert a claim, "This body has a duty to me to stay alive and perform work so I will be cared for while my body grows up."

Hence the list of the people, the creatures, the materials and substances that can claim rights to this body is endless. The family, the employer, the state, water, space, fire, air, goats, cows, sheep, grains, grass, fruits and vegetables, earth and sun, not to mention worms, mosquitoes, bugs and bacteria all can claim their rights! The vulture says: "Some day soon that body is going to be my dinner." "Oh, no," says the virus, "for generations it has been my home."

Thus, even for my own body, I am nothing more than a managing trustee. I am the dweller of this body. It is in my possession. As possessor I can say, 'my body', but only in terms of possession, definitely not in terms of ownership. Even the laws of the state recognize that bodies are entrusted. State laws prohibit suicide, reflecting the recognition that a body is a thing entrusted to the possession of a person but which the person has no right to kill. He has the right to maintain it but not to destroy it, a possessive right only to make use of it.

A possessory attitude rather than an ownership attitude toward anything is a relief whether it is towards house, money or one's own body. A possessory attitude puts the relationship with the thing claimed in factual perspective, which promotes dispassion and objectivity. The relationship is seen for what it is—non-exclusive, impermanent but at the same time a presently existing entrustment of possession to be enjoyed and properly maintained. This is the right attitude towards my mind, towards any wealth I may have, towards the people around me. To all of them I relate myself with *asakti*, with no clinging attachment, no attitude of ownership. I recognize ownership as purely notional; that possession alone is factual. I reduce all my false notional ownership relationships to factual relationships.

Asakti, non-attachment in the sense of seeing one's relationship to things objectively, is another example of *vairagya*, dispassion. Previously, in *indriyarthesu vairagyam* we saw dispassion toward sense objects highlighted. One gains dispassion toward sense objects when one recognises that sense objects do not have the capacity to produce lasting happiness or security. In *asakti* the dispassion highlighted is towards the relationship between oneself and things. It is the dispassion discovered when one sees clearly that there can be no valid nor lasting 'attachment' to anything; that is, there is no valid 'ownership' of anything.

VALUE 14

"*Anabhisvanga PUTRADARAGRHADISU*": Non-Excessive Attachment towards Son and Wife

Abhisvanga is the kind of intense attachment or affection one feels for what is particularly beloved such as *putra*, a son, *dara*, one's wife, or *grha* one's house, and *adi*, all other similar people and things usually very dear. *Abhisvanga* can be defined as *atisneha*. *Sneha* has the literal meaning of thick and sticky oil and the figurative meaning of affection. A ti means excessive. So *abhisvanga* is *atisneha*, or an excessive, sticky affection. An added particle makes the word negative. So, here *anabhisvanga* means absence of an obsessive, sticky attachment for those certain people or things generally considered very dear, *putradaragrhadisu*.

Essentially, *anabhisvanga*, in the sense here of *jnani* a value, means 'dispassionate caring'. Lord Krisna is not counselling abandonment of care or affection for family but is calling for objectivity in that caring. In the discussion of the attitude of *asakti*, absence of the notion of ownership, we saw that one cannot have a special, total claim on any person or thing. In the understanding born of *Asakti*, freedom from ownership, one will have *anabhisvanga*, lack of excessive attachment towards family, but no lack of dispassionate care and affection.

VALUE 15

"*NITYAM SAMRCITTAIVAM* Istanistopapattisu": Steadfastness of Mind

Samacittatvam istanistopapattisu simply means that one greets with 'sameness of mind' the results one likes as also the results one does not like. *Sama* means 'equal'. *Cittatvath* means 'state of mind'. *Istanistopapattisu* indicates the happening of something considered desirable or undesirable.

So, here Lord Krisna is telling Arjuna: *Nitya*, always, maintain *samacittatvath*, sameness of mind in the face of the desirable or the undesirable. Neither get elated over getting what you want nor feel dejected when you get what you do not want. Accept results as they come, factually. If an accident occurs, assess the situation with a level mind and quietly do what is required. If some venture fails, look at the facts, learn from them if you can, and do whatever is now needed. View all situations as they occur, factually, with a mind unshaken by emotional intensity—a mind that simply decides what is to be done and directs the doing of it.

When something happens that you like, don't get elated. A mind that reaches ecstasy over getting what it thinks it wants will also hit the bottom when loss or failure occurs. *Samacittatvath* is the state of mind which does not swing between elation and depression, but remains in equilibrium regardless of the situation, whether it is successful, unsuccessful, joyful, sorrowful, conducive, non-conducive.

When I face every situation with a mind which neither gets elated nor depressed, I will meet the situation objectively. The attitude of *samacittatvath* is another example of reducing subjective response to factual acceptance. More often than not, we resist accepting facts. When we refuse to accept facts, facts become problems. When we hear an unpleasant or sad news, our first response usually is outright rejection of it, either by exclaiming: "Oh, no!" or by the question "What?", a question to delay acceptance.

The following response which is attributed to a great stoic philosopher upon hearing tragic news shows reduction of facts to facts.

The philosopher who was waiting for the news of the safe arrival of a large sailing ship carrying his wife and children and all his wealth aboard, answered a knock on his door. He found a breathless messenger who announced:

"Sir, the ship carrying your wife and money has sunk!"

"What?"

"The ship has sunk!"

"So what?"

"Sir, you have lost all your wealth."

"What?"

"Your fortune is gone."

"So what?"

"Sir, nothing was salvaged; you are penniless!"

"What?"

"You are a pauper!"

"So what?"

"Sir, no one survived. You have lost your wife and children."

"What?"

"You are a childless widower".

"So what?"

When the philosopher said "What?" each time, it was not because he had not heard the words nor because he failed to understand the sentence. He had heard and he had understood, but he said "What?" because at first he refused to accept the sense of it. Since the sense was not acceptable, he said, "What?", not to the messenger really, but to himself. It was because of his initial refusal to accept the particular fact each time that made him first say "What?" But, being a philosopher, he did not hang on to non-acceptance.

"The ship is sunk, so what? There is nothing I can do about it. I am a pauper. Well, so what? I am penniless. I made money, lost it. Now I will work to make it again. My wife and children are gone. Grief and despair won't bring them back. They are gone. So what? That is a fact. I am here. That is a fact. I assimilate the facts and do what is required of me under the circumstances." There are pleasant facts and unpleasant facts. There are comfortable facts and uncomfortable facts. All the time the facts keep changing, now pleasant, now not so pleasant; now comfortable, now uncomfortable. The weather is too hot; the weather is just right; the weather is too cold. I feel healthy; I've come down with the flu. Each day brings facts of various kinds. My job is to greet all the facts with sameness of mind. I accept and enjoy the comfortable facts for what they are, the facts of the moment. Similarly, I accept without reaction the uncomfortable facts for what they are. I simply do whatever the situation calls for. If I can make an uncomfortable fact more comfortable, I do so. If I cannot, I accept and do whatever is required.

The factual response is the approach to situations of a truly practical person. One is most practical when one sees situations objectively. This is real human strength. Human strength is not found in powerful miracles but in the quiet mind of the one who faces situations as they are. Such a one is a strong person. Human weakness is the inability to accept situations, or face facts. Human strength is the strength of reducing situations to simple facts. When I strip away all my subjective projections from the facts of each situation, I will have sameness of mind in every situation. It is not the fact itself but my likes or dislikes projected onto the fact that causes my mind to react. As I reduce situations to facts without projection of my emotional reactions upon them, my mind assumes a poise that makes it easier to appreciate the vision of Vedanta. A relatively poised mind that is not muddled by projections upon itself and external situations, is necessary to appreciate the teachings of Vedanta which deals with the nature of 'facts'. Vedanta reveals the reality of the 'facts' of the objective world to be but *mithya*, 'apparent'. However, for the mind to be ready to see the 'apparentness' of that which is 'objective' (and to be ready to discover what it really is seeking is non-objectifiable, non-negatable reality), it must first strip its own subjectivity from objective reality. When I am projecting my own subjective reality based upon my likes and dislikes upon the facts of the objective world, I will be too muddled to see the truth found in the teachings of Vedanta. And it is this truth that distinguishes the apparently real and unfolds the nature of Reality itself.

A mind that is ready for the teaching of Vedanta is a mind which sees an objective fact objectively. It is a mind which does not convert a fact into a subjective problem but meets each situation with sameness of attitude, with a mental poise free from complaint. Such a mind, without subjective reaction, simply, quietly determines what needs to be done in a particular situation.

VALUE 16

"MAW CA ANANYA YOGENA BHAHTIH A VYABHICARINI": Steady Devotion towards Righteousness and God

This expresses the value of steadfast devotion to the Lord, *Paramesvara*, a devotion characterized by non-separateness from the Lord. Lord Krisna, identifying himself as the Lord, *Paramesvara*, describes the value *avyabhicarini*—non-swerving, bhaktih—devotion, *ananyayogena*—by non-combination with any other, mayi¬in me. This means a steady, unswerving devotion, due to the recognition of my non-separateness from the Lord.

Non-separateness from the Lord can be seen in two ways. In the first way, *ananyayoga*, non-separateness means: *Paramesvara thattah anyahna*, The Lord is not separate from me. This is a view which comes when I know the truth of the Lord, myself, and of creation. From this knowledge I can see that the Lord is never away from me. He is always around me; He is in me; He is outside me; He is indeed me; I am never away from the Lord; I am indeed non-separate from Him. In the second way, we can say that non-separateness is in terms of seeing the Lord as my refuge: *Paramesvara*t *anyah mama spranam nasti*, for me there is no refuge other than *Paramesvara*. The Lord is everything; He is my security; He is the source of my inspiration; by His laws come the results of my acts; He is the *karmaphaladata*, the giver of the fruits of all actions.

Devotion based on the second way of looking at the Lord is very helpful in preparing my mind for Self-knowledge in which I will see my total non-separateness from Him. It is through devotion to the Lord as *karmaphaladata*, the one who gives the results of action, that

I can maintain that poise of mind called *samacittatvath* described earlier. There it was said that *samacittatvath*, sameness of mind in the face of desirable or undesirable results, is made possible by reducing all situations to facts. Easy to say, but how do I bring about a factual attitude toward all that comes my way? This factual attitude, *samacittatvath* will come when I view all results as coming to me directly from the hands of the Lord.

Being human, my behaviour is not tightly pre-programmed by my instincts. Freedom of choice over actions has been given to me. But the results of my actions are not something which I can choose. The results come from the Lord. I can choose to act, but once I have acted, I have no further choice. I cannot prevent the result from occurring once the act is done, and that result may or may not be the result I expected or wanted.

The result of any action is always appropriate to the action, that is, the result is in accordance with the laws of the Lord, but those laws are not all known to me. The result is shaped by many laws—known laws, unknown laws, visible laws, invisible laws. I can have no knowledge or control over all the factors involved in producing a result. The actual result is always taken care of by the interplay of all the appropriate natural laws of creation. Therefore any result really comes from the Creator, the Lord.

When I view all results from my own actions or from the actions of others—as from the Lord—I can have sameness of mind towards the results. Whatever happens, I will see it as *prasada*, a blessing given to me from the Lord's hand. *Prasada* distributed from the altar is always acceptable, whatever it may be. I don't question it. Why? Because it comes from *Paramesvara*. I accept *Paramesvara* as the *karmaphaladata*. He never fails nor do His laws ever fail. Therefore, towards the operation of His laws I have an attitude of *prasada*. This graceful acceptance of whatever comes to me from the Lord is called *prasada buddhi*. There is no regret; there is no failure; there is no elation; there is no depression. The attitude is simply grateful, graceful acceptance.

Prasada buddhi, the graceful acceptance of all results brings *nityam samacittatvam*, sameness of the mind in the face of the desirable or the undesirable. Thus *nityam samacittatvam* is the result of the more basic attitude of *prasada buddhi* which itself is grounded in a steadfast devotion to the Lord. That is, seeing the Lord as the giver of the results of all actions.

If there is *mayi ananyayogena avyabhicarini bhaktih* unswerving devotion to Me (the Lord) through (seeing) nothing other than Me (the Lord) as the giver of results, there naturally will be *nityath ca samacittatvam istanistopapattisu*, sameness of mind for desirable and undesirable results. This kind of devotion frees one from any kind of reaction. One simply sees things just as they are, as simple facts. Facts become problems only because I refuse to accept them. I refuse to accept facts because I had wanted them to be different. But if, when the facts arrive, when expectation turns into result, I take that result as *prasada*, there will be no refusal of acceptance.

When we accept facts we can learn from them. Experience is a good teacher for the person with a mind clear of reactions, a mind attentive and available to be taught. But a reaction to facts interferes with learning. A reaction is a resistance to facts as they are, a resistance that comes without sanction of will or wisdom. When my attitude toward facts is built upon whether I like them or not, I will always be subject to mindless reactions in which all my wisdom and poise of mind will vanish. I cannot programme the laws of creation to tailor the ever changing situations to the measure of my shifting likes and dislikes. I can only, through devotion to the Creator, gracefully accept situations with an attitude of interest and wonder, as the environment provided by His hand for my cheerful discharge of duty. Perhaps in some cases, I can learn to be wiser in the future.

So when I have the attitude of *ananyayogena bhaktih*, non-separate devotion toward the Lord, my standpoint toward myself, toward my actions and the results that come, will be a factual attitude. I will see that as a human being enjoying free will, I can choose to act or not to act, but the results of my actions are not subject to my choice. This understanding will free me to review the results factually and choose further actions rationally.

However, when my attitude is that

(i) I am the cause of the results of my actions, and that

(ii) the acceptability of the results of my actions is determined by what I like and what I dislike.

I will have a frame of mind which responds to the world with reaction and not action. A mind in the grip of reactions loses its freedom of will to act.

A reaction to a situation is an automatic response not preceded by a thoughtful decision. Automatic responses occur sometimes from a thoughtless surrender to impulses, but more often a reaction is born of mental habits based on likes and dislikes. When I always respond to a situation in a manner determined by my likes and dislikes, there will be consistent reaction. My responses will be mechanical. I will have no control over them. When my 'actions' are really reactions, my mind will be troubled. Experience will not teach me; conflicts between thought and deed will bother me; painful emotions will build up; mood will be my master. A mind graced by devotion which sees the Lord as the giver of all the results of action will have few reactions. This is because it knows human freedom of will is given to choose actions not their results. Results come from the Lord in accordance with His laws, and because results come from Him, there is never a wrong result nor a result which one does not accept. One accepts, cheerfully, and with even mind, what comes from His hand. Such a mind, free from reactions is quiet and receptive. It can deal with negative emotions and is master over its mood. Objective and serene, a mind like this is ready to discover the fact of *ananyayoga*—the fact of one's non-separateness from the Lord and creation.

VALUE 17

"*Vivikta desa sevitvam* Love for Spending Time in Solitary

Vivikta desa sevitvam is 'love for a quiet place'. *Desa* is 'place'. *Vivikta* means 'separate' or 'solitary'. *Sevitvath* is 'inhabiting' or 'resorting to'. So, *vivikta desa sevitvam* is a value for resorting to a secluded place.

Why should love for spending time in a solitary place be listed as a value? It is not the separateness of the place that makes the value. The valuable thing is the kind of mind which is happy in such a place. A mind that appreciates quiet and solitude is a mind that has a love for being with itself. This is a beautiful attitude which is not found very often in our society. We are a society of people bent on escaping from ourselves. We try to escape because we are not satisfied with ourselves. We see ourselves as not being the way we would like to be. Therefore, we keep the mind busy so that there is no time, place or quiet in which we can be with ourselves. Even on the telephone, if there must be a waiting period, music will often be provided so the mind can be occupied!

We travel to escape from beach to mountain, sand to snow, and back again to escape from ourselves. Wanderlust is a good expression for this urge to travel. For the stay-at-home, amusement parks, movies, television, sporting events, magazines, newspapers, gala parties, etc. become the means for escape. It is not that there is anything wrong with travel or recreation; the problem is the need for escape. For some the avenue of escape may be drugs or gambling or drinking. Whether harmful or seemingly benign, the need to escape betrays reluctance on one's part to face oneself.

You can tell that activities have become an escape for you when, without the activity, you feel lost, sad, or incomplete. That occupation, which leaves you feeling incomplete when you cannot have it, becomes an escape. A given activity by itself is neither an escape nor a non-escape. It is the reason behind the activity that makes it an escape. A happy person will sing because he has nothing else to do. That is no escape. But the escaping person also will sing because there is something he cannot face, and singing occupies his mind so he does not have to look at the problem. Singing or listening to music can be either an escape or a non-escape. When people become agitated, if there are people who can sing, you will find they will begin whistling, humming or singing because they want to shake off certain thoughts. In fact, what they want to shake off is their reactions to an unwelcome thought. They think of some event sad to them or some mistake they feel they have committed; then, immediately, a whistle will start or a song will come out. This is not the song of a happy person but the song of escape. This tendency of the mind to want to escape is a universal thing. Everywhere in the world, the human mind is the same. Whether Indian or American or European, the basic mental tendencies will be the same. Cultural differences are found only in the response to these basic, universal tendencies. From culture to culture the avenues of escape will be different, determined by the nature of the society in which one finds oneself. Social factors will determine the way of escape. But the desire of the mind to escape is a universal thing. A person who enjoys being with himself in quietude is not a sad person. He is a simple, quiet, contemplative person. To be contemplative means to be able to face yourself happily. If you cannot face yourself happily, the mind will always require an escape. An escape is an occupation that engages the attention of the mind so that it does not have to be with itself.

For the one who wants Self-knowledge, it is very important to have a value for being with oneself, for quietude. This value, *vivikta desa sevitvam*, is mentioned more than once by Lord Krisna in his counsel to Arjuna. In the sixth chapter of the Gita, talking about meditation, Lord Krisna tells Arjuna

Yogi yunjita satatam atmanam rahasi sthitah, ekaki

"The yogi should dwell constantly on the Self, established in solitude, alone ..."

(*Bhagavad Gita*, Chapter VI, Verse 10)

So, I learn to be with myself by willingly taking myself to a quiet place where I take stock of myself and learn to love and accept myself. When you have the habit of repairing to a quiet place, you are learning to be with yourself. When you have learned to be with yourself, you have come to terms with yourself. Clear knowledge of yourself is now possible.

VALUE 18

"*Aratih janasamsadi*": Non-Inclination towards People and Company

Ratih means 'love for something' or 'inclination towards something'. Adding a to *ratih* makes the word indicate a lack of inclination towards something. *Jana* stands for 'people' male or female, and *samsadi* means in 'assembly' or 'collection'. So this value means a lack of craving for company, not revelling in company, not courting company.

This is not a value that calls for hatred of company. Company is not bad. It is not that one should dislike being around people. If the people are there, fine, be happy in their presence. But know that you do not require people to be happy. *Vivikta desa sevitvath*, love of quietude in which one happily is with oneself, and *aratih janasamsadi*, non-revelling in the presence of company, are companion values. They complement each other. It is not that a quiet place in itself is intrinsically something good, or that the presence of company is something bad. But the values are for a happy, non-escaping mind that loves being with itself. Such a mind is happy with itself in quietude and does not run after escape. It neither revels in nor hates company. These are two beautiful attitudes. With these values, I will never need to seek escape from being with myself, nor will I be disturbed either by the presence or absence of people. I will have composure whether I am with people or without them.

It is important to see the basis of these attitudes, to see through the values to the value underneath them. *Aratih janasamsadi* is not a value for avoiding people; nor is *vivikta desa sevitvam* a value for seeking quietude because one cannot stand people. Someone who seeks seclusion out of hatred of people is not expressing these values. Such a person is afraid of people. This fear of people is not a desirable thing in life. But the other extreme, courting the company of people all the time, trying to escape from oneself, is not any more desirable than the fear of people.

So an attitude that is desired is not hatred of people but a simple love of quietude. That is, because I love to be with myself I do not court company. This attitude establishes the right frame for a contemplative mind—for a mind given to *vicara*, inquiry. *Vicara*, inquiry, here means inquiry into the basic, profound questions about myself. Who am I? What is this creation? Who is God? What is the relationship between me, God and the creation?

Vicara, inquiry into these subtle questions, requires special sensitivity of the mind. A sensitivity beyond what is needed to inquire into the functioning or description of tangible like objects or processes. *Vicara* into something tangible like how to make bread, or even the grammar of a language is aided by having changing objects to see, to watch. One can see the *vikara* (modifications) taking place upon things, whether in a pan of dough or upon the stems of nouns and verbs.

But when the *vicara* is inquiry into the Self, we are dealing with something which, although fundamental, is not tangible. Self is not a tangible object which lends itself to trial and error methods, checked by gross perceptions. The knowledge of the Self must be seen as a whole. To appreciate the knowledge of the Self, to see the Self for the non-objectifiable wholeness which it is, requires a mind that is contemplative and sensitive.

The mind should be highly sensitive, but not the sensitivity characterized by getting hurt at every turn. How can the mind be highly sensitive and still not get hurt? The values already discussed have shown the way to sensitivity without hurt. Values come when I thoroughly understand my relationship to people, places and things around me. In that factual understanding, those situations, attitudes or events which I consider 'hurtful' lose their significance for me and thereby their 'sting'. Pride and pretence, which court hurt, drop away from me; and non-harmfulness and accommodation, which soften hurt, become natural for me. The mind that does not get hurt is an undisturbed, non-reacting, fresh and simple mind, a contemplative mind that can appreciate the whole as it unfolds in the teaching of Self-knowledge. *Vivikta desa sevitvath*, resorting to a quiet place, and *aratih janasamsadi*, absence of the need for company, are attitudes which establish such a contemplative mind, a mind ready for a contemplative life centered on Self-knowledge.

VALUE 19

"*TATTVAJNANARTHADARSANAM*": Keeping in View the Purpose of the Knowledge of Truth

Tattva means 'truth' ,'truth' in the sense of the irreducible reality of anything and everything. *Jnanam* is 'knowledge'. Artha means 'purpose' or 'end' in the sense of a goal. *Darsanam* is 'sight' or 'vision'. So *tattvajnanarthadarsanam* is 'keeping in view the purpose of the knowledge of Truth'. *Tattvajnanam* (knowledge of Truth) is the *jneyam* (the 'thing-to-be-known') in life for which the values called *jnanarth* prepare the mind.

Jnanam, as used here in the compound *tattvajnanam*, does not indicate the *jnanam* about which Arjuna inquired at the beginning of the chapter when he asked: What is *jnanath*? What is *jneyath*? There, *jnanath* indicated all the attitudes in whose presence the mind becomes the right receptacle for *jneyath*, the thing-to¬be-known. Here *Jnanath* in *tattvajnanam*, means the thing-to-be-known, i.e., the sought-for-knowledge, not a preparatory attitude.

So, what is the basic thing to be known in life? The basic knowledge to be discovered in life is the knowledge of what is real, what is fundamental. What is sought is the knowledge of the Truth, or the fundamental nature of oneself, the creation and the Creator. This knowledge of the Truth of what is—the Truth of everything—is the meaning of *tattvajnanam*. The basic knowledge of the Truth can also be called the knowledge of the Self, *atmajnanam*, because, upon inquiry, the irreducible reality of oneself turns out to be not different from the irreducible reality of God and creation. In fact, this value can be described as not losing sight of Self-knowledge as one's primary goal. It also means having an overwhelming value for that goal so that it does not become eclipsed by other goals but remains always in one's mind as the primary purpose in life, the recognised end behind all other ends that may be sought.

Self-Knowledge: What Purpose?

To discover within oneself an overwhelming value for 'keeping in view the goal of Self-knowledge', one needs to know: What does one gain from Self-knowledge? What, precisely, is the purpose served by Self-knowledge?

All human purposefulness can be classified under four headings. The collective Sanskrit name for these four headings is *purusartha* (from *purusa*, 'human being', and *artha*, 'purpose', 'that for which a human being longs and struggles'). The fourfold human aims *purusartha* in life are:

Dharma (ethical standards): the goal of conforming one's behaviour to scripturally sanctioned ethical norms in order to obtain merit or avoid demerit in this life or the next. Or, for the one who is not adherent to any particular scriptural sanctions, simply the universal set of ethical standards mandated by human free will and shaped by one's wish to be treated in a certain manner by one's fellow human beings.

Artha (security): the goal of acquiring all the things which one thinks will make one secure—money, property, possessions, power, influence, name and fame.

Kama (pleasures): the goal of enjoying the varieties of pleasures life affords—physical comforts, sensory delights, mind-pleasing escapes.

Moksa (liberation): the goal of discovering freedom from the hands of time—freedom from change, age, death, grief, loss; escape from a never ending sense of inadequacy and incompleteness, from all forms of limitation; the desire to be rid of desire itself.

Looked at from the standpoint of the fourfold human aims (*purusartha*), Self-knowledge *atmajnanam*, which is synonymous with knowledge of Truth (*tattvajnanam*) does not fit into any of the first three categories. Self-knowledge is neither mandated by scriptures for the sake of obtaining merit (*punya*) nor for the avoidance of demerit (papa). Nor is it a commonsense ethical standard serving the interest of free-willed, self-conscious beings interacting with one another. Therefore, the purpose of Self-knowledge is not to serve scriptural or commonsense ethics (dharma).

Moreover, Self-knowledge does not result in the gain of either securities (*artha*) or pleasures (*kama*). Knowledge does not produce possessions or pleasures. Actions, efforts, are required to gain securities or pleasures. Particular knowledge may be needed or useful as an aid to the effort required for a given security or pleasure but the purpose itself is fulfilled by the effort, not by the knowledge. Knowledge shapes the effort. Effort does the job. There is no knowledge, not even the knowledge of Truth, that can produce security (*artha*) or pleasure (*kama*).

Where then does Self-knowledge belong? There is only one category left and that is *moksa*, liberation, which is, in fact, where *atmajnanam* fits. Self-knowledge serves the purpose of *moksa*. The value *tattvajnanarth-adarsanam* means keeping in sight the goal of *moksa*, complete freedom from the human sense of limitation, incompleteness, inadequacy. The state of mind of the person who constantly keeps in view *moksa*, liberation, is called *mumuksutvath*; the seeker of liberation is called a *mumuksu*.

Thus, the value of *tattvajnanarthadarsanam* can also be called the value of *mumuksutvath*—the value of the human freedom-seeker who directly seeks *moksa*, liberation. A *mumuksu* never loses sight of the freedom he seeks, nor does he compromise or settle for a lesser thing like a salmon swimming out of the ocean back into the river from which it came. Where, against all odds, the fish battles the current in its single-pointed drive back to its place of origin, so too, does the *mumuksu* seek freedom. A freedom that is discovered in the knowledge of the *tattva*, the Truth of his origin.

Any human search is, basically, a search for liberation. But most people seek in places where liberation is not available. The usual seekers have not singled out that freedom itself is the fundamental human end. They instead keep their vision sighted on a house, a job, a vacation, a marriage or whatever represents a step towards completeness for them. Among these usual strugglers, some single out *moksa* as their goal when they have discovered that achievements do not bring lasting satisfaction and, perhaps, have chanced upon some book or other writing which discusses liberation. Whatever the source—a book, a travelling Swami, an informed friend—when the information about *moksa* hits ready ears, the search for information about the means to *moksa* begins. This search itself can lead a seeker over a lot of ground: from yoga to therapy, from guru to guru, in a process of negation and natural selection until the goal of *moksa* gains definition and direction; and the means to it—which is knowledge alone—becomes clear.

Knowledge is the Only Means to Freedom

Why is knowledge the only means to freedom (*moksa*)? Because the freedom sought is limitlessness itself, that choiceless human goal underlying all other human struggles for limited ends. Limitlessness is not something that can be created or produced. If limitlessness exists, it is an ever existent fact to be discovered. If my essential nature is that of a limited being, I can never become limitless. Limitlessness, by definition, can never be the end product of a process of becoming. An endless series of limited things will not constitute limitlessness. Limited means cannot produce limitlessness. Limitlessness either is or is not.

Therefore, if I am bound by essential nature, there can be no *moksa* for me. I can never be absolutely liberated. Most of the time, as I look at myself and the world around me, I judge myself to be bound, limited, inadequate, sorrow-prone. But, at the same time, there is within me that love for freedom which is so innate in everyone. A love for freedom that in occasional moments of joy or insight seems to be fulfilled as fact, contradicting all my experiences of inadequacy. Thus, even though my usual experience is that of being limited, on the basis of my innate need to be free, backed by intimations that freedom may be my nature, I am led to search for knowledge of the Truth of myself. I try to discover whether or not I am that being I want to be. If the freedom I seek is an accomplished fact, my failure to appreciate that fact can only be due to ignorance. And if my only problem is one of ignorance, search for liberation becomes a search for the knowledge which will dispel the ignorance that keeps me from knowing myself as I am.

A search for *moksa* (liberation) which has become a search for knowledge is an informed *mumuksutvath*. This is a quest for freedom characterised by recognition of the underlying basic human need to be free, by realisation from one's own experiences that one's efforts do not produce lasting freedom, and by the comprehension that it is through knowledge and knowledge alone that one does gain freedom. It is a *mumuksutvam* which has matured into *jijnasa* (a desire to know) which indicates a state of mind bent on inquiry for the sake of knowledge. What knowledge does the *mumuksu* seek? *Atmajnanam* (the knowledge of the Truth of oneself) which can also be called *tattvajnanam* (the knowledge of Truth). *Tattvajnanarthadarsanath* simply is a value for 'mature' *mumuksutvath*—a value for keeping in mind as one's primary goal *tattvajnanam*, which is synonymous with *moksa* (liberation).

Describing the discovery of the *mumuksutvam* which leads to *jijnasa*, it is said in the Upanisad:

Pariksy a lokan karmacitan brahmano nirvedamayannastyakrtah krtena Tadvijnanartham sa gurumevabhigacchet samitpaoih srotriyam brahmanistham

"Having examined worldly experiences gained through actions, the wise' mature person should gain dispassion: untreated (limitlessness) is not produced by action; for the purpose of knowing that (untreated limitlessness) one should go, with twigs in hand, solely to a teacher versed in the Vedas, clear and steady in the knowledge of the Self."

Mundaka Upanisad, Chapter IXIV, Section 2, Verse 12

The wise person described in the Upanisad, through analysis of his own experiences, has recognised that underlying all struggle for security, pleasure and merit is the basic need to discover oneself completely and free from want or limitation of any kind. He also has appreciated that no amount or kind of effort can produce the completeness he seeks. The adequate being everyone longs to find in oneself cannot be produced by a process of becoming. Limitlessness cannot be created. The only possibility is that indeed, I am limitless and am ignorant of my true nature. The resolution of ignorance is by knowledge. Therefore, if I am that which I want to be (limitless), I have to gather that fact through knowledge. There is no other way. Thus, the Brahma Sutras begin:

Atha atah brahma-jijnasa

"Thereafter, therefore, inquiry into brahman."

'Thereafter' indicates an immediately following condition after a state which has gone before. Here the state that has gone before is the discovery within oneself of a mature *mumuksutvam*. This is characterized by discrimination, dispassion, certain values and the discernment that only through knowledge of the Absolute (brahman) can liberation be gained. 'Therefore' indicates the purposive connection between the state-that-went-before and the state-that-comes-after. The succeeding state, which is the result of informed, value-based *mumuksutvam*, is *brahmajijnasa*, the desire to know brahman. Inquiry for the sake of knowing brahman is the same as an inquiry focused on *tattva*, the Truth of everything. Brahman, the Absolute, is the Truth of everything.

VALUE 20

AAdhyatmaJNANA NITYATVRAM": Stability in the Knowledge of Truth

Adhyatmajnana nityatvam, the nineteenth value in the order told by Lord Krisna to Arjuna, is discussed as the final or twentieth value for the sake of more logical analysis.

The previously discussed value, *tattvajnanarthadarsanam*, of not losing sight of the knowledge of Truth (*tattvajnanam*) as one's primary goal, is an attitude which, for its fulfillment, requires the gain of appropriate knowledge. How does one gain this appropriate knowledge—the knowledge of Truth (*tattvajnanam*) which is also the same as the knowledge of the Self (*atmajnanam*)?

Knowledge is not gained by sitting under a bodhi tree. Sitting quietly under a bodhi tree may be fine for some things. Perhaps a reflective person sitting under a tree for some time may figure out certain things about the world and its miseries, but knowledge will not come to that person simply because he sits quietly. For any knowledge to be discovered there must be a valid, effective and appropriate means available to know whatever it is that which is sought to be known. The value *adhyatmajnana nityatvam* deals with the valid, effective and appropriate means for gaining Self-knowledge. And it is Self-knowledge, *atmajnanam* alone which fulfils the value that is desire for liberation which has matured into inquiry into *tattva*, the Truth.

Adhyatma means 'centered on atma, the Self'. *Jnanam* is 'knowledge'. *Adhyatmajnanam* is the knowledge for which the subject matter is atma, oneself. *Nityatvam* indicates 'constancy'. So *adhyatma jnana nityatvath* is 'constancy in knowledge centered on the Self'. Where can one find the teaching for which the subject matter is oneself (atma)? Not in the usual disciplines of learning. Not in mathematics, physics, or chemistry; nor in anatomy, physiology or psychology. Self-knowledge is the subject matter of a tradition of teaching called upanisad or Vedanta or any name equivalent to these names. The scriptures at the end of the Vedas, where this teaching is found, are also called by the name of the teaching, upanisad. Thus, *adhyatmajnanam* (the knowledge for which the subject matter is oneself) indicates the teaching (and the books containing the teaching) called upanishad, whose subject matter is Oneself, the *tattva* (Truth) of the world and of the Lord. In fact the very word Upanishad etymologically means *adhyatmajnanam*.

The word Upanisad resolves into two prefixes (*upa* and *ni*), a verbal root (sad), and an elided *krt* affix (*kvip*). Upa means nearness. 'Nearness' can be absolute or relative. If, in context, 'absolute nearness' is an available meaning, that is the meaning which should be taken; if not, the relative meaning is understood. In the context of the word Upanisad the primary meaning, 'absolute nearness', applies. The subject matter of the whole Upanisad (establishing the context) is Oneself, atma; and atma is absolutely near, the only thing which is absolutely near for which there can be no separating distance whatsoever other than the 'distance' of ignorance. So, in context, what is indicated by *upa* is the 'absolute nearness' of *pratya gattna*, free from all *upadhi* (conditionings). *Ni* is *niscayarthakah*, 'definiteness'. 'Definiteness' about what? About *upa* (absolute nearness) which can only be atma, Oneself. Thus *ni* means definiteness about or well ascertained knowledge of atma, namely, *atmajnanam* (knowledge of atma) which can also be called *brahmavidya* (knowledge of brahman) both terms being the same in that each indicates the same non-dual absolute Reality, the *tattva* (irreducible essence) of everything. So *upani* means *annajnanain* or *brahmavidya* and the elided *kvip* agency affix indicates some verb activity on the part of this knowledge, i.e., indicates that the knowledge does something. What does this knowledge do? The meanings of the verbal root, sad, reveal the action: sad means 'wears out,' *visaranain*; or 'reaches' (in the sense of 'gains'), *gatnanatit*; or 'destroys', *avasadattant*. *Upani*, well-ascertained knowledge of Self (which is not different from *brahmavidya*) 'wears out' and 'destroys' *avidva*, ignorance, including the roots and effects of ignorance, destroying all one's error-born conclusions about oneself. What is 'reached' or 'gained' by this knowledge is Oneself as brahman from which one has been 'separated' by ignorance alone.

So the value called *adhyatmajnana nityatvam* (centered on the knowledge of the Self) is a value for constancy in the study of the scriptures known as the upanisad and other texts of Vedanta. *Nityatvam* means a constancy in scriptural study until Self-knowledge is gained, clear and free from doubt. For the gain of any knowledge, the answer to the question, "How long must I study?", has to be, "Until you know it", which means "Until you understand the subject matter." The gain of understanding is not something for which a specific time can be set. Gain of knowledge is not like gain of a result produced by an action wherein, given the relevant factors, the amount of time needed to produce a result by a particular act can be calculated based on experience. For example, in cooking one can closely calculate how long it will take to cook rice at a given temperature, at a particular pressure, using a particular cooking method. But the time for understanding cannot be similarly calculated. All that can be said for understanding is that if one wants to gain knowledge, using the proper means for gaining that knowledge, one must study until the subject matter becomes absolutely clear. It will not, of course, do you much good to study art history (because you find it easier) if the knowledge you seek is that of calculus. Such a choice would be like trying to see a rose through your ear because your hearing is sharp and your eyesight is dim. The right means of knowledge must be ascertained and used. When you have the right means to gain the knowledge you seek, it is simply a matter of continuing to use that means until the knowledge is gained and is clear and steady.

The Gain of Knowledge: Listening, Reflection, Contemplation

The study of Vedanta *sastra* (scripture), until knowledge of the Self is clear and steady, involves three things: hearing (*sravanam*), reflection (*manana*), and contemplation (*nididhyasanam*). These are the three things which constitute *adhyatmajnana nityatvam* (constancy centered on Self-knowledge). Of these, *sravanam* (hearing) is the primary means. Reflection and contemplation are concurrent but secondary means, being simply aids to *sravanath*. The basic 'hearing' or *sravanath* is listening to the words and sentences of Vedanta scripture unfolded by a teacher of Vedanta. But *sravanam* also can be the 'hearing' that occurs when one, by oneself, studies the written scriptures. *Sravanam* is study of the *sastra* (scripture) in order to find out what Vedanta has to say about oneself, about the world and about God.

Vedanta unfolds what Lord Krisna calls *jneyam* which means 'that-which-is-to be-known', that ultimate knowledge which is liberation itself. The ultimate *jneyam* of Vedanta is stated cryptically in the scriptures in aphorisms called *mahavakya*, 'great statements.' These statements occur in dialogues between teacher and student in which the teacher unfolds the meaning of the *vakya* by a teaching methodology which makes precise, in context, the intent of each word. When unfolded, the *mahavakya* reveals the *tatparya*, the 'purport' or 'vision' of Vedanta. The 'hearing' or *sravanam* includes thorough inquiry into the meaning of these statements. Study of the great statement '*Tattvamasi*' ("That thou art'), for example, requires an inquiry asking questions like: Is this just a mystic statement to be enjoyed like a fanciful poem? Is it a factual statement? What is the meaning Vedanta gives to this statement? Can one find out from the scriptures what is meant by 'that'? What is 'thou'? What is the connection between 'that' and 'thou'? What, if anything, does it mean to me right at this moment that I am a 'thou' which is 'that'?

The answers to these and similar questions are found by studying the words of the scriptures, by studying the *mahavakya* and other supporting sentences which unfold the great statements. The way of study is to listen to a teacher who is both a *srotriya* (one who is learned both in the language of the scriptures and in the methodology of teaching) and a *brahmanistha* (one who is clear and steady in the vision of the Truth of himself). By clearly creating a context for the student, such a teacher will unfold the meaning of the scriptures word by word, sentence by sentence, negating the meanings that are not there. The teacher will unfold not only the meanings of the words and sentences but also how the sentence connects to the previous sentence and how it is connected to the following sentence. The whole teaching of Vedanta is in the form of words. Therefore, one must necessarily see what the words used are meant to unfold. One must see neither more nor less, but exactly what the words are meant to unfold.

Using the words of Vedanta to 'see' myself is like using my eyes to see colour. If with my eyes open and focused I find that there is not enough light to see colour (or to see it clearly) the light should be increased. But the need for more light does not mean that it is the light which does the 'seeing'. The eyes remain the instrument that does the 'seeing'. Similarly, words and sentences, like the eyes, are the means of 'seeing'. To use these means I must throw light upon the words and sentences, analyse them, discover their exact meaning as unfolded by the scripture. These words are about me. With a fresh, open mind made ready by right attitudes, I try to discover what the words say about me. For the sake of discovery, I question the words and sentences. What do the words say about how I am connected to this world? How am I connected to the Lord if there is one? Is there, in fact, a Lord? And, if so, is the Lord the creator of the world? What is said about this world? I must be related to the world someway. Am I inside the world as part of it? Or, am I just here, and the world is here, too, but each of us is independent of the other? Is the world created? If so, is that creator a person or a principle? In *sravanam* (the 'hearing' which is study) such questions as these are addressed to the words of Vedanta dealing with the individual (*jiva*), the world (*jagat*), and the Lord (*isvara*). Vedanta scripture is studied to answer one's questions about each of these topics. In the beginning of study, these three topics are seen as a triangle with each topic enjoying its own identity, occupying its own position. But as study progresses (as the scriptural words and sentences are analysed in order to understand the nature of each of these entities) the 'triangle' disappears. The three are seen as one. The student discovers that *jiva* (individual), *jagat* (the world) and *isvara* (the Lord) have their being in one thing—one absolute non-dual Reality—and that One: *Tattvamasi* ('That thou art').

The Vision of Vedanto: Oneself

'That thou art' is the *tatparya*, the 'vision' of the Vedanta sastra. The entire Vedanta scripture is about oneself, about 'me', about what

I am. In order to understand the scripture I must clearly understand and keep in mind its basic topic, its basic vision. When the sastra, scripture talks about the world, it is talking about me; when it talks about worlds other than this world (heavens and hells to which I may go), it talks about me. The purpose of the Upanisad is not to throw light upon means and ends but to illumine the truth of all means and ends. The first part of the Vedas, the *Karmakanda* throws light on various means and ends. It is in the *Karmakanda* (the part relating to actions) that one can discover the means for going to heaven, or how to perform a ritual to bring rain or gain the birth of a son. If ends such as these are what one is interested in, the first part of the Vedas, the *Karmakanda* is the place to seek information from. The last section of Vedas, the Upanisads known as Vedanta or as the *Jnanakanda* (the part relating to knowledge) does not deal with the achievement of unachieved results. Vedanta talks about what you are, what the world is, what is meant by God, what God's nature is, how God is identical with you. Vedanta involves no means and ends. It just throws light upon what is. Throwing light upon what is, is called 'knowledge'. Knowledge is just seeing what is. Vedanta lights up the fact. Whether Vedanta talks about the world, or about creation, or about God, the Creator, or about the *devatas* or about any other subject, all discussion only throws light upon one basic fact: that there is no difference between the individual, the world and God. This non-dual fact of the identity of me, God and the world is *tattva*, the basic, irreducible Truth of everything. And, it is this *tattva*, Truth, which is revealed by the teaching of Vedanta.

The Words of Vedanta: Approach with Confidence

How does Vedanta reveal the Truth? By words. Words and sentences are the means of knowledge for *tattva*, for the Truth of everything which includes me. For knowing myself, words are the instruments, the means, even as my eyes are the means for seeing a rose. Therefore, my whole approach to using the words of Vedanta must be similar to my use of my senses. Consider how confidently one uses one's eyes. When I open my eyes to look at an object I have complete confidence that I will be able to see whether the object is there or not. I do not doubt my ability to see the object or its absence; nor do I doubt the ability of my other senses to do their jobs. If someone asks me, "Do you have any honey in your cupboard?", I go to my cupboard with great confidence in my ability to find out whether or not honey is to be found there. What is the source of my confidence? The source of my confidence is my expectation that my sense organs can do their job properly. I have my eyes and if they are not very sharp, 1 have my nose. If my nose is not enough, I have my tongue and also the sense of touch. If I see a likely jar and put my finger in it, I can say, "Oh, this stuff must be honey." If I put my sticky hand to my nose, I will be more convinced, "I think it is honey." Then if I touch my tongue with my fingers, I can conclude, "Aah! Definitely honey." From where do I get the confidence to declare, "This is honey"? I have the confidence because I know that my sense organs work.

"I see it. I have smelled it, touched it, tasted it. I know that it is honey," is *pratyaksajnanam*, 'perceptual knowledge' (knowledge obtained by direct perception through the senses). I use my senses with *sraddha*, with faith or confidence in their ability to uncover for me perceptual knowledge of the objects which they apprehend. I need to come to the words of Vedanta with the same kind of confidence with which I open my eyes, alert my ears, touch with my fingers, sniff with my nose, taste with my tongue, in order to discover the existence of a thing which is available for perception. With just such confidence I should open my mind to the words of Vedanta and see the facts these words reveal.

Vedanta: *Pramana* for Non-Negatable Knowledge

The words of *Vedantasastra* are just as much a *pramana* (means of knowledge) as are my sense organs. In fact the knowledge given me by my sense organs, upon analysis, can be dismissed. But the knowledge I gain from the words of Vedanta cannot be dismissed by any other means of knowledge. Sense organs can make known to me only the existence of things that are capable of being perceived. But what can be perceived by one means of perception or at one level (intensity or power) of a given means of perception, can be dismissed by other perceptual means or at other perceptual level of capability of the same means. What is perceived always can be dismissed. Upon sufficient examination nothing perceivable is as it appears to be, but always is resolvable into something else. The perceived 'blueness' of the sky is not really blue. The perceived daily ascent of the sun in the eastern sky does not really happen. Upon inquiry the perceived 'flatness' of the earth can be dismissed. However, the words of Vedanta give a knowledge that cannot be dismissed. The knowledge unfolded by Vedanta that there is one non-dual reality can neither be dismissed by perception nor by any perception-based logic (and all logic ultimately is traced back to a perception-base). Neither by perception nor by logic can the fact of non-duality be dismissed. This is how perception and logic play a role in the teaching and study of Vedanta. Although perception and logic may not reveal non-duality, they can never dismiss non-duality; they do not have the capacity.

Thus, *Sruti*, (the Vedic scriptures which are heard) is an independent means of knowledge. This knowledge being what it is, liberation itself, commands from one a respectful attitude toward the *pramana* (the means, the words of Vedanta) which is even greater than the respect held for one's eyes or other senses. This is true because the senses, unlike Vedanta, can deceive. The knowledge brought by one's senses is never absolutely true but, upon further analysis, is always subject to dismissal. Previously we saw (in the introduction to the discussion of these values) that experience is not knowledge; that experience does not invariably confirm and even less does it reveal Truth. Truth is gained through knowledge. Only *pramana*, a means of knowledge can reveal Truth. Further inquiry causes us to see that the means of knowledge (*pramana*) ordinarily at one's disposal, are not adequate to reveal Truth. The means of knowledge available to me, in my, body-mind assemblage, are only perceptual means which can reveal certain useful, functional 'truths' (the kind of useful information needed for daily life). But through these I cannot discover the *tattva*, the fundamental Truth which I seek.

The 'Elephant-Truth' of the Blind Men

The kind of truth which one's senses reveal is like the 'truth' which the blind men gained after each of them had felt only one part of an elephant. In this traditional story, several blind men came upon an elephant, a creature none of them had encountered before. For a few seconds before the elephant's keeper took it away, each of the blind men was able to touch or grasp some portion of the beast; and each, afterwards, was convinced that he knew what an elephant is like. They argued vigorously, among themselves. One, who had put his arms around one of the huge legs, said, "An elephant, I know very well, from my personal experience, is like a pillar". Another, who had laid his hands flat against the creature's vast side, said, "No! It is like a wall". The others had different claims. "An elephant is like a rope," said the one who had grasped the tail. "Idiots! You are all deluded. An elephant is like a sharp pointed spear," cried the one who had touched a sharp tusk. Each blind men confidently claimed knowledge on the basis of having touched the beast. In what each said there was some truth in the untruth; and the untruth was connected to the truth. Thus the knowledge each had was an untruth containing an incomplete truth, connected to truth. It is easy to see that for each of the mistaken blind men, further inquiry into his false 'truth' would lead to recognition that it was untruth or, at best, incomplete truth.

In fact every untruth is always in some sense connected to the truth (although perhaps not in such an obvious sense as a leg or trunk is connected to the elephant). It is truth when an untruth is known as untruth; in this sense every untruth is connected to truth. In another sense there is a connection because the very status of untruth is dependent upon some truth. This is the fact which the untruth contradicts or does not completely or adequately reflect. Without truth, there could be no untruth. Thus truth and untruth always have some connection. Therefore, if one inquires sufficiently into untruth the inquiry will lead to truth. If untruth were not connected in any way to truth, inquiry into the untruth would just lead to better understanding of the untruth, not to the truth. But because untruth is connected to truth, recognition of the untruth as untruth can lead to an appropriate inquiry that will uncover the truth. For example, in the classic Vedanta illustration of the 'rope-snake' in which a coil of rope is mistakenly thought to be a snake, inquiry into the nature of the 'snake' will reveal the rope—the rope being the truth of the 'snake'.

Thus the study of Vedanta (*sravanam*) includes the analysis of untruth in order that with the recognition of the untruth as untruth the proper kind of inquiry can be undertaken to reveal the Truth. The truths (sense organ data and logical conclusions based on sense data) gathered through the use of one's ordinary means of knowledge are all 'blind men's elephant-truths'. At best such 'truths' are only functional, negatable 'facts' immediately useful but subject to contradiction by other 'truths' and by complete Truth. The 'truths' of various philosophies, psychologies, religions and other belief systems also fall under the heading 'elephant-truth'—that is, they offer some truth contained in untruth and/or untruth connected to truth. These 'elephant-truths' of the other *pramana* (means of knowledge) and of the philosophies are contradicted by what is said in Vedanta sastra. Just as the fact of the complete elephant contradicts the incomplete, wrongly identified truths of its parts, so does the absolute Truth of "what is" contradicts the negatable truths of the *pramana*s . This reveals objectifiable reality and the conclusions of philosophies based on incomplete truth or untruth. Vedanta sastra contradicts the truth of one's senses and the conclusions of widely accepted belief systems, philosophies and psychologies. But what is said by Vedanta cannot be contradicted by anyone. Vedanta is not contradictable.

Sraddha: Suspension of Judgement Pending Discovery

All *pramana* require *sraddha* (faith, confidence) in their ability to deliver what is expected of them in order that one may do whatever is necessary to use the *pramana*. Eyes are the means of knowledge for seeing. To see, one must engage one's mind behind the eyes, open the eye-lids, turn one's head in the right direction and do whatever else that is necessary: perhaps, turn on the light or put on eyeglasses—whatever may be called for under the circumstances. A person who knows himself to be blind would not be motivated to try to engage his mind behind his eyes or to turn on the light. But a person who has *sraddha* (confidence) that his eyes can see will be able to surrender his mind to his eyes (and take whatever other steps may be necessary) in order that his eyes may do their job. Similarly, with *sraddha*, one must surrender to Vedanta sastra in order that it may perform its function as *pramana* for knowing oneself. Because Vedanta sastra contradicts one's usual means of knowledge, the faith (suspension of judgement pending discovery) required in the words of Vedanta is greater than the confidence needed for the operation of one's senses.

So, Vedanta being a *pramana* (means of knowledge), which contradicts other means of knowledge, one must approach Vedanta sastra with more *sraddha* (faith) than accorded to one's senses. However, the faith required is not blind belief. It is suspending the judgement pending discovery. I must come to the words of Vedanta ready to have my old ideas contradicted, prepared to grant to Vedanta the same latitude which I would give to a wise and respected friend who contradicted some observation of mine. Seeing something on the ground, I took it to be a snake and cried out, "Be careful! There is a snake." But my friend responded, "No, no! That is only a rope". Then I would not reject my friend's statement outright. Instead, hearing my friend's words, I would suspend my judgement about what I had seen for the time being, blink my eyes, and look again. I would be willing to accept a contradiction to my prior conclusion. I would again check out what my eyes had to report and then say, "Well, you are right. It is a rope." This is the type of faith with which one must approach Vedanta. An attitude which holds in abeyance old notions and prejudices—for the time being, judgements about oneself, the world and the Lord—would allow one to approach the words of Vedanta with a fresh mind.

'Hearing' is Primary; Reflection and Contemplation are Aids

So, 'hearing' (*sravana*) the great statements (*mahavakya*) of Vedanta scriptures (the *Upanisad* and other Vedanta texts) wielded as a means of knowledge by a teacher, in accordance with the teaching methodology (sampradaya of Vedanta in which a context is created for unfolding the meaning of the words of the teaching) in the primary means to gain the knowledge of Oneself (*atmajnanarim*) which is the same as the knowledge of Truth (*tattvajnanarim*). The 'hearing' or *sravanam* includes inquiry into and analysis of the meaning of the *vakya* (statements) in order to arrive at clear, ascertained knowledge of precisely what the sentences say. Concurrent with it, but secondary (and also to 'hearing' associated inquiry), are reflection (*manana*) and contemplation (*nididhyasana*). It is through 'hearing' alone that knowledge is gained, but reflection and contemplation are aids needed for 'hearing'. Even though there is 'hearing' (and the meaning of what is being heard is understood), the questioning intellect may raise doubts or habit-born obstacles may cloud understanding. Valid knowledge must be definite and clear. If doubts, vagueness or interfering habits of thought are present, reflection and contemplation will help.

Reflection is the use of reasoning to eliminate the doubts raised by the intellect challenging the knowledge of Oneself through Vedanta. In terms of knowledge the intellect has a definite role to play because it is the faculty which assimilates and accepts knowledge. With its own presumptions, its own inferences, its own certain derivative forms of knowledge, intellect poses questions to any knowledge that is gathered. Thus, it is the job of the intellect, through the use of logic, to make the knowledge gained through Vedanta free from any possible doubt put forth by other means of knowledge. The knowledge which has been 'heard'—unfolded by Vedanta—is the non-dual Oneness'. The Lord and the individual are One. I and the Supreme Being are One. I am Limitless. But my perception contradicts what has been heard. Vedanta scripture says there is One but what I see is many. My perception stands against the knowledge unfolded by Vedanta; and my reasoning, based on perceptual data, deals only with duality. So what can the intellect do when confronted with knowledge of Vedanta, the fact on non-duality? It can use its duality-based logic, to establish the fallacy of duality. The ordinary perceptual, means of knowledge cannot reveal non-duality but the 'knowledge' of 'duality' revealed by these means is negatable by the reasoning intellect itself. So in reflection (*manana*) the doubts that arise because of perceived duality are eliminated by analysis which reveals the fallacy in the thinking process that poses the doubt. Reason, inescapably perception-based, cannot reveal non-duality. But, by its own logic, it can establish that it also cannot establish duality! Through reason's negation of duality the doubts challenging the knowledge of non-duality go.

The inquiry and analysis of *manana* (reflection) also examine and dismiss the contentions of the various schools of thought which object to the knowledge of Vedanta. Many of the various philosophical systems and schools of thought pitted against Vedanta have been propounded by sharp wits. The major contenders against Vedanta are armed with logic. It is for the sake of one's own clarity that, these schools must be dismissed, the fallacies in their contentions seen the defects in their logic revealed by logic, all questions answered, all shades of meaning analysed. So in reflection one looks at all possible questions and answers them. Both the questions of one's own inquiring intellect and the arguments raised by contending schools of thought are answered. One answers all questions until the intellect can no longer raise any objections, because knowledge does not brook any doubt. There is no co-existence between knowledge and doubt, between knowledge and vagueness. So, just as one throws gold into the fire so that it comes out even purer than before, one puts one's knowledge to the test of all questioning, and doubts the systematic arguments raised be oneself and others, With this the knowledge will come out brighter that before, so that it will shine brilliantly as it shines each time it is unfolded by Vedanta scripture, untouched be anything. The knowledge itself is untouched, unpolluted by any doubt, even as the object of knowledge, the Self, is unattached (*asanga*) to anything.

It is the function of reflection (*manana*) to free the very process of thinking. Free thinking which is not stifled or chained, prepares one for the discovery of one's essential freedom by clearing away (through use of logic itself) all obstructive fallacies entertained by the intellect. It is through the free reflective thinking any distortion of reason introduced by charismatic conditioning can be recongised and eliminated. Leaders, dead or living, of various schools of thought or of various belief systems, often gain great followings. It must be seen that both ideas and beliefs that are followed by large number of people for a long period of time can be wrong. Neither the size of its following nor the length of the time entertained establishes the truth of an idea or a belief. A large following—for a long time—does not establish knowledge. 'Only a valid *pramana* (means of knowledge) establishes knowledge. Knowledge, not the conclusions or beliefs advocated by some charismatic personality, is the subject matter of Vendanta. Of we mix personality and subject matter of knowledge, both are spoiled.

Hearing and Reflection Dismiss Doubts; Contemplation Weakens Habitual Thinking

Hearing and reflection account for the elimination of all one's doubts about Vedanta. Hearing eliminates the doubts about what Vedanta scripture means. On the other hand, reflection eliminates the doubts about which is correct knowledge—that which is from Vedanta scripture or data from some other means or source. With all doubts gone, intellect no longer poses a problem. The knowledge "That thou art" ("I am Brahman; I am limitless") is accepted by intellect. When the intellect does not pose a problem, what problem can there be? There can be one remaining problem. Something called 'habitual thinking' can interfere with what is known. 'Habitual thinking' is a repetitive thought process which, although it may have had some logic behind it initially, has become 'fixed' as a habit. It is no longer linked to logic. A habit of thought is not logical, it just happens. Like a mood, one just gets into it.

The kind of 'habitual thinking' which is a problem for knowledge is sometimes called *viparita bhavana* which means 'opposite attitude'. *Viparita bhavana* is an attitude opposite to the fact revealed by the knowledge of Vedanta, an attitude reflected by habitual thinking such as: "There is security for me in these things. There is happiness for me in this situation".

A great *vairagi* (a wise person of great dispassion) with well-assimilated values requires only 'hearing' the Vedanta scripture for clear, steady knowledge. Or, if some doubt is there, reflection gets rid of the doubt. Nothing more is required after that for knowledge to be firm and clear. But for one for whom dispassion is not so well established notwithstanding hearing (*sravana*) and reflection (*manana*), there may be some problem with habitual thinking. When habit-born thoughts oppose the fact of Oneself, the knowledge of Vedanta contemplation (*nididhyasana*) is useful to eliminate habitual 'opposite thinking', contemplate. Contemplate on what you know to be the fact of yourself. Realise the fact that you lack nothing. The more familiar one is of the fact of Oneself, the less it will become the opposite attitude.

Nothing new is gained from contemplation. It is from 'hearing' the meaning of the words of Vedanta that knowledge of Oneself is gained. Contemplation, like reflection, is an aid to hearing. 'Hearing' is the means for knowing; reflection frees the knowledge from doubts; contemplation eliminates the habitual erroneous notions which obstruct the knowledge. The erroneous notions of opposite thinking are habitual rather than conclusive. Before hearing and reflection, such notions were conclusive. Before knowledge of myself it was my conclusion that, 'I am the body. Various things in the world, separate from me, make me secure, bring me happiness." But after knowledge such notions are no longer conclusive. After knowledge I know that I (limitlessness) am the only secure thing. I know that I (the non-dual Reality of Creator, creation and individual) am time-free existence, form-free awareness. I am absolute fullness which knows no gain or loss. But, even though weakened by knowledge, some of the old thinking which is born of habit may continue. And, until such habitual thinking goes, the knowledge gained remains knowledge with certain obstructions. Knowledge may be there but, stifled by obstructions. The fruit of knowledge is not enjoyed. What is it that can cause the old thought habits to go? Seeing the fact of myself. The more I see myself the less will be the hold of old thought processes. Continued *sravana*, continuously hearing the fact of myself unfolded by teacher and scripture, helps me become more familiar with seeing myself. In addition, in contemplation, I highlight what-I have seen and heard. I try, in contemplation, to see without any thinking process the meaning of certain words which I have come to know through hearing the scripture unfolded. Words that tell the fact of my nature. With the help of a word or a sound I just try to see the fact of what I have heard. This simple 'seeing' is called contemplation, *nididhyasana*.

Thus, it is by these three means, *sravana*, manna, *nididhyasana*, (hearing, reflection, contemplation) that one commits oneself to the pursuit of the nineteenth value, *adhyatma jnana nityatvam*. This is the value for constancy in the knowledge centered on the Self, which simply means constancy in the study of Vedanta sastra; and with the analysis of *adhyatma jnana nityatvam* the individual examination of each of the twenty *jnanam* values is complete.

"*JNANAM*": Value of Knowledge

Preparation for Hearing, Reflection, Contemplation

Lord Krisna called Self-knowledge *jneyam*, 'that-which-is-to-be known'. This is because in the knowledge of the Truth of oneself—released from all false sense of limitation—one discovers that one is the completely free Being one longs to be. Self-knowledge is liberation; and *sravanam* 'hearing' is the primary means for the gain of Self-knowledge. For some hearers, *sravana* may be all that is necessary; but for others *manana* (reflection) and *nididhyasana* (contemplation) are needed to make *sravana* fruitful. So the three—hearing, reflection and contemplation together are the sole means to Self-knowledge. It is recognised that of these three, 'hearing' is the principal, independent means and reflection and contemplation are aids to and dependent upon 'hearing'.

The *jnanam* values, which make the mind ready for 'hearing', reflection and contemplation, are a secondary but necessary means for the gain of Self-knowledge. The values are secondary in the sense that gain of the values alone, does not bring about Self-knowledge; but they are necessary because without the establishment, in some measure, of the *jnanam* values, the primary means ('hearing' aided by reflection and contemplation) will not work. Values are secondary to the gain of knowledge like fuel is secondary to the cooking of one's food. Fire or heat is the primary means for cooking food. But fuel or some energy source, although secondary to fire/heat, is necessary in order to enable the food to cook. Fire alone cooks, but there can be no effective fire without fuel. One gains Self-knowledge through 'hearing' alone (which includes reflection and contemplation as needed). But there can be no effective 'hearing' in a mind not graced in relative measure with the *jnanam* values. From *amanitvam*, *adambhdtvam* through *adhyadmajnana nityatvam*, and *tattvajnanarthadarsanam*, the values are necessary, making the mind ready for *sravana*. Therefore, to be prepared to be a student of Vedanta, one needs to discover within oneself, in some measure, a personal value for the twenty *jnanam* attitudes.

Understanding is the key to making the twenty values one's own personal values. Attitudes which are accepted because they have been imposed as advice, counsel, admonition or obligation are not personal values but are restraint or conditioning. Such imposed obligatory values do not make the mind ready for Self-knowledge. Only personal, assimilated values establish the mental climate for *sravanam* ('hearing'). Values become personal when "value to oneself' is seen very clearly by oneself. When I clearly see the value of a "value to me", that value becomes my personal value. But even after a value becomes personal for me, for sometime, I may have to be very alert with regard to the particular attitude. Otherwise, habit will continue to rule me. However, once understanding is there (making a value personal to me), then, after a period of alertness (a period when I deliberately take whatever actions will make the value more real for me), the value will become assimilated. An assimilated value is very natural. It is spontaneously, part of oneself. With alertness all one's personal values become one's assimilated values—a natural part of oneself, which, without effort or control, express themselves spontaneously in one's life. When in relative measure this has happened—when one sees the value to oneself of the *jnanam* values—and to some extent these attitudes are assimilated, one's mind is ready for *sravana-manana-nididhyasana*. This is the hearing-reflection-contemplation through which one gains the knowledge of Oneself. That ultimate *jneyam* 'that-which-is-to be-known,' which reveals the Truth of oneself to be time-free, form-free, full and complete existence, awareness that knows no want, no limitation, no isolation.

Epilogue: Daily Value of Values—The Effective Saint

The attitudes and ways of thinking called *jnanam* values are specified for students of Vedanta but have relevance for everyone. Reflecting a keen insight and a profound grasp of the working of the mind, the mental stances described as preparation for Vedanta comprise a mind which is a beautiful, objective instrument which is quiet, alert and effective. It is a mind ready for any study or pursuit. Such a mind, unsplit by internal conflict, undismayed by external adversity, has the best possible preparation for daily life as well as for the study of Vedanta. *Jijnasu* values enhance the quality of life, whatever one's activities may be. Daily life gains efficiency and cheerfulness—even radiance—when these values are personal, assimilated norms. One becomes a cheerful person, both saintly and effective. Generally, we consider a saintly person non-effective. The benevolence and accommodation which characterise a saint are seen as accompanied by a lack of efficiency in worldly matters. But this is not so. True saintliness makes one the most effective person possible in any situation or transaction. Why? Because such a person can be totally objective. His or her appreciation of given circumstances is not clouded by subjective conditioning. There is neither a need for self-validation through a particular interpretation of facts nor for self-fulfilment through a desired outcome. A saint clearly sees facts for what they are and can make and act upon a fact-based judgement free from subjective interpretation or need. A person not affected by the situation is the person who can be most effective in the situation. Thus, although the primary purpose of *jnanam* values (as told by Lord Krisna to Arjuna) is to prepare the mind for Self-knowledge, when the total value of these values is understood, one sees that these attitudes have the highest personal value for everyone. The *jnanam* values impartially bless and make more effective both the mind of the everyday struggler who seeks fullness in the pursuit of artha (securities) and *kama* (pleasures) and the mind of the *mumuksujijnasu* (the seeker of knowledge for the sake of liberation) who, having discerned the futility of limited ends and means, seeks fullness through the gain of Self-knowledge through the study of Vedanta.

3

Human Values and Enhancement of Human Potential

1

Management has been in existence since the dawn of civilisation, but modern-day managers widely acknowledge Fedrick Winslow Taylor as the first exponent of modern scientific approach to management and Henri Fayol as the father of administrative management. But as for perfection or sense of fulfilment in one's life and work, an individual or group needs a philosophy to guide it. The more comprehensive that philosophy, the greater is the fulfilment and welfare. Such a comprehensive philosophy was given to humanity a few thousands years ago in India. It had so far remained isolated from human collective life, and influenced only a few select spiritual seekers. This philosophy is known as Vedanta, described in the *Mundaka Upanisad* as '*Brahmavidya Sarva Vidya pratistham*'—the science of Brahman which is the basis of all science. The goal of that management was to create a complete man: a complete individual who could combine the executive dynamism and acute rationalism of administration, with the deep-rooted respect for the innate divinity of his workers and the holistic value of life.

Total Quality of Management (TQM) or Zero-Defect Management, which are common slogans in today's managerial training, are based on four factors:

(i) Man
(ii) Machine
(iii) Methods, and
(iv) Material

Even if we are perfect in the last three components, but fail to train up the Man, we are destined to fail.

According to Peter Drucker,

Manager from now on will be increasingly ineffectual ... the people with whom the executives will have to deal will be the people over whom he has no authority whatsoever.

Managing in the Next Millennium

Management is so much more than exercising rank and privilege; it's much more than making deals.

So what is needed in the future may not be a 'Manager' in typical sense. Many Executives I meet are totally baffled by what I'm thinking about...a bit revolutionary, and, in short, counter cultural.

Managing in a Time of Great Change

Noting the prelevance of many concepts of the East in new management literature, MR Thiesen perceptively remarks

The search for a better system is probably why increasingly aspects of Eastern thinking can be traced in Western Management literature.

Rhythm of Managing; p.9

It is urgent that our people treat this subject of human values as relevant, not only for the better functioning of business and corporate world but also for the better functioning of our Union and State governments, the various professional bodies, and all our citizens. It must inspire every aspect of our national life, including the management of our family.

Human Values in India: Pre- and Post-Independence Context

In the modem period, Swami Vivekananda taught our nation the great relevance of human values. Our people have a long way to go to understand implications of this teaching, and to implement it to achieve total human development in India. After Vivekananda, Gandhiji too took up this theme, and made it the sheet-anchor of his nationwide movement, as much for wresting political freedom from foreign rule, as for strengthening and unifying our national society. When we became politically free, our Constituent Assembly gave our nation a Constitution inspired by this humanistic impulse. In fact, the modern renaissance in India, inaugurated by Raja Ram Mohan

Roy in the first quarter of the nineteenth century, and matured by Sri Ramakrishna and Swami Vivekananda during the last quarter of the same century, is inspired by this humanistic vision and impulse, deriving from our own national spiritual tradition and from the cultural inheritance of the modem West. Swami Vivekananda was the one whose powerful voice awakened our nation, the one who tried to instill the sense of human values into all aspects of our national life.

So, the treatment of this subject will not be confined to just the business or industrial sector. There are innumerous constituents of national developmental activities, including the vast and ever-proliferating administrative machinery at the Union and State levels, and the ubiquitous political forces operating everywhere in ways that are good, not so good, and positively bad, in our post-independent India. All these forces need a healthy orientation, and that healthy orientation is human orientation. Even though Mahatma Gandhi gave this human orientation to our politics and to our national life, we have unfortunately forgotten it more and more, year after year, since independence. That is why we are in a political and social mess even after 70 years of freedom, and are confronted with challenging human problems in every field. These multiply in geometrical progression as we solve them in arithmetical progression. Some of the other developing countries have more respect for human values than we have here today. Our people have to sit and calmly consider this one great question—How can we infuse human values into our national life and thus overcome our accumulated problems challenging total human development?

It is obvious that something went wrong with us immediately after we became free. Our nation does not lack in any of the ingredients needed for steady national development under the spur of freedom. Our people are endowed with intelligence, varied talents, and ambition. Today we boast of being third among the nations of the world in scientific and technological man-power. But what does it mean to the nation at large? What is its impact on the condition of millions and millions of people? What is wrong with our nation that, in spite of all our talents and massive man-power resources, more than half our population is still sunk in poverty, ignorance, squalor, and suffering? Why has science and technology not given to our country that miracle which it achieved in developed countries? Why has not the blessings of science flowed from the scientist and his laboratory to the masses in a big way?

The purpose of science, as expounded by Thomas Huxley, the collaborator of Charles Darwin, in the nineteenth century, was not only for advancement of knowledge, but also 'the alleviation of human suffering'. If the first leads to the second, there is need to wed the pursuit of knowledge, i.e., education, with humanistic impulse. Unfortunately, after independence, we divorced our education, politics, and administration from this humanistic impulse; so they lost their capacity to alleviate human suffering. Some of these, especially politics, developed, on the other hand, even the capacity to aggravate human suffering, by infecting and distorting our education, administration, and labour movement. So, along with human unconcern, and always as a result of it, we witness the spiralling of social evils like bribery, corruption, tax-evasion, smuggling, lack of citizenship virtues like duty, punctuality, honest work for the remuneration one gets, and public spirit. The range of social malpractices that our people indulge in today is unprecedented, not only in our own times but in all human history. Along with the physical malnutrition of our millions, the spiritual malnutrition of the educated and well-fed classes of our nation today is writ large in every field of our national activity.

Swami Vivekananda's luminous ideals and nation-building ideas, scattered in the nine volumes of the Complete Works, contain the much needed spiritual nourishment for modern day people. Here are two sentences from his letters, which refer to our education and our dignity as citizens of free India, respectively. In a letter addressed from Chicago to his dynamic and dedicated young disciple in Madras, Alasinga Perumal, in 1894 (The Complete Works, Vol. V, p.58), he says

My heart is too full to express my feeling; you know it; you can imagine it. So long as the millions live in hunger and ignorance, I hold every man a traitor who, having been educated at their expenses, pays not the least heed to them!

Again, in a letter written to the Maharaja of Mysore on 23 June 1894, he says (ibid., Vol. IV, p.363)

This life is short, the vanities of the world are transient, but they alone live who live for others, the rest are more dead than alive.

Anyone who has studied Vivekananda's writings will be impressed by the constant stress on this human orientation. He awakened our long dormant national energies and impressed on them this humanistic touch. During our feudal past, there was very little of this human orientation; it was often- anti-human, with caste exclusiveness, untouchability, and human exploitation as its outstanding characteristics. Our upper classes missed the great opportunity then to educate and raise the common people and build up a great nation. Not only did they fail to do this, but, they also subjugated the poor and fattened themselves, by which they brought themselves and the common people under the shame of foreign domination and humiliation for centuries. Despite this unhappy experience of the immediate past, how did our educated classes slide so quickly from the ecstasy of freedom of our independence day on 15 August 1947, to rank selfishness, human unconcern, and complacency thereafter? Many of our educated countrymen today are 'dead' people, according to that dictum of Swami Vivekananda given in the letter quoted above, because they live for themselves and have forgotten to live for others, forgotten to live and work for the nation. Having got education at the cost of the nation (the fees a student actually pays for his or her education is only a fraction of his or her total educational expenses) he or she has forgotten the nation, neglected to serve it and raise the rest of the people. They have thus become traitors to the nation, as per the pungent but true words of Vivekananda quoted above. Vivekananda's teachings will show all such people in our nation today how to live in the true sense of the term. It will show how to cease to be traitors to the nation, by living for others, and by serving the common people with their knowledge and talents. His works will inject this much-needed human motivation into their actions and thoughts.

Duties and Rights

Selfishness and self-centeredness, and the evils flowing from them, have resulted in none being happy or satisfied in our country. Our people must take necessary steps to reverse this downward trend and work hard to dispel the current dismal atmosphere to make every one happy and fulfilled. This can be done by participating in the nation-building process, instead of remaining a self-centered onlooker. Our intelligentsia must possess a central passion: this is our nation, these are our people; we must do whatever we can to develop the spirit of values in our vast population. We have to take the preamble of our Constitution seriously and work devotedly to ensure 'the dignity of the individual and the unity of the nation'. The Constitution contains wonderful ideas which are suffused with human values and express the will of the nation to implement them. These are however only aspirations and promises in the Constitution itself. Their translation into social realities depends upon the free citizens of our democracy, and on their elected representatives, and the various human management institutions of the country. It is unfortunate that the Constitution failed to stress the fundamental duties of our citizens, while putting due stress on their fundamental rights. A complete philosophy of life will be a happy balance between rights and privileges, on the one hand, and duties and responsibilities, on the other.

The exclusive stress on fundamental rights has resulted in a general clamour by individuals and groups for rights and privileges from the nation. This clamour has drowned the great humanistic and ethical values of duties and responsibilities. It is time that we correct this imbalance, before the contemporary wrong attitude takes the nation down beyond retrieval.

In America, one of her thinkers had suggested that the Statue of Liberty in the east coast be supplemented by a Statue of Responsibility in the west coast. Here too, our people must consider, in the interest of a balanced education of our nation, the value of erecting a Statue of Freedom on one side and a Statue of Responsibility on the other side of Rajpath in New Delhi. It is time that all segments of our free citizens develop a sense of national responsibility and ask a question to themselves: What do we owe to our nation and how can we discharge that national responsibility? They have to realize that they have to work hard to improve their nation; they have also to learn to work together with other people; and that means that they have to achieve a certain inner growth to be able to do teamwork. We succeed in working together when we pay more stress to the common goals before us, and less on our own egos and its profit and pleasure. This is what constitutes the virtues and graces of democratic citizenship, in which individual freedom is wedded to social responsibility.

Freedom of the individual is fundamental to human growth; it is also fundamental to a democratic socio-political order. But that freedom becomes a menace, as much to the individual as to the nation and its democracy, if it fails to get inspired by a second value, namely, the sense of social responsibility. Along with this sense of social responsibility, the freedom of the individual needs to be enriched with the democratic virtues of self-discipline and a humane will. The end-result would be a character centered in a socially oriented will. It is this training in citizenship virtues and graces that makes a people, any people, capable of enriching all inter-human relations, including all management techniques with ethical and humanistic impulses and growth-oriented practical efficiency.

It is obvious that we have not wedded that sense of responsibility and self-discipline to our freedom. We as a community possess little sense of social responsibility among the peoples of the world; more so in the case of our so-called educated masses. We are not willing to respond to the great challenges before our nation. Our common people, on the other hand, have been, and are, hard-working. Our deft-fingered artisans create things of beauty and utility by hard work. But they are not able to enjoy the fruits of their honest labour; they are deprived of it by our so-called intelligentsia. Our common people have learned the work ethic; but our educated intelligentsia has not, except when it comes to their own self-interest. So, they exploit the common people, either remaining lazy themselves or by hard work for their own self-advancement. This has to change. Everyone has to learn to do a day's honest labour and then, then only, enjoy the fruit of it in the form of wages and salaries. This is the *Bhagavad Gita*'s philosophy of work, which is followed more by the people outside India, according to Swami Vivekananda, than by people within India. No nation can become great, or achieve prosperity, without its people developing a sense of self-discipline, social responsibility, and capacity and willingness to do hard, efficient, cooperative work.

Bhagavad Gita and Human Values

Some of the profoundest ideas relating to the philosophy of work are to be found in our *Bhagavad Gita*. It is unique in its stress on work-ethics. Among the great religious books of the past, this is the only one whose central theme is work—man at work, and man achieving from work a double benefit, namely, social welfare outside, and spiritual growth within. All other religious books, Indian or foreign, deal with man at worship, at prayer, at meditation, at ritual. But the *Gita* deals primarily with man at work—it may be any field of work or any profession—and presents worship, prayer, meditation, and ritual as means for man's spiritual growth and realization, on the one hand, and for increasing his work-efficiency leading to social welfare, on the other. This is Yoga, the comprehensive philosophy of life and action, capable of ensuring individual and collective human welfare. The philosophy is available to our people today to help us to achieve, through effective administrative and management techniques and better inter-human relationships, our national objectives of total human development and fulfilment for all our people, for the first time in our long history. This possibility is revealed in the testament of the last verse of the *Gita* itself, which is of great significance to us today.

It has remained a valuable testament all this while, and it is the privilege of the people of India, in this modern period, to fully implement it.

Yantra yogesvarah krsna,
yatra partho dhanur-dharah;
Tatra sri vijayo bhutih,
dhruva nitih matir mama

'Wherever there is Krisna, the master of Yoga, and Arjuna, the wielder of the bow, there, (in that society), shall be found wealth, victory, general welfare, and unwavering justice and ethical sense—this is my conviction.'

The verse refers to the confluence, in each person, of two energies needed to achieve total human welfare. The first is the energy of Yoga, the energy of vision, of calm spirituality, represented by Sri Krisna who, in the Mahabharata war, did not take part in the actual fighting, but only gave sagely guidance to Arjuna. The second is the energy of intense and efficient action, represented by Arjuna, the hero of action. This represents the combination of contemplation and action, vision and implementation, in every citizen, which the *Gita* and the Chinese philosophy of Taoism call the state of being 'sagely within and kingly without'. Herbert Spencer, in his Study of Sociology (p.403), calls it a 'uniting philanthropic energy with philosophic calm'. This is true education. When achieved by a people, all management and administration will achieve the highest level of efficiency.

The first fruit of that confluence, says the verse, is Sri, economic prosperity, that which our Constitution has set before us as the basic national objective—banishing the demon of dismal mass poverty. This needs not only knowledge and hard work, but also the capacity for dedication and team-work, which is the gift of character energy. The smile of Sri or Lakshmi, i.e., wealth, must illumine every hamlet and home in our country. That can come only after first bringing into every home the smile of Sarasvati, the goddess of knowledge; and this knowledge, to be true knowledge, must always be accompanied by character. Such knowledge, when applied to work, produces Sri or Laksmi. The relationship of Sarasvati to Laksmi is similar to the relationship of pure science to applied science; and both are needed to achieve total human welfare.

The second fruit of that confluence is *vyaya*, victory, which means success accompanying every project, every endeavour. The failures of the low level performances of many of our national projects and undertakings can be traced to the absence, in many of our people, of that confluence of hard work and character-energy with knowledge energy. And wherever success has been registered, we can detect the presence of that blessed confluence.

The third fruit of that confluence is *bhutih*, general welfare. Sri and *bhutih* together constitute welfare, which is the socio-economic and cultural objective our Constitution has placed before the nation. To enable us to achieve that high objective, we need a fourth value.

The verse refers to that fourth value as *dhruva nitih*, constant justice and ethical sense. No political system, no society, can be healthy without unwavering justice and ethical sense. This is the value called *dharma*, which holds the scale even between individuals and between groups. By favouring one individual or group and discriminating against another, we increase injustice in society, increase social discontent, and pave the way for eventual social chaos. Hence the citizens, as much as the administration, must be imbued with justice and ethical sense. This value, referred to above as *dharma*, is presented by Indian philosophy as the principle that integrates man with man in society. It is basically a by-product of the spiritual growth of the individual citizen, which is expressed as moral law, and which is reinforced by the state laws and regulations. A respect for law and the constant effort to uphold it, on the part of the citizen and of the holders of power in the state, are what make for human integration and the strength and stability of a state, more especially a democratic state like ours. It is the awakened moral sense in the citizen that expresses itself as human values and that makes the laws and regulations of the state effective. If the moral sense is absent, the laws become ineffective, as the citizens twist the laws to suit their advantage. This increases injustice in society and weakens the political and social fabric. If the moral sense is not present, social contracts become ineffective; for it is the moral sense that motivates one to stick to a contract; without it, he or she can, and will, flout it. Then the cynical remark will come true, that Moses and Jesus gave eleven commandments, but only ten were recorded, the 'thou shahs' and the 'thou shalt nots'; the unrecorded eleventh commandment says that, even if you break all the ten, only take care that you are not caught by the law!

Here's an interview that Swami Vivekananda had with the correspondent of the Sunday Times of London in 1896. (*The Complete Works of Swami Vivekananda*, Volume V, p.192, Seventh Edition):

But the basis of all systems, social or political', said the Swami with great earnestness, 'rests upon the goodness of men. No nation is great or good because Parliament enacts this or that, but because its men are great and good. I have visited China (in 1893) which had the most admirable organization of all nations. Yet, today, China is like a disorganized mob, because her men are not equal to the system contrived in the olden days. Religion goes to the root of the matter. If it is right, all is right ...

'One must admit that law, government, politics, are phases not final in any. way. There is a goal beyond them where law is not needed ... All great Masters teach the same thing. Christ saw that the basis is not law, that morality and purity are the only strength.'

Purport of Education: Human Excellence and Development

The basis of our full national development is that; the vision of 'the Dignity of the Individual and the Unity of the Nation', as enshrined in our Constitution, gets effectively implemented by the combined efforts of self-disciplined citizens and dedicated and efficient executives and employees of the Union and state and all public welfare enterprises. We classify all nations today as developed, underdeveloped, and backward. Our country belongs to the second category. How did the developed nations of today acquire the developed status? They were, some centuries ago, less developed than we are today. In the fifteenth and sixteenth centuries, there was much poverty and squalor in Europe. Then came the spread of education among the masses, hard work, co-operative work, and human concern. Thus they became developed. Modern science and technology accelerated the process. Swami Vivekananda says (Ibid., Vol. IV, pp.482-83):

From the day when education and culture, etc., began to spread gradually from patricians to plebeians (upper classes to the lower classes), grew the distinction between the modern civilization as of Western countries and the ancient civilization as of India, Egypt, Rome, etc. I see it before my eyes, a nation is advanced in proportion as education and intelligence spread among the masses. The chief cause of India's ruin had been the monopolizing of the whole education and intelligence of the land, by dint of pride and royal authority, among a handful of men. If we are to rise again, we shall have to do it in the same way, i.e. by spreading education among the masses ... Why has originality entirely forsaken the country? Why are our def t fingered artisans daily becoming extinct, unable to compete with the Europeans? By what power again has the German labourer succeeded in shaking the many century-grounded firm footing of the English labourer? Education, education, education, alone! Travelling through many cities of Europe and observing in them the comforts and education of even the poor people, there was brought to my mind the state of our own poor people, and I used to shed tears. What made the difference? Education was the answer I got. Through education, faith in one's own self, and through faith in one's own self, the inherent Brahman (the Infinite and Universal Self in all beings) is waking up in them, while the Brahman in us is gradually becoming dormant.'

Thus education on national scale, self-discipline, hard and cooperative work, and the humanistic impulse are the four means by which under-developed India can become a fully developed nation, with enormous disciplined energies released from her vast population constituting one-seventh of humanity. We can thus free ourselves from our feudal past and become a modern progressive democratic nation.

Swami Vivekananda on Human Values

Why have we not become a fully developed nation even after so many years of political freedom? The answer is that we failed to develop the above-mentioned four means of national development. Most of our educated people have negative attitudes, and along with a dismal fund of self-centeredness and callousness there is a colossal lack of human orientation. There is urgent need to develop these virtues and graces in our people, especially that of human motivation. Such a dynamic source of true education is available to all our people in the Vivekananda literature. But this education is not readily available in our educational institutions. In a democracy like ours, policy changes in education and other fields will come only through the impact of public opinion. We have, therefore, to first create that public opinion. And even for creating that informed public opinion with respect to making our education value-oriented, deriving its main inspiration from our philosophy and culture and oriented to our national purposes, we have to seek for help mostly outside our formal educational institutions. But, till such public opinion is created, and with a view to creating it, we have to resort to other sources of inspiration. Fortunately such sources are available to us in several books published in India in contemporary times. These include the Life of Swami Vivekananda by His Eastern and Western Disciples, in two volumes, and The Complete Works of Swami Vivekananda, in eight volumes, published by the Advaita Ashram, Calcutta. These are available in most bookshops, and constitute the most important source of what Vivekananda himself characterized as man-making and nation-building education. In his famous lecture delivered in Lahore on 12 November 1897 on the subject of Vedanta, Vivekananda exhorted our people to capture its *Advaitic* vision of the unity and non-duality of all existence, and work it out in the practical field of our national life, both as an individual and collectively (*The Complete Works*, Volume III, pp.427-31, Eighth Edition):

> Believe, therefore, in yourselves, and, if you want material wealth, work it out; it will come to you. If you want to be intellectual, work it out on the intellectual plane, and intellectual giants you shall be. And if you want to attain freedom, work it out on the spiritual plane, and free you shall be and shall enter into Nirvana, the Eternal Bliss. But one defect which lay in the *Advaita* was it being worked out so long on the spiritual plane only and nowhere else. Now the time has come when you have to make it practical. It shall no more be a rahasya, a secret; it shall no more live with monks in caves and forests, and in the Himalayas; it must come down to the daily every-day life of the people; it shall be worked out in the palace of the king, in the cave of the recluse; it shall be worked out in the cottage of the poor, by the beggar in the street, everywhere, anywhere it can be worked out ...
>
> Therefore, Children of the Aryas, do not sit idle. Awake, arise, and stop not till the goal is reached The time has come when this *Advaita* is to be worked out practically; let us bring it down from heaven unto the earth;, this is the present dispensation ...
>
> Ay, in this country of ours, the very birth place of the Vedanta, our masses have been hypnotized for ages into that state (of slavery). To touch them is pollution, to sit with them is pollution! Hopeless they were born, hopeless they must remain. And the result is that they

have been sinking, sinking, sinking, and have come to the last stage to which a human being can come. For what country is there in the world where man has to sleep with the cattle? And for this, blame nobody else, do not commit the mistake of the ignorant. The effect is here, and the cause is here too. We are to blame. Stand up, be bold, and take the blame on your own shoulders. Do not go about throwing mud at others; for all the faults you suffer from, you are the sole and only cause.

Young men of Lahore, understand this, therefore, this great sin, hereditary and national, is on our shoulders. There is no hope for us. You may make thousands of societies, twenty thousand political assemblages, fifty thousand institutions.

These will be of no use until there is that sympathy, that love, that heart, that thinks for all; until Buddha's heart comes once more into India, until the word of Lord Krisna are brought to their practical use, there is no hope for us ...

Therefore, young men of Lahore, raise once more that mighty banner of *Advaita*, for on no other ground can you have that wonderful love, until you see that the same Lord is present everywhere. Unfurl that banner of love! Arise, awake, and stop not till the goal is reached. Arise, arise once more, for nothing can be done without renunciation. If you want to help others, your little self must go. In the words of the Christians—you cannot serve God and mammon at the same time ... Throw away everything, even your own salvation, and go and help others ... Give up this little life of yours. What matters it if you die of starvation, you and I and thousands like us—so long as this nation lives?

The nation is sinking; the curse of unnumbered millions is on our heads—those to whom we have been giving ditch-water to drink, when they have been dying of thirst, and while the perennial river of water was flowing past; the unnumbered millions to whom we have talked of *Advaita* and whom we have invented the doctrine of lokacara (usage), to whom we have talked theoretically that we are all the same and all are one with the same Lord, without even an ounce of practice! ... Wipe off this blot. 'Arise and Awake. What matters it if this little life goes? Everyone has to die, the saint or the sinner, the rich or the poor. The body never remains for anyone. Arise and awake

> and be perfectly sincere. Our insincerity in India is awful. What we want is character, that steadiness and character that make a man cling on to a thing like grim death.

Here is the surge of the humanist passion which must inspire all our people today. They must ask themselves: Why this poverty, in our country? Why this backwardness? Why this ignorance that makes the lives of millions dismal? The answer will come: Man in India is below par; he is not yet man, but only a candidate to humanity, in the words of Victor Hugo. The philosophy by which he lives is petty, small and highly inadequate to face the modern challenges. Vivekananda wants us to utilise the opportunity provided by the modern period of human history To work out the accumulated and mounting problems of human development of millions of our people. He even wants our people to question themselves why even a dog or any other animal should go hungry in our country. In modern developed societies, not only human beings, but even dogs and cattle are well fed and looked after. We have, in Vivekananda's Vedanta, the philosophy to help us to achieve the same, or even still higher all-round development. He coined the phrase *daridra narayana*, 'God in the poor'; which, later, Mahatma Gandhi also used as a mantra to inspire our freedom movement with a humanistic motivation.

There are not only intense humanistic ideas in the Vivekananda literature, but often also radical revolutionary ones. He was a teacher of a revolutionary humanism, deeply rooted in the Indian soil. When I spoke on Swami Vivekananda: His Humanism at Chicago University in October 2002 at the invitation of that Institute, I quoted, a sentence from his speech in Madras in 1897 which sounds Marxist even before Marx was known in our country (Ibid.: 297):

> The day for these privileges and exclusive claims is gone. The duty of every aristocracy is to dig its own grave—and the sooner it does so, the better The more it delays, the more it will fester and the worse death it will die.'

Long before the advent of Marxist and other radical political and economic ideas relating to the raising of our long-oppressed common people, Swamiji had drawn our nation's attention to these problems, and provided the remedies which are in line with our age-old cultural and spiritual heritage and which derive inspiration from it. But our educated masses failed to imbibe that inspiration to the extent necessary, especially after the advent of freedom, which, had they done so, would have been a powerful stimulus to accelerate national development. But they failed to do so. They did not care to inspire themselves with the fund of human values that Vivekananda's writings had given to our nation. During his wanderings all over India as a *parivraj* aka or wandering monk, between 1891 and 1893, Vivekananda had lived with all sections of our society—our princes and our peasants, intellectuals and common people, upper classes and untouchables, Muslims and Christians. He was deeply distressed at the misery of the masses, the heartlessness of the upper classes, and the callousness of our intellectuals. After seeing at close quarters, the misery and ruin of his country's millions, he gave expression to his deep feelings in letters written a little later, from Japan, England, and America, to his disciples and friends in India. Here is one from Yokohama, Japan, written to his very faithful Chennai disciple Alasinga (Letters Ibid., Vol. V, p.10):

> I cannot write what I have in my mind about the Japs in one short letter. Only I want that a number of our young men should pay a visit to Japan every year To the Japanese, India is still the dreamland of everything high and good. And you, what are you?... Talking twaddle all your lives, vain talkers, what are you? Come, see these people and then go and hide your faces in shame. A race of retards, you lose your caste if you come out! Sitting down these hundreds of years with an ever-increasing load of crystalized superstition on your heads, for hundreds of years spending all your energy upon discussing the touchableness or untouchableness of this food or that, with all humanity crushed out of you by the continuous social tyranny of ages—what are you? And what are you doing now?... Promenading the sea-shores with books in your hands—repeating undigested stray bits of European brain work, and the whole soul bent on getting a thirty-rupees clerkship, or at best becoming a lawyer—the height of young India's ambition—and every student with a whole brood of hungry children cackling at his heels and asking for bread! Is there no water enough in the sea to drown you, books, gowns, university diplomas, and all?

> Come, be men! Kick out the priests who are always against progress; because they would never mend, their hearts would never become big. They are the offspring of centuries of superstition and tyranny. Root out priest craft first. Come, be men. Come out of your narrow holes and have a look abroad. See how nations are on the march. Do you love man? Do you love your country? Then come, let us struggle for higher and better things...
>
> How many men, unselfish thorough-going men, is Madras ready now to supply, to struggle unto life and death to bring about a new state of things sympathy for the poor, and bread to their hungry mouths, enlightenment to the people at large, and struggle unto death to make men of them who have been brought to the level of beasts by the tyranny of your forefathers?

Then, after reaching America, he wrote, pouring out his humanist passion, to the same Alasinga from Breezy Meadows, Metcalf, Massachusetts, on 20 August 1893 (Ibid.: 14-17):

> Oh, how my heart ached to think of what we think of the poor, the low, in India! They have no chance, no escape, no way to climb up. The poor, the low, the sinner, in India have no friends, no help; they cannot rise, try however they may. They sink lower and lower every day, they feel the blows showering upon them by a cruel society, and they do not know whence the blow comes. They have forgotten that they too are men. And the result is slavery. Thoughtful people within the last few years have seen it, but unfortunately laid it at the door of the Hindu religion; and to them the only way of battering is by crushing this grandest religion of the world. Hear me, my friend, I have discovered the secret through the grace of the Lord. Religion is not at fault. On the other hand, your religion teaches you that every being is only your own self multiplied. But it was the want of practical application ... the want of sympathy, the want of heart ...
>
> This state of things must be removed, not by destroying religion, but by following the great teachings of the Hindu faith, and joining, with it the wonderful sympathy of that logical development of Hinduism—Buddhism.
>
> A hundred thousand men and women, fired with the zeal of holiness, fortified with eternal faith in the Lord, and nerved to lion's courage

by their sympathy for the poor and the fallen and the downtrodden, will go over the length and breadth of the land, preaching the gospel of salvation, the gospel of help, the gospel of social raising up, the gospel of equality.

No religion on earth preaches the dignity of humanity in such a lofty strain as Hinduism, and no religion on earth treads on the necks of the poor and the low in such a fashion as Hinduism. The Lord has shown me the religion is not at fault, but it is the Pharisees and Sadducees in Hinduism, hypocrites, who invent all sorts of engines of tyranny in the shape of doctrines of paramarthika and vyavaharika (absolute and relative truth)... Well, my boy, this is the school ofmisery, which is also the school forgreatsouls and prophets for the cultivation of sympathy, of patience, and above all, of an indomitable iron will which quakes not even if the universe be pulverized at our feet ... They are children, yea, veritable children,, though they be great and high in society. Their eyes see nothing beyond their little horizon of a few yards—the routine work: eating drinking earning and begetting following each other in mathematical precision. They know nothing beyond, happy little souls; their sleep is never disturbed. Their nice little brown-studies of lives never rudely shocked by the wail of woe, of misery, of degradation and poverty, that has filled the Indian atmosphere—the result of centuries of oppression.

They little dream of the ages of tyranny—mental, moral, and physical—that have reduced the image of God (that is man) to a mere beast of burden; the emblem of the Divine Mother, (that is woman), to a slave to bear children, and life itself, a curse.

Trust not the so-called rich; they are more dead than alive. My hope lies in you—in the meek, the lowly, but the faithful...I may perish of cold and hunger in this land, but I bequeath to you, young men, this sympathy, this struggle for the poor, the ignorant, the oppressed ... Vow then to devote your whole lives to the cause of the redemption of these three hundred millions, going down and down everyday. It is not the work of a day, and the path is full of most deadly thorns. But Parthasarathi (The Charioteer of Arjuna) is ready to be our Sarathi, we know that and in His name and with eternal faith in Him, set fire to the mountains of misery that have been heaped upon India for ages—and it shall be burnt down.

Thousands and thousands of our youth heard the above call by reading Vivekananda literature during the first half of the last century. They responded to it by joining the hard and protracted struggle for India's political freedom and social upliftment of the downtrodden masses under Gandhiji and other great leaders. Who is to implement that vision and redeem that promise? If our youth in the post-independence decades had studied the strenghthening, purifying, and unifying Vivekananda thought and got re-educated, they would have achieved self-discipline, national dedication, and character-strength. Thus educated, they would have entered our Union and state services, banks, schools, colleges, universities, and other various service institutions, as employees. They would have become the blessed instruments for redeeming that promise; our nation would have marched ahead and become a fully developed nation within these years. But it is a great tragedy that it did not happen. Most of our educated masses became, instead, content to remain at the low level of seeing 'nothing beyond their horizon of a few yards—the routine work: eating, drinking earning and begetting, following each other in mathematical precision' , as graphically and truly depicted by Vivekananda in the letter quoted above. Almost all such people became obsessed only with the three 'p's, namely, pay, prospect, and promotion! Accordingly, '*their nice little brown studies of lives never rudely shocked by the wail of woe, of misery, of degradation and poverty, that has filled the Indian atmosphere*', as in the poignant words of Swamiji quoted earlier.

This self-centeredness came to us even through some of our other religious books such as the *Smrtis* or Hindu law books. Years ago, I remember to have read a prayer by a house-holder in one of them: it is typical of our widespread self-centered attitudes. It says: '0 god, give me a son'. This in itself is harmless; but the next line discloses the small mind behind. It says: 'And, 0 God, give a daughter to my neighbour!' He wants the trouble of bringing up a daughter to be put on the shoulders of his neighbour, from whom he can get his daughter-in-law on his own terms! When our people pray in temples, it is always a 'give me this' or a 'give me that'. Do they ever pray for the welfare of the common people? Do they ever pray that dismal poverty should end and that they themselves be made the blessed instruments for that great purpose?

In Vivekananda's presentation of religion, you find a different approach and tone, as was seen in some of his words quoted earlier. Here is another passage, which will educate our men and women to become more heroic, the last paragraph of which the teacher-founders of the Delhi School of Economics, Dr V.K.R.V. Rao and his colleagues, chose as a motto to inscribe in the School's Vivekananda Auditorium in the 1950s (Ibid., Vol. V, pp.135-36):

> I must see my machine in strong working order and, then, knowing sure that I have put in a lever for the good of humanity in India at least, which no power on earth can drive back, I will sleep, without caring what will be next.
>
> And may I be born again and again, and suffer thousands of miseries, so that I may worship the only God that exists, the only God I believe in, the sum total of all souls — and above all, my God the wicked, my God the miserable, my God the poor of all races, of all species, is the special object of my worship. (author query: check the quote for completeness of idea).

Vivekananda giving the Pedantic human orientation to our culture and religion finds an inspiring expression in an event connected with his last visit to Varanasi, the most ancient and holy city of India. There he had inspired a few young men with his Pedantic message of renunciation and service. Renunciation of the little genetically centered ego and manifestation of the real Self, the Atman, the by¬product of which is a spontaneous mood of dedication and service. He saw thousands of pilgrims from all parts of India thronging to Varanasi, bathing in the holy Ganga, and worshipping in the ancient and holy Visvanatha temple. He was inspired by seeing the immense faith and devotion of the people. But he was also deeply distressed to see that, when these pilgrims fell sick, there was no provision to care for them and treat them, and they were left to suffer and die in the streets and lanes. He pointed out this misery to his young disciples and addressed them: 'Learn to see your Siva not only in the temple but also, in a more tangible form, in these suffering humanity, and serve them in a spirit of worship; that is true religion.'

The young disciples were inspired by this Vedantic vision and technique. Sri Ramakrishna had taught Narendra (Vivekananda) and other young disciples a few years earlier: 'Every Jiva is Siva; service of the Jiva is, therefore, worship of Siva.' Immediately they set to implement this vision and technique of *tyaga* and *seva*, renunciation and service. They began in an ad-hoc manner, in the verandas of friendly houses, with a quarter rupee as capital, and later, through a regular medical institution. This slowly developed into what you see today as the Ramakrishna Mission Sevashrama (Home of Service, Varanasi). Till a few decades ago, it was the only good hospital caring for the people of Varanasi and the students and staff of the Benaras Hindu University. The same is the history of the Ramakrishna Mission Sevashrama at Kankhal, Haridwar, and the Ramakrishna Mission Sevashrama at Vrindaban. As medical service institutions they are small in size; but the vision and the philosophy behind them are lofty and immense in significance, making the subject of human values that are the very soul of religion and socio-political action.

Quantitative Expansion Calls for Qualitative Enrichment

Human orientation is what makes a static system of administration and management dynamic. Here the heart is touched, not, the mere intellect. It is when heart responds to heart that a static bureaucracy and management, be it in government or in service institutions like banking, become transformed into dynamic developmental administration and management. There is an appropriate strategy in everything. Our people, and even our foreign collaborators in industry, often complain that nothing moves in our bureaucracy. How many well-conceived developmental plans and programmes in our country get stifled by our wooden bureaucracy! All this will change when all our public service activities become infused with an enlightened citizenship-awareness and humanistic motive. Every file in front will then evoke in the employee sitting on the office chair, the human response to the human urges and needs of people, living far and near; which the file represents.

When human urges and aspirations for a better life invade the hearts of millions of people whose life had been dismal and stagnant for centuries, they become aroused by the economic and social possibilities of the modern revolutionary age. They resolve to take advantage of them and set to work for their betterment. They keenly feel the need for finance and capital; and the bank goes to their help with finance and thus sets in motion the developmental process. Earlier, there was the ubiquitous money lender. In spite of his high interest rates, which have ruined many families, his role was also social service. However, his motive was not service, but high profit; a motive relevant to a static socio-economic order only. It was not meant to produce new wealth, not meant for socio-economic development, but merely to shuffle existing poverty and wealth among the population. In this context appeared the institution of modern banking. In its earlier stages, it was established by a few people, who were mostly money-lenders-turned businessmen or industrialists, with a view to finding finance, for their own or their friends' business or industrial ventures. The scope of such banking was very restricted and was not capable of playing a national role. That restricted role of banking changed in the wake of political freedom and the nation-wide initiation of socio-economic development activities. This led to nationalisation and the quick spread of banking institutions, first in urban, then in rural areas and this process is being accelerated year by year.

The growth of banking services into every nook and corner of the nation is only a quantitative expansion. Such quantitative expansion calls for a Pari Passu qualitative enrichment. Our quantitative expansion has been colossal, since independence, with respect to our Union and State bureaucracies and other service institutions. But what our proliferating institutions need urgently today is qualitative enrichment. This calls for the infusion of human values in their operations. And these human values do not proceed from buildings and equipments, rules and regulations, organizations and systems. They unfold from the depth of the human personality. They manifest under the guidance of an adequate philosophy of life, but get stifled and blunted under the guidance of a wrong philosophy of life and work. Values are not mechanical, says the agnostic thinker Bertrand Russell (Impact of Science on Society, p.77):

> The Machine is the modern form of Satan, and its worship is the modern diabolism... Whatever else may be mechanical, values are not, and this is something which no political philosopher must forget.

Indian wisdom, as expressed in Vedanta, holds that a philosophy of values is a part of, and derives from, a philosophy of man in all heights and depths. It holds that man creates values from within himself in the context of his interactions with nature and society without. Out of the two, he only manipulates nature, but he both manipulates, and enters, and is manipulated and entered into by other human beings in society. It is while doing so that he becomes the focus of values and experiences fulfilment. Thus values are specifically the products of evolution at the human stage, and are spiritual in nature, in the sense that they arise from the inner spiritual nature of man.

Human Values in the Light of Vedantic Concept of *Purusartha*

It is a wrong philosophy of life that resulted in human unconcern and brought about the centuries-long degradation in India. This was exposed by Vivekananda in the passages quoted earlier. In the same passages, he also gave us the correct philosophy, the adequate philosophy, which can lift us and put us on the road to human happiness and welfare, both individual and collective; and that is the *Advaitic* vision, the understanding of our basic oneness, and the spirit of love and dedication and service that flows from it. The *Advaita* Vedanta inspires us with a positive outlook, exhorts us to live and work with zest, and transforms our self-interest into enlightened self-interest. Unlike many religious ideologies, Indian or foreign, Vedanta does not look down upon man's seeking of material or sensory values.

It is instructive to study human values in the light of the comprehensive Hindu concept of the four *Purusartha*, i.e., values sought after by *purusa* or man. These are *dharma*, *artha*, *kama*, and *moksa*. In its scale of values, Vedanta finds an honoured place for all desires and urges of man, from the material and sensory to the moral, ethical, aesthetic, and super-sensory or transcendental. The Sanskrit word and concept *kama*, desire, constitutes the entire range of human cravings and satisfactions at the sensory level; it is the first of the *purusartha*. The second *purusartha* is *artha*, wealth, which is the instrument for the satisfaction of *kama*. The third *purusartha* is known as *dharma*, which means ethical sense, and which helps to discipline and regulate the pursuit of the first and the second, so that all persons in a society get the opportunity to satisfy their urge for them. Human values in management and administration proceed from this third *purusartha* of *dharma*; though third in order from the point of view of human experience, it is put first in all enumerations, due to its primacy and importance. This *dharma* is essentially what manifests spontaneously as a by-product of man's inner growth, of man's spiritual growth, from the freedom of individuality to the freedom and social responsibility of personality. The first is *vyaktitva*, the second is *vikasita vyaktitva*. These terms, person and personality, are defined by the British biologist and humanist, Sir Julian Huxley thus: Persons are individuals who transcend their organic individuality in conscious (social) participation. ' This growth from individuality to personality is a spiritual growth which transforms a mere *grhastha* or householder, who is genetically limited in his or her sympathies and interests, into a citizen whose sympathies and interests become nationwide, and also international, cutting across all genetic and other limitations. This is not mere *vyaktitva*, individuality, but *vikasita*, i.e., expanded, beyond physical or genetic limitations. It is this second step in spiritual growth– the first step being individuality itself, i.e., awareness of one's individual identity, dignity, and worth—that makes for enlightened citizenship in a democracy.

Human values manifest spontaneously in man as person, but only artificially and with effort in man as mere individual. When man as a person, as an enlightened citizen, becomes an employee of public institutions like banks or government secretariat offices, human values become manifest, and qualitatively enrich the work of those institutions. Such a person will not think of himself or herself as a mere employee, but as a free citizen of India called by the nation to perform a particular service to the people. This is what transforms work into a mission, into a national commitment; and this is also what enhances the dignity of the worker, from being a mere employee, or paid servant, into an instrument of human purpose. A clerk's work, done with a clerk's mind, makes that clerk and his work small; but the same work, done with a citizen's mind and attitude, elevates both the work and the worker. This is the philosophy of work as taught in the *Bhagavad Gita*. It is echoed in an oft-quoted sentence of the British thinker, Bernard Shaw:

This is the true joy in life—to be used for a purpose which you consider mighty; to be a force of nature, and not a clod of ailments and grievances, ever complaining that the world does not devote itself to making you happy!

It is this attitudinal transformation, this enlightened citizenship attitude, that must invade the hearts and minds of all our present ad hoc and nominal, citizens, in general, and also of all the millions of employees of all our secretariats, banks, and other public service institutions, in particular. This is the importance of that third *purusartha* or value referred to earlier, namely, *dharma*. *Dharma* in this context, does not mean any dogma or creed or theological belief or religious ritual, but only the growth of man from a self-centered individual, seeking only his or her own freedom and self-interest, to a free and socially responsible person, seeking one's freedom and self-interest in the context of the freedom and self-interest of all others in society.

In this, we see the genetically limited *grhastha* or householder growing, becoming spiritually evolved, into a true citizen. This growth is much needed by all in India, for, since several centuries, we have degenerated into being good *grhastha* but bad citizens. The *grhastha* as citizen, endowed with awareness by his or her social responsibility, and discharging it well, is highly praised in the Hindu tradition. In the glowing words of the *Manu-Smrti* (3.77-78):

Yatha vayum samarsritya sarve jivanti jantavah;
Tatha grhasthamasriya vartante sarva asramah

Just as all creatures live depending on air, so do all *asrama*, (namely, *brahmacari* or student, *vanaprastha* or forest-dweller after retirement, and *yati* or all renouncing monk or nun) exist depending on the *grhastha* or citizen-householder.

Yasmat trayo' pyasramino jnanenannena canvaham;
Grhasthenaiva dharyante, tasmat jyesthasrami grhi

Because of the fact that the three other *asrama* are always supported and nourished with knowledge and food by the *grhastha* alone, therefore the *grhastha* is the most excellent *asrama*.

Vedanta philosophy, therefore, treats these three, namely *dharma*, *artha*, and *kama* as the *trivarga*, the triple set, always going together to ensure the happiness and welfare of all. Their presence together in any society makes for material progress, cultural development, and general welfare of its diverse population.

Vedanta designated the fourth and last *purusartha* with the word *moksa*, which means full spiritual freedom. It is a super-sensory and trans-social dimension of experience, but not supernatural. Unlike Christianity and all other Semitic religions which uphold the supernatural and thus come into conflict with physical sciences, there is no concept of the supernatural in Vedanta. Its concept of nature, of *prakrti*, is wide enough to embrace the two dimensions of one and the same reality, namely, the dimensions of the physical and the secular—*apara prakrti*, and the super physical and the spiritual—*para prakrti*. It is the unique state of joyous aloneness (in contrast to painful loneliness), in which man ceases to be gregarious. 'In the last stage of life's journey, man walks in single file', says Dr S. Radhakrishnan. Meditation is like climbing the Everest. We start as a crowd at the base camp, the number decreases steadily as the climbing progresses, and, at the very summit, we proceed in single file. Meditation, in daily spiritual life, represents this experience of aloneness, of non-gregariousness.

Thus trans-social, the *moksa* value, has tremendous invisible impact on society. It strengthens the power of *dharma* to achieve human integration in society, be it through citizenship confined to a nation, or that same citizenship reaching out to the international and human dimensions. For, *dharma* is only that *moksa* ideal and experience expressed in and through the social context. Vedanta has expounded this concept of the four *purusartha* by keeping in view humanity as a whole, and not as segments like nation, caste, or creed. *Artha* and *kama*, under the guidance of dharma, are wholesome; but they become harmful without that guidance. Sri Krisna praises such *kama* in the *Gita* (7.11):

Dharmaviruddho bhutesu kamo ' smi bharatarsabha

'I am that kama in all beings that is unopposed to dharma'.

This dissatisfaction with, and going beyond, the *kama* and *artha* to *dharma* and *moksa* values is uniquely a human capacity. Without that extra step, human life stagnates, and the pursuit of *kama* and *artha* becomes abnormal and unhealthy as much for the individual concerned as for the society. It is the pursuit of *dharma* and *moksa* that lifts human life above the animal life: *dharmena hinah, pasubhih samanah*—'bereft of dharma, man is just an animal', says an oft-quoted verse of the Hindu tradition. In his *Gita Rahasya* (p.156), Lokamanya Tilak quotes the following words of the materialist English philosopher, John Stuart Mill, which would be appropriate in this context:

> It is better to be a human dissatisfied than a pig satisfied; better to be a Socrates dissatisfied than a fool satisfied. And if the fool, or the pig, is of a different opinion, it is because they only know their own side of the question.

The Hindu spiritual tradition teaches us (*Manu-Smrti*, 4.176):

Parityajet artha-kamau
you syatam dharma-varjitau;
Dharmam capyasukhodarkam
loka-vikrustameva ca

Give up those *arthas* and *kamas* (wealth and sensory carvings) which are opposed to *dharma*; and (give up) even that *dharma* which results in one's own unhappiness (like donating all wealth without thought for the care of one's children) and in the suffering of the people.

Thus earning wealth by right means and honest labour is *dharmic*; but greed, and its disposition to dishonesty and unscrupulousness, is opposed to *dharma*. Being opposed to *dharma* means it is opposed to general social welfare and one's own inner spiritual growth. It is *dharma* that equalises a strong man and a weak man in society. If the restraint of *dharma* is not there, the strong will have all the *kama* and *artha*, and the weak will be deprived of even elementary human satisfaction, as was prevalent in our feudal social order, where the have-nots were left to live a near-animal life. This is what we have to change totally in our democracy, by infusing moral, ethical, and human values into our society.

Indian Concepts of Sarasvati and Laksmi: Their True Significance

I wish to point out that our people have to learn afresh the true meaning and significance of the two important Hindu concepts of Sarasvati and Laksmi. Sarasvati stands for knowledge—not the dead knowledge crammed and stuffed into the brain—but knowledge which is the product of investigation into the truth of nature and of man. Laksmi, similarly, means not just wealth, but wealth invested in productive enterprises. It means wealth and welfare resulting from the application of knowledge through efficient and co-operative work. Sarasvati accordingly represents, in modern knowledge and language, pure science, and Laksmi represents applied science. Thus Laksmi flows from Sarasvati. The two are not jealous sisters, who avoided each other, as was our perverted belief in the decadent period of our history. The same decadent period also taught us that the worship of these beautiful goddesses consists mainly in doing rituals before their images or pictures, and not in the tapas of knowledge seeking, and in the tapas, of hard work in the fields, factories, workshops, and offices.

This is the lesson that our nation has to learn today in a big way, so that we may succeed in banishing the demons of ignorance and poverty from our land, which was once known as the land of wisdom and wealth. Modern Western history teaches us this truth that these two goddesses are friendly sisters. First comes the worship of Sarasvati through scientific research and the acquisition, assimilation, and distribution of knowledge. This is followed by the worship of Laksmi, through the application of knowledge in all fields of human development and welfare. The integrated play of the energies of Sarasvati and Laksmi in a society is what the last verse of the *Gita* expounds, as I had explained earlier.

Our country needs to manifest more and more energy, in the true form of worship of Sarasvati, by the steady spread of education and enlightenment among our people. Imagine the mental energy resources that will become available to our nation, if our. whole population is educated at least up to the eighth standard; or better still if every one completes at least the higher secondary level. Widespread education will ensure unprecedented productive and other economic activities, which will result in an unprecedented expansion of employment opportunities and banking services as well. All revolution in banking and productive enterprises, which represents the play of Laksmi, depends upon a prior revolution in education and research, which is the play of Sarasvati.

Management Philosophies and Techniques: American versus Japanese

Before the world war, India learned the technique of modern management mostly from the United Kingdom. In the post-war years, India turned to the United States for this and many other spheres of knowledge and techniques. Now we are getting this knowledge from many other nations as well. As we progress and enter deeper and deeper into the processes of modern industrialisation, the subject of management assumes increasing importance. We face the problems of efficiently tackling the organisation and management of our ever-expanding developmental monetary investments, of out vast material resources, and of our ever-expanding work force in our offices, factories, workshops, and educational, hospital, and other service institutions. There is a quick transition taking place in our expanding industry from hereditary to professional management cadres. This has called for the need for management training, for the fulfilment of which more and more institutes and schools of management training are coming up in all parts of our country.

One salutary development in this field, discernible during the past few years, is the interest in, what is called, the philosophy of management, on the one hand, and on the other the question whether India has any philosophy of her own on the subject of management.

Every nation, every culture, has its own approach to the subject of management, as well as to other forms of group life and activity. Today, there are two great nations, which are highly specialised in the field of management and have their own philosophies relating to it: America and Japan. Many in India do not know that their own country also has its own philosophy of administration and management. But today there seems to be a ray of hope. Many of our people are eager to learn about it. I have come across books of various Indian writers expounding this subject, basing their treatment on the great Yoga philosophy and technique of the *Bhagavad Gita*.

This new interest in India's own philosophy and approach is stimulated by our people witnessing, during the post-war years, the amazing phenomenon of the management philosophy and techniques of an Occidental or Western country like America which had been dominating the whole world for many decades, now yielding to the management philosophy and techniques of an Oriental or Eastern country like Japan. We can see a plethora of books published on management by American writers, comparing the two management systems, and praising the Japanese system as more efficient. I wish to draw your attention to one such book which, in content and style, makes fascinating reading, The Art of Japanese Management by Richard Tanner Pascale and Anthony G Athos. The Washington Post rightly observes, 'If there is one major lesson to be learned from the Japanese business structure, it is how to manage.' The 'Introduction' to this book by the Managing Director of a reputed American company has this to say about the deficiencies of the American system:

> This is an important book; its importance derives from both its timing and its contents. We are, I believe, at the beginning of a period where significant new research into the practice of management is essential. The Academic journals, the business press, and the popular media, have all recently speculated on the managerial causes of weak competitive performance by American enterprise. Top managements, the business schools that train them, and the consultants who advise them, have all been faulted for a destructive preoccupation with analytical technique—too narrow in its conception and too short term in its application ...

> The weaknesses in American management that have been at fault in our declining international competitiveness have not been so much an over-reliance on analysis and technique, as a failure to fit the application of technique into a broader, more complete, and more coherent concept that enables organizations to perform in a superior way and to endure over time. The authors present such a concept, called 'the 7-S model'.

The 7-S model is later presented by the authors as: Strategy, Structure, System, Staff, Style, Skill, with Superordinate goals inserted between the first three mechanical items and the last three human items. By superordinate goals, the Japanese mean the shared values and goals that bind together the fabric of all successful enduring corporations. They constitute the *dharma*, the corpus of spiritual values, of any human group. The 'Introduction' further states:

> In describing the 7-S model, Pascale and Athos do not disparage the analytical methodologies that have been developed, taught, and applied during the three decades. These methods have contributed importantly to the formulation of business strategies, the development of effective organization structures, and the definition of useful systems for managing businesses large and small. About this there is no doubt. But the authors present a framework of management that blends thinking about style, skills, staff, and superordinate goals, with notions of strategy, structure, and systems, into an interdependent reinforcing network. It is the absence of or conflicts within, this complete network, the authors argue, that accounts for weak corporate performance. This point is made and illustrated with numerous examples and comparisons between Japanese and American management practices.

The authors state in the beginning of their book that 'man is limited not so much by his tools as by his vision'. They continue (pp.22-25):

> 'The principle objectives of this book can be stated simply.
>
> First, regardless of society or culture, mankind has discovered only a limited number of tools for making organizations work...

Second, managerial reality is not an absolute: rather, it is socially and culturally determined...

Third, firms, which perform well year after year, whether Japanese or American, tend to have a lot in common...

Let us briefly consider how we got where we are...

The Industrial Revolution, with its invention of mass production, diminished the importance of the skilled trades and the social affiliation obtained through them. The emergence of the concept of factors of production' (land, labour, and capital) had revolutionary implications for the Western view of humankind. Humans (the labour content) were no longer an inextricable part of the organic whole of society. Rather, the person, as labourer, became an objectified and standardized component of the production process. Not surprisingly, this view of labour ' tended to divorce and as a social and spiritual being from his productive' role at work. Correspondingly, this rearmed the lingering lesson of the centuries that one's spiritual and social life should reside outside the work place. This concept has persisted in Western thinking to this day and as we will see, it is one of the sources of our present problem...

The principal difference between Eastern Institutions and those in the West is that ours turned to organizational structure and formal systems to cope with these challenges. In contrast, Eastern institutions, while until recently advancing more slowly in thinking about organizational forms and formal systems, paid much more attention to social and spiritual means...

Eastern societies were so populous, and because spiritual, public, and private matters were so integrated, their organizations tended to regard the task of control in the context of the whole of human needs, rather than as a more narrow transaction between labour and capital. They were generally more sophisticated than the West in utilizing social and spiritual forces for the organization's benefit, and in accenting the responsibilities to their employees that went with such broad influence'.

While discussing the successful managerial philosophy and practices of one of the Japanese companies, the Matsushita Electric

Company, the authors introduce a whole section entitled 'Spiritual Values' (Ibid.: 49-52):

> "Spiritual" is an unlikely term in a narrative or corporate life, yet nothing less suffices to capture the strong belief system that underlies Matsushita's Philosophy...
>
> The Matsushita philosophy provides a basis of meaning beyond the products it produces. Matsushita was the first company in Japan to have a song and a code of values. "It seems silly to Westerners", says one executive, "but every morning at 8 a.m. all across Japan, there are 87,000 people reciting the code of values and singing together. It's like we are all community." Matsushita foresaw that a lifetime's organizational experience shapes one's character indelibly. It was unthinkable, in his view, that work, which occupies at least half of our waking hours, should be denied its powerful role. The firm, therefore, had an inescapable responsibility to help the employee's inner selves. This responsibility could best be realized by tying the corporation to society and the individual, by insisting the management serve as trainers and developers of character, not just as exploiters of human resources.
>
> Some Western minds will find these ideas at best remote, at worst delusive. But such a connection between philosophy and hard-headed business objectives is one that the Japanese take as natural. One observer notes that Matsushita provides two distinct kinds of training. One is basic skills training, but the second and more fundamental one is training in Matsushita values. These values are inculcated through a long apprenticeship across one's career. The newly hired are exposed to them continually. As a member of any working group, each person is asked, at least once every other month, to give a ten-minute talk to his group on the firm's values and its relationship to society. It is said that nothing is so powerful in persuading oneself as having to persuade others...

The basic principles, beliefs, and values of the firm are as follows.

Basic Business Principles

To recognize our responsibilities as industrialists, to foster progress to promote the general welfare of society, and to devote ourselves to the further development of world culture.

Employee's Creed

Progress and development can be realized only through the combined efforts and cooperation of each member of our Company. Each of us, therefore, shall keep the idea constantly in mind, as we devote ourselves to the continuous improvement of our Company.

'The Seven Spiritual' Values

1. National Service through Industry
2. Fairness
3. Harmony and Cooperation
4. Struggle for Betterment
5. Courtesy and Humility
6. Adjustment and Assimilation
7. Gratitude

These values, taken to heart, provide a spiritual fabric of great importance... The Director of a major Matsushita subsidiary comments:

> Matsushita's management philosophy is very important to us. It enables us to match Western efficiency without being one bit less Japanese. Perhaps the ultimate triumph of Matsushita is the balancing of the rationalism of the West with the spiritualism of the East.

Referring to the need for all management to deal differently with human resources from material resources, organization, and style, the authors say (Ibid.: 105):

> The inherent preferences of organization are clarity, certainty, and perfection. The inherent nature of human relationships involves ambiguity, uncertainty, and imperfection. How one honors, balances, and integrates the needs of both is the real trick of management.'

I had expounded earlier the science of spiritual growth from individuality, *vyaktitva*, to personality, *vikasita vyaktitva*, as understood in Vedanta. Sri Ramakrishna (1836-1886) calls it the growth of *kacaami*, 'unripe I', into *pakaami*, 'ripe I'. Bertrand Russell compares individuality, or *kacaami*, to a billiard ball whose relationship to another billiard ball is only coexistence or collision.

But men must learn to understand each other and work in harmony with each other, in co-operation and team spirit. This is achieved by the spiritual growth from individuality to personality, from *kacaami* to *pakaami*. It is based on the *Advaitic* vision of a basic spiritual unity. Western outlook is dominated by logical dualism and contradiction introduced by Aristotle and Descartes. Expounding the difference between this dualistic Western and monistic Far Eastern (and also Indian) views of 'self' and 'individuality', the authors state (Ibid.: 121-25):

> There are few concepts as deeply embedded in the Western minds as the concept of 'self Our philosophy, language, and psychology are filled with it. We see our 'selves' as distinct entities, separate from all others in most important respects, with separate beliefs, talents, and experience. In Japan, each person is, believed to possess a unique spirit, soul, mind, and heart—but this self (or 'self-concept) is seen as an impediment to growth. People are regarded less as individuals than as collaborators in the context of their roles. One's separate 'identity' is not singled out as the primary sign of personal development throughout the life cycle, as it is in the West...
>
> The Japanese perceive the drawing of lines between self and 'others' as arbitrary. Their culture emphasizes reciprocal influences; ours tend to emphasize separateness. Westerners struggle to develop and then retain separate identity in the race of invading influences. The Japanese tend to develop an 'inclusive identity' that incorporates those close to them...
>
> For cultural reasons, dependence is a disquieting word for Westerners; for practical reasons, excessive independence is, too... What is needed, conceptually, is a clearer notion of interdependence that permits us .to preserve the best of independence and dependence without getting the worst of both. The Japanese accomplish this through the concept of Wa. Technically, Wa means group harmony. But its full meaning encompasses a range of English words—unity, cohesiveness, team spirit.

Highlighting the importance of the current change from the concept of 'Personnel Management' to the concept of 'Human Resource Management', the authors remark (Ibid.: 193):

> What is needed in the West is a non-deified, nonreligious 'spiritualism' that enables a firm's superordinate goals to respond truly to the inner meanings that many people seek in their work—or, alternatively, seek in their lives and could find at work, if only that were more culturally acceptable.
>
> Western institutions are, in fact, backing into this role. Two forces are at work: employees seeking more meaning for their jobs and demanding more concern from the corporation, and legislative pressures enforcing a broad range of personnel services, including employee rights to counselling. In response to these forces, most major firms now describe these activities as 'Human Resource Management' instead of 'Personnel'—it is to be hoped, the first step in adopting a larger perspective.

In the concluding chapter, the authors speak of American national culture, and American industrial management sub-culture, as the two root causes of that country's recent management decline. Comparing this with the Japanese management philosophy and techniques, the authors conclude (Ibid.: 204):

> What we saw was that generally we were very similar to the Japanese on all the 'hard-ball' strategy, structure, and systems. Our major differences are in the 'soft-ball' S's—skills, style, staff, and superordinate goals. Their culture gives them advantages in the 'softer' S's because of its approach to ambiguity, uncertainty, and imperfection, and to interdependence as the most approved mode of relationship. We saw that their development of language and forms of discourse especially their indirection, permit high development of skills we seldom achieve or honour. Their careful attention to their human resources, from the initial recruitment all the way through retirement, made us look as wasteful of our people, as we have been of our other resources. We saw how the boss-subordinate relationship encourages a degree of effective collaboration that we might envy, and how consensus is used to accomplish smooth implementation, which often eludes us. In short, we saw that, by comparison, we were all too often grossly underdeveloped in our sophistication about 'man-in' organization', and powerfully disadvantaged by our culture.

The authors warn, in the last but one sentence of their book, that 'the task is not to imitate cosmetically, but to evolve organically'.

What this Comparison Means to India

All aspects of management and administration in India, including our relevant training institutions, will do well to sit back calmly and ponder over what the philosophy and technique of Japanese management means to us. As Eastern countries, both have a common spiritual background. We should remember that Zen meditation, which gave Japan trained and disciplined minds, is an Indian contribution which India herself, in recent centuries, failed to utilize and profit from. We depended solely on an amalgam of rituals and ceremonies, magic and miracles, and superstition in religion, and stuffing of minds, in education, neglecting the vital discipline training of the mind in both. A little thought will reveal to us the close kinship of the Japanese philosophy and technique to our own philosophy and value system. This revelation will impart a dynamism and direction to our administration and management, now sadly lacking, when a good percentage of our people grasp it and become inspired by it. They will then realize the implications of certain truths that stare at us. While Japan has very few natural resources, our country has plenty of them. In intelligence and ability too, we are not below the Japanese or Americans. Yet, both of them are far ahead of us in economic and social development. We are still an undeveloped and developing nation, even after years of political freedom, economic planning, and crores of investment.

Pondering over these facts, it will become obvious that some vital element is lacking in us. That vital element is trained and disciplined and socially oriented minds and hearts. At the beginning of chapter four of the *Gita* Sri Krisna states that the great philosophy of a dynamic and comprehensive spirituality called Yoga, expounded by him in chapters two and three, became gradually diluted and lost yoga nastah parantapa. Commenting on this Sankaracharya elucidates that 'it was lost when it fell into the hands of weaklings and people bereft of disciplined and trained minds and hearts': *durbalan ajitendriyan prapya*. If and when that long missing element is supplied, our nation can not only reach the level of the Japanese economic and social performance, but even out do it. It is on this vital missing link that we have to concentrate our national attention and identify and introduce it in our education, religion and inter-human situations.

The first thing that will strike us then will be the fact that many of our people are not aware of their own philosophy of life and work, and that we have been, and still are, imitating cosmetically Western philosophy and methods. Such awareness could have made us evolve organically on our own, on the basis of our own philosophy and culture. Hence our actions have been ad hoc, and under the tyranny of the immediate present. Most of us know only the weak and ugly aspects, the popular *desacara* and *lokacara* aspects, of our country's culture and religion; and these are obsolete and irrelevant in the modem age. This limited understanding has made our people apologetic and bereft of self-respect. It has weakened our national resolve and capacity to seek and assimilate the real philosophical and spiritual elements of our own culture and, in that strength, to seek and assimilate the best aspects of Western and other cultures, and not merely imitate their cheap elements.

Our people should slowly grasp the *Advaitic* vision, the vision of oneness, of non-separateness, as given earlier in Vivekananda's fiery words, and assimilate the dynamic philosophy of calm, silent, cooperative work as taught in our *Bhagavad Gita*—the attitude referred to in the third chapter entitled Karma Yoga: *parasparam bhavayantah sreyah param avapsyatha*, 'by mutuality and cooperation, all shall achieve the highest welfare'. This will help us learn to respect the dignity and inherent worth of oneself and others as sparks of the One Divine Atman, and we shall capture a high level of self-discipline, human concern, and practical efficiency. This basic human transformation will invest all aspects of our administration and management with tremendous dynamism and humanistic orientation. All management and administration derive from the prevailing social attitudes and outlook, and these are not conducive to efficient management.

A nation cannot become great without self-discipline. And self-discipline is the mark of a free man, as indiscipline is the mark of a slave. That we are still a highly indisciplined people, and also riddled with petty jealousies, only shows that we have not shed our slave mentality, though external political freedom has come to us. Unliberated India had more free people than free India has. This tragedy is the result of not using that freedom, which came to us after centuries of political slavery and social humiliation, to energetically work to transform Indian society from an undeveloped to a highly developed one. Our people used their undoubtedly high intelligence only to advance themselves, in total neglect of the nation. They forgot that such lives are empty, in spite of having more or less money or power, such people, in the words of Vivekananda quoted earlier, are more dead than alive. One hope-inspiring sign on the horizon of our nation, since the last four or five years, is that this truth of what constitutes human worth and human excellence is dawning on an increasing number of our people. This must lead us to a 'discovery of India', as Jawaharlal Nehru termed it in his own case, and making that discovery flow into an energetic effort to re-shaping modem India in the light of her lofty philosophy and spirituality and rich culture.

Efficiency of administration and management depends as much on the quality of the employees as on that of administrative heads and managers and executives.

If our people as a whole are imbued with self-respect, a sense of honour, self-discipline, and citizenship virtues, and all our managers and employees are drawn from the common citizen pool of the nation, the entire administration and management techniques and processes will undergo a revolutionary transformation. It will become an efficient science and art of drawing out the best from oneself, and from others, in a dynamic effort at total human development, growth, and fulfilment. That will transform our country from being merely the largest democracy, in view of our mere population strength, into the greatest democracy, in view of our people getting endowed with keen minds, and large hearts, and efficient hands.

Unliberated people, like immature children, are difficult to manage; but free and responsible people are easy to manage. All management involves commanding and obeying. But, in a democracy, all commanding should avoid injuring the self-respect of the one commanded. And all obeying should be on the basis of one's freedom and self-respect, and never degrade into cringing. It is only in this context that inter-human relationships in the management situation can evoke the best from the other person. Such free and responsible people will be naturally endowed with the citizenship virtues and graces of duty and punctuality, cooperation and commitment. Such employees will not even need supervision of their work, for supervision militates against a person's sense of honour. And all truly free and responsible people are always endowed with this great virtue of personal honour and self-respect. Our employees, in a majority of cases, are still found wanting in these virtues, in spite of their being free citizens of a free nation. They lack the virtues of duty and punctuality, because they lack a sense of true freedom and personal honour.

It is educative to know how employees of other free nations behave with a sense of human values and social responsibility, and how they look at our ways. Here are two such illustrations:

This happened at the Ramakrishna Mission Institute of Culture, Calcutta, twenty years ago. We had a British citizen as a manager of our International Scholars and Guest Houses. One day, she came up full of joy and said that she had received a letter from the British Government in London, stating that she had just become eligible to receive her old-age pension according to the relevant British law and that they were enclosing the first cheque of that pension. Even though she herself had no idea of her eligibility for that pension; the staff in the relevant British Government office in far-away London had kept track of her case and given her due, without her, having to ask for it!

Here we can see a living example of human values in administration. What a contrast it is in our own country! Here, thousands of persons in her position would not only fail to get their dues spontaneously on time from the government and other service institutions, but would have to keep knocking from office to office for months and years! What a distance our management and administration have to travel from the current callousness and human unconcern to spontaneous human responses to human situations! This is the elementary spiritual growth that we have to achieve in our country in a big and pervasive way as responsible citizens. And I am sure that in the near future our people will achieve that growth, which is the fruit of true education and true religion in one.

A Japanese visitor to our country was struck by the widespread wearing of wrist watches by our people, including even our clerks, rickshaw pullers, and other low-paid citizens. He remarked to his Indian friend: 'In spite of Japan being more economically advanced than India, we Japanese do not consume most of what our industry produces like wrist watches and clocks, but largely export them for strengthening our economy; and what strikes me further in India is that everyone here wears a watch, but nobody is punctual. The watch seems to be more a status symbol than a useful instrument of punctuality!'

As a first step to toning up management in our banks and other similar institutions, and instilling a measure of self-discipline in all employees, it is worth while to consider introduction of a programme of commencing the day's work with all the staff, from Manager to the peon, sitting together or in small groups, in silent meditation for five to ten minutes. With the mind dwelling on God as the one Self in all beings, these few minutes could be devoted to the thought of dedicating one's life and work to that reality, through devoted service to all beings in the chosen field of one's work.

India: Its Historic Uniqueness

In the last century, India experienced an expansion of her energies. The first obvious sign was Swami Vivekananda's intellectual and spiritual impact on the dynamic modern West. Following our own philosophy, science, and art of management and administration, we have to build up the human values of our vast nation and render our distinctive service to the rest of the world. And the world is waiting for it. By 2020 AD, we have to work unitedly to make India a great world power, but a world power with a unique historically acquired character of her own, namely, a power for the diffusion of spiritual and human values, a power for international peace, co-operation, and welfare. This must be the one passion of our people which saw great achievements and changes in the scientific, political, and social fields of human endeavour, including our freedom and the freedom of all colonial oppressed peoples of the world. In her long history of over five thousand years, even when she had often developed mighty empires with economic and military strength, India maintained uniformly peaceful international relations, without any instance of military aggression on other nations. But she has, silently and effectively, invaded the hearts and minds of other nations, in her own way, namely, through inspiring ideas and ideals and through great spiritual personalities like Buddha. And for this she became internationally renowned as the land of wisdom and humanism. Swami Vivekananda refers to this unique impact of India on contemporary civilizations in these words (The Complete Works, Volume III, pp.105-6):

> The debt which the world owes to our Motherland is immense ... In ancient and in modern times, seeds of great truth and power have been cast abroad by the advancing tides of national life; but, mark you, my friends, it has been always with the blast of war trumpets, and with the march of embattled cohorts. Each idea had to be soaked in a deluge of blood ... This, in the main, other nations have taught; but India has, for thousands of years, peacefully existed. Here activity prevailed when even Greece did not exist, and Rome was not thought of ... Even earlier; when history has no record, and tradition dares not peer into the gloom of that intense past, even from then until now, ideas after ideas have marched out from her, but every word has been spoken with a blessing behind it, and peace before it. We, of all nations of the world, have never been a conquering race, and that blessing is on our head, and therefore we 'live'.

Again (Ibid.: 109),:

> At the beginning of this century, Schopenhauer, the great German philosopher studying, not from a very clear translation of the Vedas made from an old translation into Persian, and thence by a young Frenchman into Latin, says: "In the whole world, there is no study so beneficial and so elevating as that of the Upanisads. It has been the solace of my life, it will be the solace of my death. "This great German sage foretold that: "The world is about to see a revolution in thought more extensive and more powerful than that which was

> witnessed by the Renaissance of Greek literature", and today his predictions are coming to pass. Those who keep their eyes open, those who understand the workings in the minds of the different nations of the West, those who are thinkers and study the different nations, will find the immense change that has been produced in the tone, the procedure, in the methods, and in the literature of the world, by this slow, never-ceasing permeation of Indian thought.

Again, speaking about the spiritual dimensions of Indian culture, Swamiji says (Ibid.: 148-49):

> This continent is illumined with brave and gigantic minds and intelligences which think of this so-called infinite universe as only a mud puddle; beyond and still beyond they go. Time, even infinite time, is to them but non-existence. Beyond and beyond time they go. Space is nothing to them; beyond that they want to go; and this going beyond the phenomenal is the very soul of religion.
>
> The characteristic of my nation is this transcedentalism, this struggle to go beyond, this daring to tear the veil off the face of nature and have, at any risk, at any price, a glimpse of the beyond ... Do you want to enthuse them? Then here is the way to do so. You talk of politics, of social regeneration; you talk of money making and commercialism—all these will roll off like water from a duck's back. This spirituality, then, is what you have to teach the world.
>
> Have we to learn anything else? Have we to learn anything from the world? We have, perhaps, to gain a little in material knowledge, in the power of organization, in the ability to handle powers, organizing powers, in bringing the best results out of the smallest of causes ... But if any one preaches in India the idea of eating and drinking and making merry, if any one wants to apotheosize the material world into a God, that man is a liar ... The Indian mind does not want to listen to him.

And pleading for making Vedanta practical, and pointing out the tremendous practical efficiency and character energy that will flow to all our people from such a total practical orientation of this great philosophy, he says (Ibid.: 244-45):

> Centuries and centuries, a thousand years of crushing a tyranny of castes and kings, and foreigners, and your own people, have taken out of all your strength, my brethren. Your backbone is broken, you

are like downtrodden worms. Who will give you strength? Let me tell you, strength, strength, is what we want. And the first step in getting strength is to uphold the Upanisads, and believe, I am the Soul—(the Atman), "me the sword cannot cut; no weapons pierce; me the fire cannot burn; me the air cannot dry; I am the Omnipotent. I am the Omnicient. "So repeat these blessed saving words. Do not say we are weak; we can do anything and everything ... This is the strength that you get from the Upanisads; this the faith that you get from there.

These conceptions of the Vedanta must come out, must remain not only in the forest, not only in the cave, but they must come out to work at the Bar and the Bench, in the Pulpit, in the cottage of the poor man, with fishermen that are catching fish, and with the students that are studying. They call to every man, woman, and child, whatever be their occupation, wherever they may be. And what is there to fear? How can the fishermen and all these carry out the ideals of the Upanisads? The way has been shown. It is infinite; religion is infinite, none can go beyond it; and whatever you do sincerely is good for you. Even the least thing well done brings marvellous results. Therefore, let every one do what little he can. If the fisherman thinks he is the Spirit (the Atman), he will be a better fisherman; if the student thinks he is the Spirit, he will be a better student. If the lawyer thinks that he is the Spirit, he will be a better lawyer, and so on... But that does not mean that there should be these (special) privileges. They should be knocked on the head. If you teach Vedanta to the fisherman, he will say, I am as good a man as you; I am a fisherman, you are a philosopher; but I have the same God in me as you have in you. And that is what we want; no privilege for any one, equal chances for all. Let every one be taught that the Divine is within, and every one will work out his own salvation.

Liberty is the First Condition for Growth

We are passing through, as I said earlier, the most revolutionary period of our long history. We can successfully come out of this fire of transition and maintain our millennia-long historic continuity into the future, if our people understand the spiritual strength behind our rich age-old culture and the philosophy that has sustained it, namely, the Vedanta. The appeal of that Vedanta comes to our people today through the lion-roar of Vivekananda (Ibid.: 93):

> Let every man and woman and child, without respect of caste or birth, weakness or strength, hear and learn that, behind the strong and the weak, behind the high and the low, behind every one, there is that Infinite soul (the Atman), assuring the infinite possibility and the infinite capacity of all to become great and good. Let us proclaim to every Soul: Uttisthata, jagrata, prapya varan nibodhara: Arise, Awake, and stop not till the goal is reached" (*Katha Upanisad*, 3.14). Arise, Awake! Awake from this hypnotism of weakness. None is really weak. The soul is infinite, omnipotent, and omniscient. Stand up, assert yourself, proclaim the God within you; do not deny Him! Too much of inactivity, too much of weakness, too much of hypnotism, has been and is upon our race. 0 ye modern Hindus, dehypnotize yourselves. The way to do that is found in our own sacred books.

Mauryan Emperor Asoka of the third century before Christ in his edicts scattered in lands extending from Mysore in the South to Tajikistan, Afghanistan, and Pakistan, in the North-West, proclaimed the policy of 'silencing the war drums (*yuddha-bheri*)' and 'sounding the kettle drums (*dharma-bheri*)' of humanism and peace. Recalling this historically acquired unique international peace policy of Asoka, Swamiji says (Ibid.: 276):

> There have been great conquering races in the world. We also have been great conquerors. The story of our conquest has been described by the noble emperor of India, Asoka, as the conquest of religion and spirituality.

In the modern age, many Western thinkers have referred appreciatively to this Indian contribution to international peace and harmony. American historian Will Durant, in his ten-volume *Story of Civilization,* Volume One, entitled *Our Oriental Heritage*, presents what the modern world can expect from India, in these words (p.633):

> It is true that even across the Himalayan barrier, India has sent to us such questionable gifts as grammar and logic, philosophy and fables, hypnotism and chess, and above all, our numerals and our decimal system. But these are not the essence of her spirit; they are trifles compared to what we may learn from her in the future. As invention, industry, and trade bind the continents together, or as they fling us

> into conflict with Asia, we shall study its civilizations more closely, and shall absorb, even in enmity, some of its ways and thoughts. Perhaps, in return for conquest, arrogance, and spoliation, India will teach us the tolerance and gentleness of the mature mind, the quiet content of the unacquisitive soul, the calm of the understanding spirit, and a unifting, pacifying love for all living beings.'

If this tribute to India by Will Durant tickles our national vanity, it should also awaken our sense of national and international responsibility. This is still more so when we listen to the British historian late Arnold Toynbee on what the world expects from India. ('Introduction' to Sri Ramakrishna: His Unique Message by Rev Swami Ghananandji).

> Sri Ramakrishna message was unique in being expressed in action. The message itself was the perennial message of Hinduism. As Rev. Swami Ghanananda points out. Hinduism is unique among the historic higher religions in holding that neither Hinduism nor any other religion is a unique representation of the truth or a unique way of salvation...
>
> Sri Ramakrishna made his appearance and delivered his message at the time and the place at which he and his message were needed. This message could hardly have been delivered by anyone who had not been brought up in the Hindu religious tradition. Sri Ramakrishna was born in Bengal in 1836. He was born into a world that, in his lifetime, was, for the first time, being united on a literally world-wide scale. Today we are still living in this transitional chapter of the world's history; but it is already becoming clear that a chapter, which had a Western beginning, will have to have an Indian ending, if it is not to end in the self-destruction of the human race ... At this supremely dangerous moment in human history, the only way of salvation for mankind is an Indian way. The Emperor Asoka's and Mahatma Gandhi's principle of non-violence and Sri Ramakrishna's testimony to the harmony of religions here we have the attitude and the spirit that can make it possible for the human race to grow together into a single family—and, in the Atomic age, this is the only alternative to destroying ourselves.

Conclusion

I cannot conclude this chapter better than by presenting to you the powerful Vedantic exhortation of. Vivekananda to all people, irrespective of caste, creed, race, or sex. It is an exhortation conveying a truth about the wholesome impact of human values, not only on administration and management, but also on the flowering of character in spiritual realization and fulfilment (Ibid.: 93):

> Teach yourselves, teach every one, his real nature. Call upon the sleeping soul and see how it awakes. Power will come, glory will come, goodness will come, purity will come, and everything that is excellent will come, when this sleeping soul is roused to self-conscious activity.
>
> Purity, patience and perseverance are the three things essential to success in life...

These three basic needs are solely based on Human Value and the leading factor of the same.

4

Human Values and Enhancement of Human Potential

2

Human values are necessary in today's management. Business is no longer confined to a national state but is really borderless. Hence business from the international viewpoint cannot be regulated by governments unless international agreements can be reached. In this 'lawless land' the responsibility of the executive is greater than ever. Which values does one promote in her/his actions and decisions? Which responsibility does one take? On a national level we find similar concerns with ethics and values in management. Being a generator and facilitator of human material wealth, does one's responsibility towards human values end there? We do believe that the manager of today has a wider responsibility than that. We believe that it is in the interest of the managers themselves to have a heightened awareness of the values of humankind and also promote them.

Human Values: What are they?

Like most basic areas of human knowledge and experience, the concept of human values defies definition. Yet it can be instinctively felt, cognitively grasped and discussed as a shareable experience, and thus made a valid area of enquiry. This enquiry is a major undercurrent of the intellectual literature of all the ancient civilizations and of the later day philosophers, scholars and great leaders of social and political movements. The profusion of ideas, divergent approaches and intermixing of several strands of thought make the effort of conceptualising human values a daunting task for modern scholarship. However, for a clearer understanding of the scope, significance and interrelationship of these ideas it is necessary to have a conceptual framework for classifying them. In the following paragraphs we make a humble attempt at this difficult academic endeavour.

Classical literature does not make a distinction between values and human values. Perhaps there was no need for it then. Philosophical ideas on value enquiry were directed towards finding the nature, meaning and purpose of human existence. In the present century, search for a theory of values has become a separate branch of modern philosophy and is called axiology. Although the different realms of this value enquiry covers all areas of human concern like ethics, religion, art, science, social science, law, etc., no separate or special significance is attached to the term human values.

We would like to call one main approach to this classical value enquiry as the ideal-normative approach. In Western tradition it is represented by Plato's formulation of the absolute values of Truth, Goodness and Beauty. They are conceived as having independent existence of their own and are used as ideal norms for value judgement at the relative level of human existence. In the Indian tradition, absolute values are related to the absolute reality whose nature is described as Sat, Chit and Anand. Attainment of a state of eternal bliss by the realisation of identity of the individual self with the universal Self of this absolute reality is the highest and ultimate object of human striving.

Closely related to this absolutist perception is the theistic view which may be called a sub-group of the idealistic-normative approach. It is based on a metaphysical belief system which accepts the reality of a divine cosmic order and faith in the authority of a creator God who is also the upholder of all values. The basis of all ethical, social and other human values is sought in the enduring truths, either revealed or obtained through super conscious insights of sages, contained in the sacred religious literatures. Although differing in their belief systems, rituals and customs, the world's great religions largely agree on the basic moral values, conceptions of personal virtues and social group behaviour based on humanistic values of love, brotherhood, caring and sharing. Many leaders of the Indian renaissance, like Swami Vivekananda, Sri Aurobindo, Rabindranath Tagore and Mahatma Gandhi, were inspired by the absolutist-theistic value system and used it as the basis for their efforts towards the spiritual, social and political rejuvenation of Indian society.

In recent times, the term 'human values' has been used to denote this theistic approach to value system (Chakraborty, 1995; Swami Ranganathanand, 1991). This is perhaps because of the need to highlight the universal humanistic aspects of this value approach, as against the merely speculative, mystical, or life-denying ascetic aspects. In the modern interpretation of theistic value approach, the authors have shown its relevance and significance to managers and other professionals. Another reason for the use of the adjective 'human' before these values may be to distinguish this value approach from the modern, so-called scientific, approach to human phenomena and associated values. Interpreted in its narrow sense, this scientific approach robs man of the dignity of his divine association, his spiritual nature and reduces him to a biological organism of a random collection of atoms. It denies any meaning and purpose to life and rejects all considerations of faith, belief, feeling and intuitive religious perceptions. This mechanistic, deterministic interpretation makes man merely a malleable automaton, which can be 'programmed' to meet the demands of the existing socio-technological order, through manipulation of his lower order needs and desires.

In another sub-group of the idealistic-normative approach to human values, we would like to place all the different strands of humanistic thoughts, ranging from love and compassion of Buddha to the radical humanism of Marx. Included in this sub-group are the ideas of humanists having varying degrees of theistic, non-theistic and atheistic leanings but attaching prime importance to man and to human values. As Fromm (1981: 148) points out "There is a remarkable kinship in the ideas of the Buddha, Eckhart, Marx, and Schweitzer: their radical demand for giving up the having orientation; their insistence on complete independence; their metaphysical skepticism; their godless religiosity, and their demand for social activity in the spirit of care and human solidarity". These humanist ideas and movements developed as protests against oppressive constraints on human spirit of freedom, creativity and dignity, which were imposed by religious dogmas or by dehumanising social or technological orders of their day. They developed a new ethics of man, based on inter-linking of humaneness, love and respect for life, the joy of sharing and caring, and the faith in man to shape his own destiny. They find deep reflections in the literary traditions of both the East and the West over the last few centuries (Bharati, 1990). This gave rise to different kinds of social and political theories, like liberalism and socialism, for the betterment of humankind, particularly of the oppressed and the exploited. In recent times it has led to the declaration of Universal Human Rights by the United Nations. The term 'human values' has generally been understood in this context of humanistic thoughts.

We would like to call the second main approach to human values as the empirical-purposive approach. This was adopted by modern psychologists and other social scientists like Rokeach (1973), Schwartz (1994) and Mukherjee (1965). It views values as distinct component of the total human personality, which guide or affect attitude and behaviour of the individual and social groups. In Schwartz's view, values are "responses to three universal requirements with which all individuals and societies must cope: needs of individual biological organisms, requisites of coordinated social interaction and requirements for smooth functioning and survival of groups" (Schwartz, 1994: 21). This approach is non-normative and is neither based on any religious, philosophical system of ideas or world view nor on any social-political ideology. Identification of values, their classification, and search for inter-relationships between them is based on empirical methods of observation, attitude surveys, statistical validation techniques, etc. Conceptualisation of human values based on the findings of empirical research is fast becoming a distinct area of social science research.

These empirical studies and researches on human values are not merely idealistic or intellectual exercises. They are purposive in the sense that the knowledge gained by them is sought to be utilised for practical purposes in diverse areas like, management science (leadership and team building, human resource development, etc.) and socio-political policy decisions (welfare programmes, race relations, positive action programmes for minorities, population control programmes, environmental policy, etc.).Another way of classifying the different approaches to human values could be according to the level of aggregation they focus their attention on. These levels may be called the individual, the sociological and the ecological.

The first level focuses on the individual human being, taken as an independent entity. Some illustrative value terms referring to this level are survival values, character, personal virtues, aesthetic appreciation, human rights, salvation, self-realization, etc. At the second level, individual values are subordinated to the sociological values. It is concerned with operation of values at the collective level of human society. It includes values associated with family and other social institutions and professions like caring and sharing, sense of social responsibility, social and economic justice, sarvodaya, values of humanity and human inter-connectedness, etc. Similarly, the ecological level subordinates the first two and consists of values from the standpoint of human beings as a part of the total ecological system. In the reports commissioned by the Club of Rome, there is a concern for developing a "new world consciousness...a new ethic in the use of material resources, a new attitude towards nature, based on harmony rather than on conquest...a sense of identification with future generations" (Mesaroric and Pestel, 1974: 148) to avoid global catastrophe caused by unrestrained economic growth. "For the first time a demand is being made for an ethical change, not as a consequence of ethical belief but as the rational consequence of economic analysis "(Fromm, 1988: 149). Human values and perceptions from this perspective focus on the inter-dependency of human beings and nature and include expressive terms like respect for and harmony with nature concept of Mother Earth, sustainability, conservation, etc.

We thus arrive at a two-dimensional matrix for classification of the concept of human values. One dimension of this matrix consists of the different approaches and the other of the three levels of aggregation, shown as the horizontal and the vertical columns in the table below.

Table 4.1

Two-dimensional Classification Framework of Human Values

Approach Level Theistic Humanistic	*Ideal-normative Empirical-purposive*
Individual	XXX
Sociological	XX
Ecological	X

It needs to be emphasised that the categories in this proposed classification scheme are far from exclusive. In fact they very much overlap. For example, many humanistic approaches have theistic foundations and many items of the empirical approach are reformulations of the idealistic approach. What is implied in the classification is the identification of the main emphasis or main focus of the approach. The entries in the matrix indicate what we consider to be the main level(s) of aggregation which a particular approach focuses on. In our view, the theistic approach focuses mainly on the individual level in its quest for making a "good" man, whereas the humanistic approach is concerned with both the "good" man and the "good" society. This is not to deny the sociological and ecological concerns of the theistic approach. We however feel that these concerns are secondary to that of the individual. On the other hand, the different empirical approaches together cover all the three, individual, social and ecological levels.

The progression in the above matrix, both in the vertical and horizontal directions, has a chronological order. The earliest human value perceptions were related to the individual level. The growing complexities and tensions of human societies enlarged the scope to include the sociological considerations as its second focus. And the disastrous impact of the rapid technological developments, coupled with the population explosion of the present age has made ecological concern as the third focus. Once again this chronological flow has no exclusivity. The philosophical speculations and beliefs of the earliest civilisations, including the aboriginal civilisations in existence today, have remarkable sensitivity and insights about nature and man's relation to it. However, it is only in recent times that the theme has acquired an urgency to prompt development of a concerted approach to human values in relation to ecology. Similarly, many of the later day humanistic values have been traced to the earliest Upanisadic idealistic-theistic views on life and its values (Devaraj, 1988). Yet there is a general chronological flow from the absolutist, theistic view of human values to the humanist view, and finally to the present day empirical view.

Can Human Values be Taught?

The questions of interest to us are can human values be taught to modern managers in any systematic way and, if so, to what effectiveness. I, myself along with Swami Someswaranananda have since 2002 been giving workshops on the theme "Enhancement of Human Potential and Human Values." We have done these workshops both on in-house basis in many companies and as open workshops for managers from different companies and academics, especially in India, but also from abroad. The impetus for this development is said to have come from managers at various management development programmes given at our Ramakrishna-Vivekananda International Foundation, New Delhi and Vivekananda Centre for Indian Management, Indore, asking for Indian insights that could be valuable for organizations and management.

Keeping in view the need of the hour and alarming erosion in human values among the entire class of workers and executives of the country and abroad, leading corporate bodies have taken up the premier role of bringing a revolution in the field of management research and studies. Their aim is to produce the best executives and managers of the country who will be well developed totally based on 'Indian Management Excellence', Indian traditional sciences and values. Indian traditional sciences and scriptures corresponding to the management sciences have to be applied through the short term and prolonged inventional and supplementary research and training module. And for this, organized and structural training is required to be provided to corporate managers, executives and management officials at large.

In this context, we have designed the brief of a module of Management Development Programme on the basis of Indian context and Indian traditional sciences, or what we called 'Indian Management Excellence' (IME). Corresponding module has been named 'Excellence of Human Potential Programme' (EHPP). The theme of the module is to create awareness about the human potentials among management executives, and to make them understand the truth of life, the science of life and life-light for enabling them towards innovative and effective management. By this, management executives will be more capable and be able to render highly qualitative and truly responsive work through the avenue of enriched dynamism with value based enthusiasm towards the ultimate goal of total fulfilment of humankind.

It is claimed that Indian values are found in the deep-structure of the Indian psyche, as reflected in these sources. The basic idea is purification of the mind, partly through a mind-stilling technique, and partly through practice of nourishing noble thoughts (e.g., fearlessness, creativity, raj asik model of leadership, compassion, friendliness, humbleness), and rejecting wicked ones (e.g., greed, jealousy, arrogance). Such practice will reveal the "divine", or "higher self", within the individual who will be able to perceive the same in others. The goal is that in a management setting these practices will have repercussions on business life. More specifically, in respect of the individual, improved cooperation, non-attachment to the selfish rewards of the work, increased creativity, service to the customer, improved quality, creating an ethico-moral soundness, cultivating self-discipline and self-restraint, and enhancing generosity.

The content of the workshops varies according to the duration. There are three modules, the first one lasting three days, and the next two lasting two days each. Each module elaborates different principles. Module I, also called the "foundation module", develops the basic concepts and practices. It is argued that managerial effectiveness is dependent on a sound values system, undergirding the superstructure of skills, which in turn emanates from a pure mind.

The factors influencing a pure mind are discussed in terms of higher and lower self, isolation and re-identification with the latter and the former respectively, the *guna*, *karma*, *samskaras*, *nishkam karma* and other theories. The first steps of the mind-stilling technique relating to these principles are given at this stage. Module II focuses on leadership and teamwork and elaborates on a number of principles from Vedantic and Buddhist literature connected to the theme. Additional steps in the mind-stilling technique are also introduced. Module III covers the topics stress, counselling and communication. The main issue here is to identify with one's innermost self, which is *ananda*, as the basic remedy for stress-generating influences. A few more steps are included on the mind-stilling process in this module.

The workshops are promoted directly and indirectly; directly through mailing of pamphlets to select companies, and indirectly through the network of previous course participants of the workshops. Initiatives for the in-house workshops can come from the top management, HRD (personnel) department, open workshop participants who want to bring in the workshop to the company, persons who have come in contact with the ideas, etc. Participation at the workshops is mostly on voluntary basis, but there could be occasions when managers are asked by the CEO or someone else senior to attend.

Following the categorization of human values as mentioned above, these workshops would fall into the "ideal-normative" approach, with theistic learning. The source of the values taught at the workshops is derived from the sacred texts of Indian intellectual literature, and the values have an eternal and universal character to a great extent. It is normative in the sense that the values are something people ought to have from the ideal perspective. The basic foundation of values is taken to be divine, implying a theistic approach, but the humanistic elements are found in caring values, concern for others, love and compassion. The level of focus is mainly on the individual in terms of personal virtues. It is stated that in order to change the environment we must start with ourselves. Thus, more aggregated human levels (organizational, political, societal, ecological, global) are not neglected, but the starting point is always the individual.

Workshops Examined

We had a workshop in NTPC in its New Delhi-Badarpur Plant. NTPC being market leader in the power sector in India and as one of is leading companies in the country has shown the path towards this pursuit. All the participants were Managers belonging to senior management cadres. The ranks attending the workshops can vary—some can have pure peer-groups and some others have superior-subordinate relationship at the same workshop. The annual international workshop, on the other hand, attracts top and senior practitioners, academia, consultants, and government officials from India and abroad. The respondents whose plans of action would be analysed thus represent a cross section of highly educated, motivated and successful persons in their chosen spheres of activity.

Analysis of the plans of action, meant to understand the intentions of the participants and make inferences from their statements about the extent to which these workshops have influenced human values in managers, is done meticulously. The intended actions are analysed with reference to (a) the contents of the workshop, and (b) the purpose of, and the direction in which the participants want to make use of the contents, inputs, knowledge and skills they have learnt from the workshops.

Content Analysis

A content analysis of the responses shows that the most frequent item figuring in almost all the course participants' plan of action is the resolve to practice the mind-stilling and breathing exercises taught in the course, as an essential experiential practice for *Chitta-Shuddhi* and for communion with the higher Self. Its enthusiastic reception may have also been prompted by the urgent need for maintaining a calm mind in the tension-ridden life of practicing managers.

The next most common resolve relates to the practice of a cluster of values and value-principles emphasised in the course. It includes,

(i) cultivation of values related to higher self and suppression of disvalues associated with lower self, (ii) practice of *nishkam karma* (self-less action) in work-life as well as personal life, (iii) practice of giving model of life based on the concept of five fold debts (*deva rin, rishi rin, pitri rin, nri rin,* and *bhuta rin*) (iv) cultivation of *satwaguna* over *rajoguna*, and (v) introspection to examine, and to rearrange one's career goals, life styles, attitudes and value systems in the light of the above noted paradigm of higher values.

Some responses indicate a desire to propagate and share the ideas learnt in the course with members of the family as well as members of the work-group. A smaller number of responses show the desire to learn more about these ideas by reading the sacred wisdom literature of India, like *Tattabodh*, *Gita*, *Upanisads*, writings of Vivekananda, etc.

One can conclude from this content analysis that the value concepts of Indian psycho-spiritual tradition have been well received. They have had a positive impact on the participants as indicated by their resolve to internalise them and to use them as a basis for self-development.

Conclusion

This innovative approach to value education for practising managers and to focus on human potentials is impressive. We have culled out selected psycho-spiritual values from the traditional wisdom literature of India, suitably reinterpreted them and woven them together to form a coherent theory of human values. This theory is then utilised to explain the problems and tensions of both personal and work life of professionals and to indicate the way for a better quality of life. This approach finds deep resonance in the hearts and minds of Indian managers is evident from our observations of the course and the enthusiasm of the participants, and, at times, deeply moving articulations at the conclusion of the workshops.

Such response undoubtedly provides a fertile soil for reexamining ad developing one's human values. To that extent, it is evident that the workshops have been effective in influencing the human values of the course participants. However, it is difficult to reach any conclusion as to what extent the course objectives have been interiorised by the participants and the general learning effects of the workshops in the daily lives of the participants. What are the effects in the managers' work and family lives, and do their decisions reflect an increased awareness of human values? Neither can we draw any conclusions about the duration of the effects, i.e. whether it will last for a day or week and then vanish, or, if the effects are stable and enduring.

It is also evident from the responses and the stated objectives of the course that the main focus is on the self; self-awareness, self-analysis and self-development. It is consistent with the view that the individual is the cornerstone of all changes and transformations at the organizational as well as the societal levels. While the necessity of this self-development as a precondition for the value transformation in society may not be in doubt, the emphasis on it may convey the age that it is also sufficient for all the value problems of today's living. At the organizational level the difficulty may be posed in terms of two distinct, though related, categories of intra-personal and interpersonal values. The latter are of vital significance to managers' organizational role of a team leader, a change agent or a member of a work group. A heightened sensitivity to personal virtues, which is very effective at the intro-personal level, in itself may not be sufficient for values needed for effectiveness at the inter-personal level. Additional emphasis on humanistic values like human warmth, friendliness, acceptance of the other person as he/she is, trust, empathy, etc., may help bring about a better value balance. As indicated in our study, the emphasis on the inter and intra-personal levels, as also the extent to which other approaches to human values should be emphasized, may have to be adjusted, depending on the type of organization that is approached.

The manager significantly affects, and is affected by, the value culture of the society, through the mediating agency of organizations and other social institutions. Proper appreciation of this value dynamics requires understanding, and interiorisation of the operation of human values at the societal and ecological levels of our categorization. It is not clear as to what extent values at these levels can be developed and nourished through the present structure and approach of the human value workshops. An evaluation of the immediate impact of workshops, the long-term benefits and the influence on different levels of human values may help clarify the position. Understanding this, could lead to suggestions for expansion and alteration of the course contents as well as the methodology of the workshops.

5

Reformation of Indian Organizations

India ranks among the top industrialized countries. It has also recently joined the ranks of nuclear powers. Thus, one would expect Indian industries and businesses in general to be effective, efficient, and satisfying to their customers, clients as well as employees. But this seems to be on the contrary. Visitors from abroad as well as Indians are appalled at the inefficiency and lax work-culture that prevails in our organizations in general. Asked to rate the level of effectiveness and efficiency of their own organization, many Indian executives and managers indicate a range of 30 to 60 per cent. The quality of many goods produced within the country is such that there is a general hankering in India for imported goods. The daily life of teens can be characterized as a constant battle with the inefficiencies and hurdles of the systems and procedures of the organizations they have to deal with. A general lack of a service mentality appears to be the dominant characteristic of Indian organizations. The front-line workers go about their work, uncommitted to their organizations, and seem to regard their jobs just as a means towards making a living, with no obligation to put out and produce.

Managers and management academics ought to wonder if the quality of products and services available in this country are reflective of its industrial-business acumen at its entry into the twenty-first century. For all the progress India has made in industry and commerce, which is no doubt considerable, quality is not evident in its daily business transactions. Most people seem to be content to console themselves by saying, "What can we do, we are a poor country!" It is not that India lacks technology, or technical know-how, or raw materials, or manpower. In fact, India's manpower is the envy of many intelligent, educated, trained countries. But there has been a constant brain-drain. Thus, a relevant question for behavioural scientists, and change agents is how to bring positive change to the front lines and bottom levels of organizations, and induce high commitment and high performance at all levels. Even going up a few levels in the organizations, it would appear that our changed gentry, our changed technology, our changed techniques have not yielded results to justify our confidence in such techniques that have come to us as 'received knowledge' from the developed countries. My recent review of more than a hundred change efforts in India as well as the developing world as a whole (Srinivas, 1995a; 1995b), leads me to feel disheartened in my faith in these techniques of change. Judging from the organizational development efforts that have taken place in India in the last many years, I am inclined to conclude that the more we have tried to change things at the top, the more they have remained the same at the bottom. Thus, there is no doubt that the change models and the paradigms we have been using need a critical reexamination. Perhaps we need a paradigm or paradigms that suit the ethos of the people, the ethos of the culture. I have elsewhere (Srinivas, 1994) presented an argument that culture specificity is imperative for organizational renewal and development in the Indian context.

We have certain basic realities of Indian society—caste, clan, corruption, and coalitions, that behavioural science models do not easily recognize. Professors Jai Sinha and Rajen Gupta have pointed these out some time back (Sinha, 1988 and 1994; Gupta, 1991 and 1995). Unfortunately, recognising and taking into account these realities would make us politically incorrect in the current national climate. Many behavioural scientists whom I have had a chance to interact with in India have opined that the ground realities are fast disappearing and will soon vanish with the advent of the electronic media like Star TV. Therefore, any attempt to take these into account will only take us backward, not forward. For them progress consists of marching to the beats of received wisdom while ignoring the ground realities, as they consider these to be on their way out. The reason why they think in such black-and-white, either-or terms, and not want to blend the east and the west, baffles me. Especially when our heritage says *Aa noh bhadraha, kritano yanta vishwwtha* (*Rig Veda*)—'let noble thoughts come to us from all quarters'.

My personal visits to many executives and managers in their chambers, and having seen them 'in performance' leads me to conclude that at the senior levels we have what Westwood and Chan (1995) call 'headship', not leadership. At the middle and junior levels we have sahibship. This is how the colonial masters managed. Headship, like the head of a large joint family of the olden days, is not bad if exercised for the good of the many (*bahujana hitaya*). But there are no visible examples of enlightened headship, not in sufficient numbers, documented. The very notion itself is distanced, as there are many instances of self-centered headship occupants, particularly in the political scene, who are 'making hay while the sun is shining'. Instances of sahibship are evident all too often. This has resulted in the managerial class as a whole losing trust and respect from the lower levels. The subordinates look upon their superiors with cynicism and indifference, and are outrightly disobedient. The degree of deterioration in the work-culture is so deep that I do not think that trust in and respect for authority can be rebuilt through techniques of Organizational Change formulated in the developed world. I think we as change agents, need to develop paradigms which help us reestablish legitimate authority in organizations.

There seem to be many arguments why positive change cannot be brought about at the lower levels of our organizations but my observations lead me to believe that the main problem is with managerial orientation and style. To quote India's grand old industrialist the late JRD Tata, "*There is a belief in our country that our culture and our character cannot allow our people to attain consistently high standards; that shoddiness and carelessness are our God-given ways of life. But if with faith in them, you ask our men for their best, they rise to a belief in their work and create a momentum towards improvement. Often I have seen men who were considered ordinary, rise to extraordinary heights*" (Lala, 1992). While talking to a couple of CEOs in Mumbai, I found them endorsing JRD by narrating personal experiences that led them to develop similar beliefs. If men who are considered ordinary have to rise to extraordinary heights, JRD's insight needs to be utilized in practice. But with the prevailing hierarchy in Indian organizations this insight cannot be put into practice by any mantra in the acquired wisdom. But there are other mantras, if only we look outside the box. But looking outside the box could make it uncomfortable for our rational, left brain or intellectual mind, schooled in western thinking.

One of my observations related to headship and sahibship turns out to be an affirmation of a statement made over a hundred years ago, "*Three men cannot act in concert in India for five minutes. Each one struggles for power.*" None other than our respected sage Swami Vivekananda made that statement. Our newspapers vouch the veracity of this national blemish everyday. On the other hand, I have seen men change and transform, and work to realize goals that were unattainable earlier. But this effort for change and transformation has been achieved under a different paradigm than that upon which the technology of organizational development is built. Brief mention will be made below of these dramatic changes and transformations.

Remarkable Organizational Transformations

Some remarkable changes and transformations have taken place in India. These are based on a paradigm different from that of the mainstream western behavioural science and its change agentry. The first of these came to my attention during a recent opportunity I had to go to some tiny villages and hamlets along the border of Gujarat and Rajasthan. The villagers who at one time had been feuding, helpless and resigned to fate, had come alive and made a complete turnaround. They were now functioning as empowered adults making value-based, business-wise, proactive, in-concert decisions. They had learned to cooperate and collaborate for individual as well as collective benefit. The self-discipline and sense of empowerment among youth, women and the aged were unbelievable. I saw a similar transformation of individuals and groups at a *Vaghri* community (vegetable sellers having a low social status) urban ghetto in Ahmedabad. This socially low ranked group had pulled itself up, and the individuals had improved their personal sense of self worth, and were brimming with pride at their achievements. Similar changes have taken place in thousands of villages in fanning and fishermen communities across Maharashtra, Gujarat and other states (Srivastava, 1998).

How has this change and transformation, this group solidarity and commitment to achievement, come about? It is through the Swadhyaya (Self-study or Self learning) movement that was started by Panduranga Shastri Athavle, who has been recognized with the prestigious Magsaysay and Templeton awards. *Swadhyaya* is a process of self-development and discovery of one's identity in a spiritual sense (Sheth, 1994). It is also known as the 'silent movement'. The personal discipline achieved by the followers of this movement was evident to me in the behaviour of a very large crowd of over a lakh of people on the grounds of Gujarat University in Ahmedabad. The movement and its approaches have been depicted in story form in a movie called *Antarnaad* directed by Shyam Benegal. Regrettably, Indian sociologists and behavioural scientists in general have not shown much interest in documenting these amazing transformations and achievements, with some exceptions such as Ramashray Roy (1993) and Narayan Sheth (1994), and Shaw and his colleagues (Shaw et al., 1998) [Also see Rahnema, 1991, Copp and Copp, 1991, and Srivastava, 1998].

To me, the *Swadhyaya* movement was an indication of what is possible in this country in current times. It shows that it is still possible to raise the consciousness and commitment of the masses; for them to be empowered. *Swadhyaya* has demonstrated that spirituality has a profound effect on the human mind and should not be ignored in the pursuit of 'concerted efforts' towards change. The movement has achieved a sea change in over 150,000 villages, spread across all the provinces from Maharastra to West Bengal. *Swadhyaya* has utilized *Bhakti* (devotion), for people to empower themselves. To me it was also a demonstration that psychological growth and development can precede and cause economic and material development, and not the other way around as the Maslowian hierarchy of needs suggests. The principles of *Swadhyaya*, I believe, can be adapted in organization level change interventions. I saw glimpses of the outcomes of such an adaptation in some industrial organizations I visited in the industrial township of Hallol near Baroda. It may be noted that the *Swadhyaya* movement has some parallels with the notions of 'caring capitalism' and transcendental values evidenced by some 'social venture' organizations in the United States (Srinivas, 1998).

Yet another example of indigenous creativity that I have seen is that of *Edukeertan* (or industrial *keertan*). It is cognitive re-education through multiple senses, using a combination of devotional music, story telling, humour, mime, histrionics, drama, dance, etc. I observed it first hand in a textile mill in Bombay. The participants were the rank and file employees of the mill, all sitting cross-legged, Indian style, on a carpet on the floor. The trainer/change-agent was an industrial engineer turned *keertankar*, dressed in the traditional garb of *dhoti*, turban, long coat, and, of course, with a harmonium and cymbals. A transparency projector was the concession to modern times. Through songs, stories of ancient lore, with images that were suggestive of the holy and the sacred, and with audience participation, the messages of quality control and productivity were delivered in a traditional manner. The participants, at the end of the day, seemed convinced to the core. Each one of them made a vow to take responsibility of their jobs, for quality production, including all ancillary activities. What transpired was so powerful that I felt I had witnessed a miracle or a happening. This trainer has offered programs on productivity, quality control, interpersonal relations and self-development, more than a thousand times in different locations. And the programs are in the regional languages of Marathi, Gujarati and Hindi, and some times in English. These have also been a success in Tanzania and Malaysia. Doordarshan has reportedly made a documentary of these programs.

Indigenous Approaches to High-Commitment and High-Performance

Some incredible 'high-commitment, high-performance' organizations have been developed, again based on a different paradigm than that of the mainstream Organisational Development.

One such organization is Yash Paper Mills of Ayodhya. A barely literate workforce of 200 employees working in three shifts, have been organized as eight work groups. Their functional identity is in Hindi language. That is, each group is known as a Sangh (e.g., Kachha maal vyapar sangh, raw materials procurement association). Each Sangh is headed by a Sahayak (manager), and also elects a Pramukh (foreman), for a one-year term. The mental images and feelings these Hindi terms evoke are one of collaborative alignment. A Sahayak is a helper (not a manager or boss), a Pramukh means an important person, not a lead-hand. And Sangh is an association, not a department. Each Sangh holds a meeting once a week to discuss current and forthcoming production runs and makes decisions with respect to problems encountered or anticipated. Unresolvable issues are taken to the weekly meeting of the *Sahayaks*. What is not resolved at that level goes to the Managing Director. And it is interesting to note that no issue had gone to him in three years. The first shift in the morning holds a prayer meeting where they sing the Sanskrit sloka "*Twameva Maata, Twameva Pita* ...." while facing the statue of the triumvirate of *Vishwakarma* (God of production), Gandhi and Swami Vivekananda. Some Muslim employees also join in these prayers, as it is an invocation of blessings for the day's productive endeavour. The prayer ceremony includes hoisting the national flag and singing of a company anthem that has been etched and erected at the spot. The bonus is distributed equally to all. And again, everyone is equal in the lunch room, standing in queue, helping himself, and washing his own plate after he has eaten.

The company also keeps the workers informed of the feedback from the market. They bring in their distributors/wholesalers once a year, for 2 to 3 days, in a *mela* style, and have them interact with the employees and make presentations to them on market conditions. The employees also get dealer perspectives on comparative quality and how their own products stack up with those of others. It may be noted that this company is not a 'green site' company. It used to be a traditional union-management organisation, riddled with confrontation. It took them three painful years to switch over to the new system. The union's presence is still there. But it is an enlightened presence. In economic terms how has the company performed in the new system? In objective, financial terms, it has done better, and the trend seems to be improving and showing better and better performance. The qualitative data indicates high commitment by the employees, even at the lowest level. Just two consultants helped to change Yash Mills over to the new system. One of them is an industrial engineer and the other a spiritually inclined poet and corporate advisor. The Yash Company makes a splendid case study in indigenous creativity. But, unfortunately no behavioural scientist with change-agentry credentials has looked into this company.

Another example is that of Saravana Bhavan in Chennai (Gustaysson, 1997). It is a chain of fast food restaurants. The company practices a 'care and share' relationship with its employees who are treated as an extended family. The salaries match the best in the industry, and to top this, there are ample benefits like work uniforms, children's school fees, books, and school uniforms. For a girl child, the company makes monthly savings deposits to mature in time for her marriage. The parents of the employees are sent an allowance. The Managing Director is affectionately referred to as *Annachi*' (elder brother). It is 'nurturant-task leadership' (Sinha, 1980) writ all over the employment relationship.

Another MD also held in affection by the employees is KC Schroff of Excel Industries, known to the company employees as 'Kaka' (uncle). This is among the top ten companies in the Indian chemicals industry. Schroff sits at a MD size desk in a large shed, surrounded by scores of clerical employees. He uses the same cafeteria as they do. He wants his employees to see him and be able to talk to him. He is truly a morale builder, a loyalty builder, a commitment builder. Both Saravana Bhavan and Excel Industries can be labeled as 'familial' organizations—a type that Gupta (1995) has identified as desirable in the Indian context. Schroff's leadership philosophy seems to have been reinforced by *Vipassana* meditation training. And for many years now Excel has been sponsoring 8 to 10 of its employees from across the levels to a 10-day *Vipassana* meditation training camp. *Vipassana's* potential for phenomenal transformative change at the individual level has become well known through experiments made at Tihar Jail in Delhi. I had an opportunity to witness one of these training sessions and talk to some prison inmates who had gone through this training at the Baroda Central Jail. (The prison had previously held several *Vipassana* meditation courses for the inmates as well as for the correctional officers.) The prison looked as if it was in the midst of a festival. The sprawling compound, the walkways and the living quarters were meticulously clean. (I could not help but wish that the reverse was true, that this cleanliness was in the outside, and what was outside was contained within the tall walls of the Jail.) There was minimum security inside the compound. I talked to some of the prisoners as well as the correctional staff who had undergone *Vipassana* training earlier. They appeared at peace with themselves and with the world. The inmates extolled the training as having transformed them and their view of the world (When I was leaving I found out that many of them were convicted murderers). The Superintendent was all praise for the *Vipassana* training. He said that it had made the prison governance much easier, with cooperation from the prisoners in place of antagonism of the pre-training days. He also indicated that the Jail industry production (candles, soaps, clothing, etc.) had jumped up by 25 to 30 per cent annually. He attributed this to the change that had come about in the prisoners as a result of the *Vipassana* training program. I am told that the widely known Tihar Jail *Vipassana* meditation got its inspiration from the beginnings at Baroda Jail. Interestingly, I also came across some company CEOs who had experienced a personal transformation through *Vipassana* meditation training, and had been sending others in their organization for such programs. As a result, several of these employees I talked to had experienced much personal growth. Consequently, they were practising role excellence. I also attended a three-day conference at the Vipassana head quarters in Igatpuri and ran into many company executives and management consultants who vouched for *Vipassana*. The organizational benefits of *Vipassana* meditation has been jointly documented by a CEO and an MD (Shaw and Patel, 1998). My curiosity led me to go through a 10-day course myself very recently. It was tough, very tough. I hung in there and made it. I believe it has much potential for leadership training and personal transformation that needs to precede organizational level changes. And it is culture congruent, whereas T-group training and the like are not. It is deeper at the intrapersonal level whereas T-group training is more at the interpersonal level and more superficial.

Vipassana is not the only meditation technique that is being introduced in Indian organizations. There is also the *Rajayoga* technique of the *Brahmakumaris* which has found its way in many organizations in India as well as outside the country. Then there is the *Vedanta* based meditation that includes alternate nostril breathing that goes by the neutral label 'mind stilling', that we have been teaching managers and executives. I visited a divisional office of the IPCL in Bombay which had set apart a room and a designated time for people to come and practise mind-stilling meditation for which most of them had been offered training on a voluntary basis. I talked to a random sample across the hierarchic levels, and most reported individual benefits of reduced stress and decreased health problems. Some reported a more collaborative, more trustful climate in the workplace. Systematic research in this area is going on in the United States, Sweden and Norway (Gustaysson, 1992; Harting et al., 1995; Schmidt-Wilk et al., 1996). It is needless to say that no systematic research is going on in India. Nevertheless many companies in India, including some large corporations are abandoning behavioural scientists in favour of meditation techniques. The list of companies is impressive—TISCO, TELCO, IOC, NTPC, IPCL, CIL, IFFCO, NFCL, SBI, Ambuja Bengal, Salora International, Bhilwara Group, Godrej and Boyce, Atul Chemicals, and so on. It speaks of a trust, a belief and a demand in the corporate world for culture-specific approaches for effecting a transformation and change in their office atmosphere. It would thus seem that what the premier business schools in India are teaching is not going well in the field. Unfortunately, this has brought in many charlatans into management consulting and change agentry. I believe it is imperative that the behavioural science anchored change agents in India should make a serious attempt to examine the research literature on meditation and other yoga psychology based approaches (e.g. Patanjali's Ashtanga Yoga), and seek to integrate them with the received knowledge.

The examples cited above of indigenous approaches to organizational change and development, and the yield in terms of high employee-commitment and high-performance in Indian organizations should make us ponder upon our culture's ground realities. It should make us wonder if our approach to developing our organizations is the same as in the West. It should make us take note of and accept the internal characteristics of our society, its innate modes of thought, its cherished values and beliefs. We should be asking the question whether the incorporation of Indian ethos values in our managerial thinking can help us move away from sahibship-management and enable them to nurture high-commitment and high-performance in their organizations. It is possible that the ineffectiveness, bureaucracy and alienation of Indian organizations may be related to their being discordant with their deeply held culturally cherished values. It is possible that the Yash Paper Mills, the *Swadhyaya* movement, the *Vipassana* and other schools of meditation seek to achieve this value alignment, and hence their appeal to achievement/task oriented executives and managers. Employees everywhere relish tasks and activities that are congruent with their individual and social values. They hate or anguish over tasks that are otherwise. When they are forced into activities that are not congruent, only some courageous souls refuse to comply and face the consequences or quit the organization, but most people work in a compliant manner, afflicted with alienation. Perhaps this could be an explanation of the poor work culture that plagues Indian organizations. The remarkable changes narrated above have come about through an appeal and value re-education: Values are the soul and substance of the Indian psyche. There is much to discover about how organizational effectiveness in India can be enhanced through culturally appropriate paradigms.

East is East and West is West

Much of the psychological knowledge we have is culture bound. It was developed mostly in the Euro-American society based on its issues and approached with its own world views. So much so, Amir and Sharon (1987) were unable to replicate in Israel some of the more central studies of contemporary American social psychology. Out of the thirty attempts to replicate, twenty could not succeed. Only six were fully successful and four more were partially replicated. Similarly, Berry (1974) while studying French-Canadian/English-Canadian relations, tried using an implicit model derived from Black-American/White-American research. But he found it inappropriate to import American socio-psychological concepts to Canada. This led him to pose an important question. The point that is being made here is, if there are difficulties in transporting theories, methods and findings from the United States to Canada, how much more likely are there to be problems when larger cultural contexts are involved? More such questions can certainly be added. Can Japanese achievement be understood in terms of American achievement motivation theory? Can Freudian theory be used to understand father-son conflicts in Melanesia? It is obvious that there are limits to the trans-cultural portability of knowledge. Even research findings seem to be subject to the cultural socialization effects of the researchers. For example, surveys of human values carried out by Hofstede and Rokeach on the one hand, and those carried out by a Chinese Value Survey group on the other, arrived at different findings. While the first three dimensions found were the same in both the Western and the Eastern surveys, the fourth was different. The Western surveys were concerned with certainty, preference for laws, rules, safety and security measures, but not with the issues of virtue. Consequently they found an 'uncertainty avoidance' dimension. The Chinese survey with its Eastern acceptance and comfort with uncertainty did not enquire in this respect. It enquired with respect to virtue, thrift, perseverance, tradition and 'face', and discovered a virtue dimension of 'Confucian dynamism'. The researcher's biases came through in their findings! Thus, we cannot but agree with Hofstede (1992) who commented on these findings: "*... not only values and practices but even theories are products of culturally determined socialization. This should make us modest when we try to transfer, for example, Western types of education and management or training packages to people in a Third World country. Not only the tools but also the categories available for thinking may be unfit for the other environment.*"

Thoughts: Eastern and Western

A paradigm is a conceptual framework. It structures a virtual reality. Once the paradigm is accepted, its basic assumptions are not questioned. Effort is then directed at developing conceptual elaboration, test hypotheses, and develop means for enhancing desired ends, improve diagnostic and intervention tools, establish, criteria for assessment and create assessment tools. Paradigms are thus lampposts for advancement in thinking and for new discoveries. It must be recognized that while they are useful, paradigms are not valid for all time, as is well known with the paradigms of science, (Grof, 1983). While they are accepted, they create demands on practitioners and researchers. Four paradigms are noted below (See Ajaya, 1983). But first let us take stock of their respective world views in relevant dimensions.

World Views

The Western world view holds that man is a limited organism having a one time existence and is separate, autonomous, more solid and atomized (made up of a set of discrete traits, abilities, values and motives). Man is a 'sensate' being, this-worldly, hedonistic, utilitarian, empirical, secular, humanistic. Change, evolution or growth is through mutations according to science, through 'grace' or mercy of the Lord according to religion. This is still the dominant or majority view today, although under the surface there appear to be some fundamental changes such as the emergence of transpersonal psychology and reticent recognition of alternate and indigenous therapies.

The Indian Vedantic thought views consciousness as primary. Matter is the effect rather than cause of consciousness (The ordinary waking state is only a lower level of consciousness). Life is a process of refining the consciousness. Through personal effort and discipline one can directly experience Truth, release, liberation, nirvana. The self is conceived as fluid and interdependent with role and personality being superficial. It is easily changed when one is not caught up at that level of being. Self-examination and pursuit of personal growth are fundamental. It is an inward journey, a therapeutic evolution from cognitive shortcomings to mental breadth, to universal consciousness when one recognizes that the concerns and needs of all people are the same (Florsheim, 1990; Rama et al., 1976; Ajaya, 1976).

Reductianist: Views

This is a thought based on the Western world view. The dominant notion here is 'that which is'. It is fundamentally of a material nature; a complex phenomenon which can be understood by breaking it down into its more basic material components. In this paradigm human consciousness is not primary; rather, it is the result of the interaction of material entities. Here this paradigm views the physical and biological sciences as models for mental phenomena. Thus the reductionist attempts to understand human beings in terms of more primitive modes of functioning. Any change in the behaviour of humans needs to be sought in stimulus-response terms, in 'behaviour-mod' terms and in terms of schedules of reinforcement, extrinsic rewards, path-goal structuring and use of power and politics to obtain conformity and compliance and manipulative use of stimuli to elicit desired responses.

Humanistic Views

This is a view that has grown from and is still linked in part to the reductionist paradigm and thus not altogether distinct and separate from it. It emerged as a slight revision and a sort of protest against the degraded position accorded to human life by the reductionists. This paradigm holds that individual human experience is quite unique and must be studied and valued in its own right rather than reducing it to any sort of components, or regarding it as inferior to any other phenomenon. While no transcendent or universal consciousness is recognized, it is held that each human being is motivated toward actualizing one's latent potentials; that such motivation is a biologically driven need. This humanistic paradigm is concerned with what the upper limits of normal human functioning are, and how normal humans can fully realize their upper limits. Qualities such as creativity, empathy, trust in human nature, assertiveness, openness to experience (including sensory pleasure and emotional states), will and sensitivity to interpersonal relations are held to be important for a satisfactory and meaningful life. In the move towards being one's true self, individuals need to break loose from the habituated pattern of thinking, reorient themselves, discover their potentialities and upper limits through experimentation with new behaviours, and then become established with new cognitive structure and associated behavioural patterns. The change-agent becomes a role-model, and the quality of the relationship with the change-agent plays a significant role in this transformation. The change-agent creates a warm, supportive, trustful climate and models, and encourages behaviours that are desirable for the client's reality.

Dualistic Thoughts

The dualist thought is based on the assumption that the universe is fundamentally made up of interacting complimentary qualities. Both materialistic phenomena and consciousness exist as fundamental duality. Human existence is that of individualized, delimited consciousness involved with material phenomena. A transcendent consciousness also exists which is unidentified with material phenomena. The individualized consciousness is evolving towards a more complete experience of transcendent consciousness, but can never fully experience the comprehensive or transcendent consciousness. To the extent that the individualized consciousness involves itself with the material phenomena, it will experience a mixture of pleasure and pain. And to the extent that the human being realizes or positively relates to a more transcendent state of consciousness, he/she experiences such qualities as joy, contentment, knowledge, and truth. Jungian psychology, yoga psychology, general systems theory and Taoistic thinking are, to an extent, based on the dualistic perspective. Also, some denominations of Hinduism, some sects of Christianity and Islam subscribe to this dualistic paradigm. Induction of change, growth and development under this paradigm are through conversion of faith (much as in 'born again' religious conversions), and through charismatic, visionary, powerful, benevolent and paternalistic leaders. Change models based on dualistic paradigms also seem to obtain positive results. For example, Nadkarni (1992) has developed a model under the dualistic paradigm using a combination of devotional music, story telling, humour, mime, histrionics, drama, dance, etc. It seems to be very successful and has had literally hundreds of applications, although there is no information on its long-term effects. Nadkarni aligns desired behaviours with religious and scriptural stories and elevates productivity to the position of a goddess. His approach seems to appeal to the right brain thinking that Perry has pointed out as desirable in Africa: "*Begin with material aim at the emotions... (provide) a shared holistic experience based on all the channels of experience which include sight, sound and touching/feeling. Continue with material showing wholes and relationships. Explain the order, structure, logic of the material and conclude with a return to the emotional material*" (Perry, 1993). The fact that the prescription written for Africa seems to be working well in India shows that the dualistic paradigm models have a wider applicability. The trainer Rajaram (Kathawala) Nadkarni unfortunately has passed away without anybody apprenticing him to pick up his techniques and without any behavioural scientist or sociologist studying and assessing his methods. The katha technique, of course, is based upon the dualistic paradigm. At the same time his technique was culturally appropriate. The ancient technique of *ekottaropaya* (technique of just-one-more-thing), instead of extolling a 'new way', is presented as just an extension of an age old idea that has stood the test of time, something that for long has been held in esteem and even considered hallowed. For example, 'quality' is elevated to the status of a hallowed goddess, just one more in the long list of venerated goddesses. In his words in Hindi, *Gunavatta ek Devi hai, Isku aaradhana karna chahiye...* (Quality is a Goddess, she should be worshipped...) He asks the participants to join him in a chorus of acclamation, acknowledgment and public veneration of this one-more goddess, *Bolo Sri Saraswati Bhagavatiki Jai, Bolo Sri Gunavatta Shaktiki Jai* (Hail to goddess Saraswati and hail to goddess of Quality); *Doshasura Mardini Gunavatta Devi ki Jai.* (Hail to goddess Quality who is the destroyer of the Defect Demon). In contrast to this alignment of the new with the old, the accepted and the respected, a change-agent in the United States is compelled to label the new as new; that even the new can be true, and that it is true because it is new. The premise is that time makes ancient good uncouth. But in the Indian society with its long history and traditions, it may make more sense to align new ideas with the honoured past, as a clearer articulation of what is already present in established truths. It may be noted that Mahatma Gandhi utilized this technique of one-more thing to introduce a concept that motivated millions of people to join the national independence struggle. He linked the concepts of *satya* (truth) with *agraha* (indignation) and came up with the concept of *satyagraha*, a confrontational method for changing an intolerant situation with a dominant oppressor. *Satyagraha* concept combined strength, courage and obstinacy of behaviour of the underdog with the much-valued cultural characteristics of humility and goodwill towards the oppressor.

Monistic Thoughts

While the dualistic paradigm proposes two fundamental principles that interact to create the universe, the monistic paradigm begins with the assumption that there is only one fundamental principle, consciousness. The monistic paradigm premises simply that unitary consciousness is all that exists. It holds that while the phenomenal world appears to exist, it is insubstantial and exists only as an illusory manifestation of unitary consciousness, like a mirage or a dream existence. While dualism accepts that the perceiver and the perceived are different, one being the subject and the other the object, monism postulates that there is neither the perceiver nor the perceived, neither subject nor object; what may appear to be two is actually one. This paradigm takes its stand in a non-sensory experience and considers sensory data to be of little value in conveying knowledge of the fundamental reality. This view is quite shocking both to the reductionists and to the dualists. Hindu world, especially the *Vedanta* school, Jainism, Buddhism and the Afro-centric world view fall under the monistic paradigm. This view paradigm accepts a fundamental equality in the human psyche; one is the same as others (or not too different from others). It also accepts that power distances are only apparent and superficial; that there are cause-effect chains; that one has to suffer the consequences of one's conduct; that ignorance is the cause of erroneous behaviour, not evil nature; that the 'present' or 'here and now' is as important a determinant of the future as the past has been a determinant of the present. According to the monistic paradigm change is inevitable and inherently positive and one can and should change one's conduct and behaviours in order to grow. The paradigm accepts that one is inherently equipped to open the doors to one's own positive growth; that both intellectual-analytical as well as emotion-laden methods are acceptable and valid in the pursuit of growth and development. The Jungian, Yoga and transpersonal psychology also fall under this paradigm. It has recently come to be recognized that this perspective has important implications for psychotherapy.

A noteworthy attempt to develop an organizational change model and techniques under the monistic paradigm is that of Prof SK Chakraborty of IIM, Calcutta and Swami Someswaranandaji. Based on Indian psycho-philosophies of Vedanta and Yoga, this is indeed a pioneering effort. Executive testimonials indicate that this approach fits in very well with the world view of the cultural milieu and that considerable success has been experienced (Jhunjhanwala et al., 1987). This approach emphasizes the development of equanimity or stability of mind as a way of coping with the workaday world where the gamut of emotions run from excitement, exuberance, fulfilment, frustration and depression. The concept of mental composure is held to be the key to analysis and resolution of organizational irritations and imperfections. Composure leads to shedding of the egoism of "me" and unconditional extending of the self to others.

Conclusion

Having chalked out some principle paradigms, we might note that the field of OD has been operating under the humanistic paradigm since its inception while much has changed in the scientific and ideational or value communities. Discoveries in neurosciences, medical thought, physics and other disciplines have all come to recognize the Eastern perspectives. Recent thinking in physics, neurology, computing and other sciences has recognized that real phenomena are not confined to those that can only be objectively observed and measured. There is a hierarchy of realities –some of them manifest, and some hidden under ordinary circumstances, directly observable only in certain special states of consciousness. The sciences have thus broken out of the Newtonian paradigm. The field of OD needs to break out of its founding Lewinian paradigm.

Although not based on OD, applications, research evidence on monistic paradigm based *Yoga* therapy outcomes, have been documented with respect to behavioural as well as cognitive changes and generally enhanced mental health. This has been done not only in India where a supportive world view prevails but also in a prison population in the United States (Balodhi, 1986; Wilson, 1991; Rama et al., 1976). The monistic Yoga therapy has also been combined with reductionistic EEG biofeedback and the outcomes have been positive (Balodhi, 1983). Carl Jung viewed religion as playing a central role in the psychological transformation of individuals (Coward, 1989). The religio-spiritual world views and cultural ideologies make it obvious that human beings have not lived by 'bread alone' nor are they likely to. Individuals and societies are inspired by spiritualism and religion, cultural hopes, dreams, ideals and inspirations. All the great achievements of mankind were motivated by such intangibles. Organizational renewal and revitalization can surely be based on such intangibles! Dualistic and monistic transpersonal OD approaches may serve to be unifying and synergistic, particularly in caste and class ridden societies, that are nevertheless home grounds with supportive world views. It should perhaps be explicitly mentioned here that while we have advocated the formulation and utilization of indigenous models of OD, we are not averse to adaptations of the Western techniques or a creative synthesis of Eastern and Western ideas. It must also be recognized that developing and practising OD under the dualistic and monistic paradigms will not be without issues and problems of its own. For, in monistic as well as dualistic thinking, the core beliefs in their details are complex and even contradictory. It would then be difficult for change-agents to suggest a particular technique or method as an appropriate one in a given situation. Also, since time is endless and cyclical, and growth and change are assumed to occur over an extended period of time, it may be difficult to initiate timely action or seek to function by time lines. Additionally, aspired goals and ideals of a people may not be their actual goals and values in daily life. For example, while the 'ideal self' ought to be extending outward, it is usually limited in practice, going no further than the extended family or the clan or some such in-group. Breaking loose from this narrow practice to move in the direction advocated in the dualistic and monistic paradigms is not likely to be easy for individuals.

In the practice of OD as a discipline in India, we have reached a choice point. We can continue to think in terms of the reductionist-humanistic paradigm and continue to apply currently established OD techniques in our social contexts without a proper fit. Or, we can actively seek to formulate models and techniques that are culturally relevant for synergistic organizational renewal. Organizational vitalization and revitalization are task-group therapy.

Organizational renewal is psycho-social therapy. Organizational development is psycho-social hygiene. Can its rationale and techniques afford not to be linked to the cultural values and beliefs that are indigenous to a nation and culture? Let us emerge from darkness to light. *Tamaso Maa Jotirgamaya*.

6

Corporate Governance

An Ethical Approach

Corporate Governance and Corporate Performance

Good corporate governance must include the framework of strong performance orientation. Conformation with good governance is a hygiene factor—performance is important. Good governance needs to incorporate leadership and management imperatives that can lead to strong financial and strategic performance. Corporate governance and performance are not mutually exclusive. On the contrary, the companies with sustained sterling performances are usually the paragons of governance also.

I would like to describe some of the initiatives and tools we use to promote performance culture.

Economic Value Added, or EVA, in short, is the residual profit after the cost of capital used has been deducted. EVA is used as the principal financial metric in our Group. A large number of our employees are on a performance linked variable remuneration system which is linked to EVA improvement in the business. Variable remuneration forms a large part of their total remuneration package. There is no limit to the upside and downside of the variable remuneration. To promote a long term viewpoint, not all the variable remuneration is paid out in the year it is earned: some of it is held in reserve. The next year, the bonus earned is added to the reserve and a portion of that sum is paid out, and so on. The variable remuneration is modified by applying an individual performance factor based on individual performance, and gauged through a balanced scorecard approach.

We have a strong performance management system in place. We force-rank all our managers, we reward performers disproportionately and put the laggards under the scanner. The best talent in the group is identified through a structured process and monitored carefully. Rewards and recognition are used to spur both the individual and team performance. There is very strong emphasis on performance, which needs to be attained within the framework of our cherished values.

Corporate Governance regulation is here to stay. Regulations do have a major role to play. It is, however, dangerous to have statutes in the area of process. We need to be careful not to go overboard in terms of over regulation that affects entrepreneurship and performance to the extent that they become 'weapons of mass distraction'.

Profit Motive in Industry: Its Evils

The Trade Union Movement was a counter-challenge thrown at the dominant profit motive of the capitalist. But that challenge too, however, was dominated by the same profit motive, but on behalf of the working class. This was sought to be achieved by collective bargaining, which also involved strikes by the unions and lockouts by the managements, wherever necessary. Such a situation also involved much loss of productivity, detrimental to the society as a whole, the interests of which found very little place in the worker-capitalist confrontation. Such a confrontation also did not permit human values to emerge out of the production process.

Exploitation of man by man is the bitter fruit of profit motive. By extending that motive as the dominant consideration of the Unions also, the evils of modern industrialism only became enhanced.

At a time when introduction of ethical values in an economic enterprise was but a cry in the wilderness, R.H. Tawney, in his book Religion and the Rise of Capitalism, observed:

> *A reasonable estimate of economic organization must allow for the fact that, unless industry is to be paralyzed by recurrent revolts on the part of outraged human nature, it must satisfy criteria which are not purely economic.*

The social irresponsibility of capitalist economics has been expressed vividly by several writers who are advocates of technology with a human face. E.F. Schumacher is a passionate advocate of technology with a human face, and also of the importance of greater stress on intermediate technology for all developing countries like ours. In his thoughtful book *Small is Beautiful*, with its significant sub-title 'A Study of Economics as if People Mattered', he says (pp.37-40):

> *In the current vocabulary of condemnation, there are few words as final and conclusive as the word 'uneconomic'. If an activity has been branded as uneconomic, its right to existence is not merely questioned but energetically denied... Call a thing immoral or ugly, soul-destroying or a degradation of man, peril to the peace of the world or to the well-being of human generation; so long as you have not shown it to be 'uneconomic', you have not really questioned its right to exist, grow, and prosper*
>
> *Something is uneconomic when it fails to earn an adequate profit in terms of money... The judgment of economics, in other words, is an extremely fragmentary judgment; out of large number of aspects which in real life have to be seen adjudged together, before a decision can be taken, economics supplied only one, whether a thing yields a money profit to those who undertake it or not...*
>
> *It is great error to assume, for instance, that the methodology of economics is normally applied to determine whether an activity carried on by a group within society yields a profit to society as a whole...*
>
> *Economics deals with goods and services from the point of view of the market, where willing buyer meets willing seller... The market is the institutionalization of individualism and non-responsibility. Neither buyer nor seller is responsible for anything but himself..*
>
> *To be relieved of all responsibility except to oneself means, of course, an enormous simplification of business...*
>
> *In the market place, for practical reasons, innumerable qualitative distinctions which are of vital importance for man and society are suppressed... To the extent that economic thinking is based on the market, it takes the sacredness out of life, because there can be nothing sacred in something that has a price. Not surprisingly, therefore, if*

economic thinking pervaded the whole of society, even simple non-economic values like beauty, health or cleanliness can survive only if they prove to be 'economic'.

Offering a critique of such a fragmentary economic approach and motivation in terms of such non-economic values highly prized by man, Schemacher remarks (ibid, p.68):

What is the meaning of democracy, freedom, human dignity, standard of living, self-realization, fulfilment? Is it a matter of goods or of people? Of course, it is a matter of people. But people can be themselves only in small comprehensible groups. Therefore, we must learn to think in terms of an articulated structure that can cope with a multiplicity of small-scale units. If economic thinking cannot grasp this, it is useless. If it cannot get beyond its vast abstractions, the national income, the rate of growth, capital-output ration, input-output analysis, labour-mobility, capital accumulation; if it cannot get beyond all these and make contact with the human realities of poverty, frustration, alienation, despair, breakdown, crime, escapism, stress, congestions, ugliness, and spiritual death, then let us scrap economics and start afresh.

Stating that it is the intrusion of human freedom and responsibility that makes economics metaphysically different from physics, and that all real human problems, arise from the antinomy of order and freedom, Schumacher calls for a blending of both in a healthy business corporation (Ibid.: 234):

With order, planning, predictability, central control, accountancy, instructions to the underlings, obedience, discipline—without these, nothing fruitful can happen, because everything disintegrates. And yet—without the magnanimity of disorder, the happy abandon, the entrepreneurship venturing into the unknown and incalculable, without the risk and the gamble, the creative imagination rushing where bureaucratic angels fear to tread—without these, life is a mockery and a disgrace.

Psycho-Social Evolution and Ethics

Nineteenth century capitalism received its stimulus from the materialism of that century's physics and biology. As presented by Thomas Huxley, collaborator of Darwin: whereas ethics means the making of as many as possible fit to survive, biology expounds evolution as struggle for existence and survival of the fittest. Nineteenth century capitalism translated this human term into colonialism. It exploded into the two catastrophic world wars. But just as twentieth century physics has ceased to be materialistic in the crude sense as understood in the last century, the revolutionary advances in the science of biology in the twentieth century made ethics central to evolution at the human stage.

Speaking on "The Evolutionary Vision", the late Sir Julian Huxley, noted biologist, and grandson of Thomas Huxley, gave a spiritual orientation to the evolutionary process (*Evolution After Darwin*, Vol III, p.215):

Man's evolution is not biological but psycho-social. It operates by the mechanism of cultural tradition, which involves the cumulative self-reproduction and self-variation of mental activities and their products. Accordingly, major steps in the human phase of evolution are achieved by breakthroughs to new dominant patterns of mental organization of knowledge, ideas, and beliefs-ideological instead of physiological or biological organization.

In the light of these revolutionary ideas of twentieth century biology, discussing the aim of human evolution, or evolution at the human stage, Sir Julian Huxley says (Ibid.: 20):

In the light of our present knowledge, man's most comprehensive aim is seen not as mere survival, not as numerical increased, not as increased complexity of organization, or increased control over his environment, but as greater fulfilment—the fuller realization of more possibilities by human species collectively and more of its component members individually.

And pleading for a scientific study of the scope of this concept of fulfilment, Huxley says (Ibid.: 21):

Once greater fulfilment is recognized as man's ultimate or dominant aim, we shall need a science of human possibilities to help guide the long course of psychosocial evolution that lies ahead.

India is fortunate to have such a science of human possibilities as the central theme of her *Bhagavad Gita*.

Capitalism lays stress on quantity. Ethical and spiritual values lay stress on quality. And Huxley, in his lecture on 'The Evolutionary Vision', speaks of quality emerging as the criterion of evolution at the human stage, in place of quantity which dominated the organic or the pre-human phase of evolution. (Ibid.: 257):

I spoke of quality. This must be the dominant concept of our new belief system—quality and richness as against quantity and uniformity.

Discussing the subject of economic utility in the light of this new belief-system, Huxley says (Ibid.: 259):

Once we truly believe ...that man's destiny is to make possible greater fulfilment for human beings and fuller achievement by human societies, utility in the customary sense becomes subordinate. Quantity of material production, of course, is necessary as the basis for the satisfaction of elementary human needs—but only up to a certain degree. More than a certain number of calories or cocktails or TV sets or washing machines per person is not merely unnecessary, but bad. Quantity of material production is a means to a further end, not an end in itself.

And highlighting quality as the dynamics of human evolution, Huxley concludes (Ibid.: 260-61):

Thus the evolutionary vision...illumines our existence in a simple, but almost overwhelming way.. It shows us our destiny and out day. It shows us mind enthroned above matter, quantity subordinate to quality.

Dominance of Service over Profit Motive

Since the Second World War, there has been deep thinking in various parts of the world on the nature and scope of modem industrial organization. A wave of disillusionment had set in about all aspects of modem industry and technology. This had created in its wake a wave of humanistic thinking and a reassessment of the role of both profit-motivated capitalism and trade unionism in human development and fulfilment. Dehumanization arising from debasement of work and the worker, the converting of work into a battleground of self-assertion and self-interest, the huge size of modem industrial corporations and their impersonal functioning, and their ruthless drive for technological thoroughness without caring for human cost—all these present serious challenges to human wisdom all over the world. Modem industry has also to face the challenge of all types of environmental pollution affecting human welfare.

To put profit before people is to debase the people. It makes the profit so gained dismal, and the work performed increasingly boring and meaningless. Beyond a certain point, a worker cannot find satisfaction with high monetary returns alone. For his spiritual satisfaction, he needs the stimulus of involvement of his heart and mind, along with that of his hands, in his work. He needs to know that what he does is of significance to himself and his fellow humans. In the absence of these, the worker becomes increasingly mechanized and dehumanized. Modem industry distorts the human psyche by breeding the evils of alienation, frustration, and general unfulfilment in millions of working people, and thereby distorts the social situations as well. Work plays a significant part in human development and fulfilment. If a dominate profit motive debases the work and the worker, a dominate service motive elevates both. Service motive can make even humdrum work pleasant and significant by spiritually enriching and nourishing the worker inwardly.

The *Bhagavad Gita* and Corporate Governance

The *Bhagavad Gita* is acknowledged to be the longest philosophical poem expounding the greatest philosophy of work. Work and worker constitute its central theme. The *Gita* presents work as the means for *abhyudaya*, material and social welfare of the worker, and through him of his society, and of his *nihsreyasa*, spiritual growth and fulfilment. The latter is the product of the worker's consciousness of his work as service conducive to the welfare of society. The *Gita* also exhorts the worker to gradually rise to the level of viewing such service as worship of the Divine in man. This is the famous *buddhi yoga*, Yoga of Enlightened Reason, of the *Gita* which Sri Krisna expounds and eulogizes in verses 48 to 51 of its second chapter.

Yogasthah kuru karmani sangam tyaktva dhananjaya;
Siddys, asiddyoh samo bhutva, samatvam yoga ucyate

Giving up attachment, equal-minded in success and failure, do all work,
O Arjuna, established in the yoga (of buddhi); this evenness of mind is called yoga.'
Durena hyavaram karma buddhi yogat dhananjay; Buddhau saranam anvicha, krpanah phalahetavah
Work (prompted by the profit motive and for mere sensate satisfactions) is far inferior, 0 Arjuna, to (work done under the guidance of) the yoga of buddhi; resort to (this) buddhi; small-minded and short-sighted are they who work (only) for selfish advantage.
Buddhi-yukto jahatiha ubhe sukrta duskrte;
Tasmat yogaya yujyasva yogah karmasu kausalam
The man endowed with buddhi (enlightened Reason) goes beyond (the relativity of) both the merit and demerit of all work. In this very life; strive, therefore, to acquire the yoga (of buddhi); yoga is spoken of as dexterity in work.
Karmajam buddhiyuktah hi phalam tyaktva manisinah; Jaewabandhva vinirmuktah padam gacchantyanamayan
Wise people endowed with (the yoga of) buddhi, detached from the fruits derived from work, and freed for ever from the bondage of existence, attain to that state of life which is beyond all evil.

Not only workers and managements in industry, but also all politics and administration, will have to imbibe the spirit of this *buddhi yoga*. It would help mankind to realize the objective of human development and fulfilment, of a national and international socio-political order based on social justice and social peace, of a polity free from all kinds of exploitation, not merely economic, but also political, intellectual, and religious. That the *buddhi yoga* of the *Gita* has the power to bring about peace and justice in the world at large was voiced in a speech by no less a person than the Secretary General of the UNO, the late Dr Hammarskj old, when he translated and commended the sentiments of verse 49 referred above.

Socialist Vision

The challenge to this capitalistic thought has come from modern socialism of the communist and socialist varieties. The constant and common theme of both types of socialism is the end to exploitation of man by man. The main difference between communists and socialists relate to the socialist non-acceptance of economic determinism and the class-war advocated by communists. The socialist vision of a non-exploitative society has been an influence in India for over 100 years, beginning with Swami Vivekananda. In fact, the main socialist ideas have influenced Indian thinking of man and society from the time of the *Upanisads* nearly four thousand years ago. The *Upanisads* and the *Gita* expound the spiritual equality of man in the light of the one Atman, Divine Self, present in all. The teaching against greed in all world religions is socialistic in its operation. The Gita gives an ethical orientation to the concept of *yajna*, or sacrifice, in its third chapter (3.13):

Bhunjate to tvagham papa ye pacantyatma-karanat

Those sinners who cook (and eat) only for themselves, verily, eat only sin.

Swami Vivekananda has described the modern age as the age of the emergence of the *sudras*, of the proletariat. Says he (*Letters of Swami Vivekananda*, 1948 Edition, p.352):

I am a socialist, not because I think it a perfect system, but half loaf is better than no bread.

The other systems have been tried and found wanting; let, this one be tried—if for nothing else, for the novelty of the thing. A redistribution of pain and pleasure is better than always the same persons having the pains and pleasures. The sum total of good and evil in the world remains ever the same. The yoke will be lifted from shoulder to shoulder by new systems, that is all.

Let every dog have his day aim—this is miserable world, so that, after this experience of so-called happiness, they will all come to the Lord and give up this vanity of a world and governments and all other botherations.

Speaking on the future of India at Chennai in 1897, Swami Vivekananda had said (*The Complete Works of Swami Vivekananda*, Volume III, 1960 Edition, pp.294-297):

'The days of exclusive privileges and exclusive claims are gone, gone for ever from the soil of India, and it is one of the great blessings of the British Rule in India. Even to the Mohammedan Rule we owe that great blessing, the destruction of exclusive privilege... The duty of every aristocracy is to dig its own grave; and the sooner it does so, the better. The more it delays; the more it will fester, and the worse death it will die. '

According to R.P. Masani, Dadabhoy Naoroji, the outstanding economic thinker and political leader of the pre-Gandhian India National Congress had attended the International Socialistic Congress at Amsterdam in 1904 and cultivated some association with the British Socialistic pattern. Gandhiji, Jawaharlal Nehru, Vinoba Bhave and Indira Gandhi, apart from hundreds of other thinkers and political leaders have been advocates of citizen's freedom. Even the Indian communists, in participating in the democratic parliamentary institutions in India, have adjured the extremist lines of ideologies and programmes. And recently, the European Communist parties have also abandoned their earlier doctrinaire approaches. The influence of Indian culture and philosophy has softened the rigidities of Marxism in the Indian context. It has opened the way for a socialism with ethical and human motivations, in tune with the spiritual inheritance of the Indian people.

Freedom versus Equality in Corporate Governance

The central problem of socialism has been the squaring of the two great urges of man, namely, freedom and equality. In normal circumstances, both cannot co-exist. In the human context, stress on freedom tends to increase inequality, and stress on equality tends to decrease freedom. The French Revolution stressed freedom and the Russian Revolution stressed equality. In the economic sphere, capitalism upholds freedom and denies equality, while Marxism upholds equality and restricts freedom. India is faced with the challenge of combining these two great values of freedom and equality. Our country is arriving to usher in socialistic equality in the context of democratic freedom. While doing so, she is encroaching on some peripheral aspects of Fundamental Rights, with respect to freedom, only with a view of strengthening and implementing the Directive Principle of the Constitution with respect to equality.

This is inescapable in the context of along-established feudal social system, and in the interests of its early replacement by a democratic social order. For freedom, in a feudal context, means only freedom of wealth and monopoly to exploit the weak and the helpless. But the freedom offered in the Fundamental Rights will shine in all its glory in India only after the Directive Principles have achieved a satisfactory measure of levelling up of the common people. Curtailing of the freedom to exploit others is the surest way to enhance all-round freedom. And freedom is the first condition of growth, proclaims Swami Vivekananda, who also presents this value as the supreme gift of Vedanta.

It is obvious that a mere economic or political approach can never help the nation to effect this union of freedom and equality. It needs a spiritual approach which, fortunately, is available to our people from our philosophers and spiritual teachers, both ancient and modern. The genius for synthesis, characteristic of Indian wisdom, when it begins to affect the thinking of our people in a pervasive way, can be expected to make our politics, administration, and society achieve this happy blend of democratic freedom with socialistic equality.

Indian Message of Dharma

It is against this thought background of ancient *Vedanta*, twentieth century science, and modem human experience, that we have to view economic activities of industrial corporations and business ventures in modern India. New scientific truths take time to influence social thinking and action; and much of our current socio-economic thinking and action is still influenced by nineteenth century science. Ethical values, what India calls dharma, are inseparable from any ordered human society. Bereft of them, man becomes reduced to a beast, says Indian wisdom: *dharmena hinah pasubhih samanah*. Dharma as the principle of integration of man with man in a society does not mean religion in the sense of creed, doctrine, or ritual, nor any scheme of other-worldly salvation. A mere accumulation of bricks does not constitute a building. It needs cement to unite brick with brick to build the integrated structure. Similarly, a mere aggregation of men does not constitute society. Dharma is the value that unites man-to-man to form the integrated organization which is society. Dharma stresses the idea of mutuality and inter¬dependence of man in society. Man needs the context of other human beings for his very humanization. This is how Sri Krisna expounds dharma in the *Karma Parva* of the *Mahabharata* (8.45.50):

Dharanat dharma ityahuh, dharmo dharyate prajah. (If the citizen protects and holds the Dharma, Dharma will protect the citizen. If the citizen will hold the Dharma then society will hold the Dharma. If society holds the Dharma then the Nation will also hold the Dharma well. Ultimately the nation will also be Protected by the Dharma)

Purusartha

Indian philosophy considers *kama*—sensate satisfaction, and *artha*—wealth, which are the means to karma, as valid human pursuits or *purusartha*. But it considers *lobha*—greed and *moha*—delusion, arising from unchecked desire, as unethical, because they are anti-social. To restrain these two pursuits from becoming anti-social, Indian philosophy presents a third vital human pursuit, or *purusartha*, namely, *dharma*-ethical sense. It is dharma that helps all people, not just a few powerful and clever ones, to experience the maximum *kama* and *artha*. And Sri Krisna, the human manifestation of the one divine self in all beings, endorses this validity of *kama* in the Gita (7.11).

Dharma—viruddho bhutesu kamo' smi bharatarsabha

I am that *kama*, sensual desire, in all beings, which is unopposed to *dharma*.

Indian philosophy refers to dharma, *artha* and *kama* as the *trivarga*, the inseparable group of three, and treats them as the universal warp and woof of all ordered human society. It presents, *moksha*—absolute freedom of the spirit, as the fourth *purusartha*, and as an optional trans-social pursuit meant for those few who desire, and dare to go deeper into the spiritual dimensions of life and realize one's true nature in all its glory. For all the rest, this *moksha* experience comes within the limitations of the social context, as dharma. *Dharma*, thus, is the confluence of the social and the trans-social; every sacred and secular literature of India sings its glory. Indian culture is rooted in, and inspired by, this great value of *dharma*.

Moral versus Psycho-Social Evolution in Corporate Sector

It is the echo of this great value that we get in the concept of psycho-social evolution of twenty first century biology referred to earlier. Modern biology says that with the most versatile organ, namely, the cerebral system, given to man by nature, evolution at the human stage, has ceased to be primarily organic, and has become psycho-social. It demands that man, with the help of his cerebral system, detach his psyche or self from the organic system and make it grow and expand, in ethical awareness and social feeling, so as to realize its oneness with other psyches in society. Here we get an echo of the *anasakti-yoga* of the *Gita*. All greed, delusion, and exploitation proceed from the self, when centred in, and attached to, the organic system. By psycho-social evolution, man grows spiritually and becomes capable of showing affection to his fellow man, of communicating with each other, of working in a team. It is at this deeper level that he becomes capable of realizing the value of dharma, ethical sense from within himself, and expressing himself naturally and spontaneously, in moods and acts of service, and also becomes incapable of exploiting other human beings.

Our national cultural ethos will not allow our people to drift into the worship of, what several modern economic thinkers refer to as, the false god of GNP, of an unchecked pursuit of organic satisfactions, of a mad rush after material affluence. Our philosophy tells us how and why these have to be pursued, and when and how to stop, and what higher things there are to pursue. If our own tested cultural values guide us in our economic pursuits in the modem period, we shall be satisfied with a measure of decent material and social welfare for all our people.

Social Purpose of Industrial Corporations

When economic activity is conducted in the light of this philosophy of man and society, it ceases to be primarily a profit making venture. Profit-making does remain as one of its important motivations; but it becomes subordinated to the service motivation.

This is the ethical role of a modem corporation, the word 'modem' breathing the spirit of modem science, of modem humanistic values and urges, and the trials and tribulations of industrial experiences of the post-war period. Our country is fortunately placed, as we are in the early stages of our industrial development. Our industry has to learn from the dismal post-war experiences and warnings of British and Western European industry, and take steps to define a new role for our managements and trade unions, and set a new national purpose for our corporations. A new revolution in trade unionism will follow a new concept of industrial corporation, in which the profit motive of the employer, which gave rise to the counter profit motive of the employee, gives way to the service motive. This will provide a national partnership between management and labour, not for exploiting the corporation for mutual advantage, which may happen only in a capitalist system, but for the service of all the constituent parties concerned. It will flow from a social purposes clause to be inserted in the corporation's aims and objects, and incorporated in the nation's Company Law itself.

Role of Labour-Management Partnership in Corporate Governance

When we thus make profit motive secondary and service motive as primary, we convert both the management and labour of a corporation into what they really are, namely, citizens of free India engaged in a partnership within a national productive enterprise. This management-labour partnership then becomes the custodian of the wider interests of society. And it is in this venerated role as free and responsible citizens, with its wider national horizons and awareness of national responsibilities, that the representatives of labour now being inducted to the managements become a source of strength to the corporation. Such a process will hasten the conversion of the corporation into a trust for the good of society. It is in such a socially responsible corporation, inspired with this ethical and human motivation, that workers can be expected to play responsive and responsible role from the shop floor to the board room. Such a corporation comprising the workers, the investors and the shareholders, the state, the consumer, and the community at large will emerge for good. A corporation's obligations are two-fold—internal and external. Internal—to the corporation, for its continuance and development; to its employees, for their human dignity, development of skill, promotion, and security; and to its investors and shareholders, for a reasonable return on their investment. External—to the state, by way of taxes due; the consumers, for supply of quality goods at reasonable prices, to the community at large, by suitable welfare measures. The ethics of a modern corporation will also include responsibility for producing only such goods as are beneficial for humanity and needed for its development and fulfilment.

Mass Production versus Production by the Masses

The presence of a large segment of public sector corporations in our country which are dissociated from the vice of the exploitations associated with the private sector, and controlling the commanding heights of the national economy, is a vital factor that give our technology a human face. Public and private sector industries have to realize that private affluence and public squalor in our country are a standing challenge to our political system and to our social conscience. We have also to safeguard ourselves against the current materialistic philosophy behind modern production techniques. This is more so as it stimulates the insatiable human cravings and create ecological problems, and mutilates man and distorts the social situation.

Introducing into our industry ethical values and giving our technology a human face, also involves, as suggested by Schumacher, adoption of intermediate and small-scale technologies, which are labour intensive, in place of high technology where it is not relevant. Using the scanty capital resources available to start thousands of small work units, and giving gainful employment to millions, constitutes the ethics of industrial enterprise in our country today.

This follows the wise lead given by Gandhiji: 'not mass production, but production by the masses.'

Conclusion

Public sector corporations have a great responsibility, therefore, to uphold ethical and human values in industry. Along with achieving production efficiently and raising profits, it would set an example to all private sector corporations in our country. When ethical and human values inspire industrial and business corporations in India, we will see the end of exploitation of man by man, and by money power, in our country. This will help to fulfil Gandhiji's dream, in spirit, if not in letter, of the principle of trusteeship inspiring industrial and business activities in India. There are already some small industrial ventures in our country, sponsored by some members of Gandhiji's constructive work movement. These function under the trusteeship principle advocated by Gandhiji. It is heartening to find that such ventures, with slight variations, are functioning in some of the Western countries as well. Writing in the *Harijan* of 31 March 1946, Gandhiji said:

> *Supposing India becomes a free country tomorrow, all the capitalists will have an, opportunity of becoming statutory trustees. But such a statute will not be imposed from above. It will have to come from below. When the people understand the implications of trusteeship, and the atmosphere is ripe for it, the people themselves, beginning with Gram Panchayats, will began to introduce such statutes, such a thing coming from below is easy to swallow. Coming from above, it is liable to prove a dead-weight.*

I would like to conclude by emphasizing that corporate governance is not just another management or social fad. It is the ultimate management tool. Good corporate governance is a journey and not a destination. It is a very rewarding journey for those who choose the right path. Above all, corporate governance is both about doing things right and doing the right thing.

7

Transnational and Transcultural Differences

Values in Tension

Our moral intuitions frequently blur when we cross our nation's boundaries and leave for Hong Kong or New York. Without the backdrop of approximate moral consensus that exists within a culture, and without the laws and judicial procedures that define standards of minimal conduct, moral clarity is elusive. When we ask whether it is permissible to make new investments in nations where civil and political rights are violated, or to hire only male managers in Saudi Arabia, our intuitions may fail us. When we ask whether it is permissible to comply with the less restrictive environmental or occupational health laws in host countries, or to fill management and senior technical positions in a host nation with nationals from that home country, we must abandon norms that are merely nation-specific and move to principles that transcend national boundaries.

But do such 'transcending' principles exist? Can we find guideposts to lead us through the maze of cultural differences? At a minimum, any search for guideposts will require more than good intentions. Even the best-informed, best-intentioned executive must rethink intuitions in mixed cultural contexts. Even when those intuitions are fundamentally sound, they have been honed in home-culture contexts. The same intuitions that serve well in a homogeneous context can fail when home and host norms conflict. Hence even the traditional litmus test, "How would you respond if your actions were written up on the front page of the newspaper?", is an unreliable guide. For in international context there exist strikingly different sets of newspaper readers.

Although issues of global corporate ethics constitute an ethical swamp, there are ways through the swamp. Ethical imperialism or a simplistic "do in Tokyo exactly as we do in New York" policy is clearly a wrong turn. Instead, we need an approach in which companies respect the 'moral free space' of cultures and industries even as they stick firmly to their own core values—an ethics code. Moral free space refers to the right of any community, be it a culture, company, or industry, to shape—at least within limits—its own business values. Failing to respect it can have disastrous consequences. In 1993, a large US computer products company insisted on using exactly the same anti-sexual harassment exercises for Muslim managers in the Middle East as they earlier used with American employees in California. In doing so, the company trumpeted its global 'ethical consistency'. The result was ludicrous. The instructors' presentation baffled and offended the participants. The US trainers knew nothing about the strict conventions governing gender relationships in Muslim culture. Because they used the same training formula as at home, they failed to respect the moral free space of their hosts. Moreover, the message they wanted to send—to avoid coercion and sexual discrimination—was lost. Clearly sexual discrimination does occur in these countries but eliminating it means respecting and understanding the differences.

Host country law is a notoriously unreliable guide. Many nation states have difficulty efficiently regulating foreign transnational corporations, and unscrupulous companies sometimes exploit their problems to their own advantage. As James Brooke noted in the New York Times, virtually every country from Morocco to the Congo on Africa's west coast has been approached by companies who want cheap sites for dumping waste. In 1988, officials in Guinea Bissau, one of the world's poorest nations, agreed to bury fifteen million tons of toxic wastes from European tanneries and pharmaceutical companies. The companies agreed to pay about $120 million, which is only slightly less than the country's entire gross national product.

Brooke also described how in Nigeria in 1987 five European ships unloaded toxic waste containing dangerous poisons such as polychlorinated biphenyls. Workers wearing thongs and shorts unloaded the barrels for $2.50-a-day and placed them in a residential area in the town of Kiko. They were not told about the contents of the barrels.

We may denounce host country governments who permit such abuses, but the fact is that many countries are unable to police transnational corporations adequately. Clearly, neither a simple-minded extension of home morality, nor an appeal to host-country law, can be the answer.

Cultural Relativism is Not the Answer

One answer to the question we are raising is as old as philosophical discussion, and as old as Sophistry. Its label is 'cultural relativism' and it is a view that holds that cultures define ethics, and that, in turn, there are no universal 'rights' and 'wrongs'. According to cultural relativism, if Indonesia tolerates the bribery of public officials, then so what? Indonesia's bribery is no worse than Denmark or Singapore's refusal to bribe. If Switzerland fails to find insider trading morally repugnant, then so what? Swiss liberality in investment policy is no worse than U.S. fair-mindedness—or at least that is the claim of cultural relativism.

The concept of cultural relativism is fairly simple to grasp, and often tempting when business opportunities are at stake. Consider a recent example. The SS United States was arguably the, most luxurious ocean liner when it cruised the oceans during the 1950s. By the 1990s its sailing days were over, but a group of investors considered refurbishing it for luxury cruising. But it was loaded with asbestos and would have cost about $100 million to remove it under current U.S. standards. So it was towed to Turkey in 1992 where the cost of removing the asbestos was only two million dollars. Turkish officials refused to allow the removal because of the danger of cancer. In October 1993 it was towed to the Black Sea port of Sebastopol where standards are lax. It had more than one half million square feet of carcinogenic asbestos removed for much less than $100 million. Few would argue in this case that Sebastopol's laws established adequate ethical standards for shipyard workers.

Unfortunately, managers too often fall into the trap of confusing cultural relativism with a more defensible value, namely, tolerance. Tolerance and relativism are related, but differ dramatically in what they imply. What most of us have in mind when we shy away from absolute moral pronouncements and endorse tolerance is the opposite of relativism. When we deny that one country should dictate morality for another and we encourage respect for the customs of foreign peoples, we are pointing to a universal, transcultural value. In other words, if we believe that the United States ought not to force its modern democratic method of government on Muslim countries, then we similarly believe that all other countries ought not to impose democratic methods on Muslim countries. And, in turn, we expect Muslim countries not to impose their form of government on other, non-Muslim countries. In this way tolerance is a universalizable moral value, and a far cry from relativism.

Tolerance supports moral free space, and, in turn, the right of a culture, company, or industry to have some control over defining its own values. It helps us to see that 'different' does not always mean 'worse'. For example, while research shows that Hong Kong managers are less sensitive to the issue of bribery than Western managers, it also shows them to be far more sensitive to the issue of failing to give credit for the contributions of subordinates (a practice rampant in many Western corporations).

Cultural relativism, in contrast, is inconsistent with tolerance, and should be rejected. Its main problem is that certain cultural differences clash with globally-accepted conceptions of value. The defence of those differences leads to a reduction ad absurdum. To seriously maintain cultural relativism, one must be prepared to tolerate all cultural differences. If one nation endorses piracy (as some nations in history have), then one must grant piracy the same moral status as a doctrine of anti-piracy. Or, consider the dramatic example of crime prevention in ancient Rome. In ancient Rome it was the practice to kill all the slaves in a household in the event that one slave murdered the master. All slaves were lined up and summarily executed without trial. They were executed whether they were young or old, male or female, and whether or not they were involved in, or had any knowledge about the murder. In some instances involving large households, the practices resulted in the execution of three to four hundred innocent persons. While the practice was justified on the grounds that it deterred future plots against the master, few of us today could embrace such reasoning. And in the light of heinous practices such as this, few of us can cling to theoretical relativism that would tolerate these or even worse practices. Hence, if we reject relativism in the extreme instances, then morality in the international sphere must be something more than an unprincipled 'do as the Romans do'. It does not follow that all questions of moral differences among cultures can be solved by measuring them against a rigid, universal yardstick. But it means that morality has some, albeit imperfect, relevance to transcultural contexts.

Still another reason for rejecting cultural relativism is that the vast majority of people in every culture are not relativists when it comes to at least one value, namely, economic efficiency. While people around the world differ about what has economic value, most prefer to give up less of what has economic value for them, in order to get something that has more economic value. This shared respect for efficiency has powerful implications for ethical conduct in business, since some forms of ethical conduct encourage efficiency while others discourage it.

Consider the current statistics on software piracy. The ratio of pirated software to legitimately purchased software varies dramatically from country to country. For example, in Italy the ratio of pirated to purchased software is roughly eight times that of Great Britain or the United States and four times that of Germany, Now what is remarkable here is that the laws are virtually identical in all the countries surveyed. They all have laws against software piracy, but in some the rate is sky high, while in others it is low. What accounts for the difference? Most of the difference must be attributed to a difference in perspective taken by the users of software about the ethics of piracy. And what does this have to do with the value of efficiency? Ask yourself, "In which country will the bright entrepreneur decide to invent and market new, path-breaking software?" Hence, some international environments enhance the shared value of efficiency while others retard it.

Absolutism is Not the Answer

The stark alternative to cultural relativism is 'absolutism'. Absolutism claims an authoritative list of ethical truths exists, that these truths are expressed in a single moral language, and that they require the same ethical behaviour around the world. Were absolutism true, it would rule out the possibility of two conflicting ethical positions in different cultures being equally valid. Absolutism obviously clashes with the idea of moral free space. Its problems, however, are numerous.

First, absolutism clashes with our deep intuitions about the need to respect different cultural traditions. Consider the well-known differences that separate styles of values around the world. One of the main dichotomies in ethics practiced globally is between loyalty-oriented' and 'rights-oriented' approaches. The former focuses on loyalty and organizational relationships. It uses family, friendship, religion, the corporation, and the nation to define other ethics. The Japanese, for example, define business ethics far more in terms of loyalty to their corporation, their nation, and their business networks, than do Americans. The latter, rights-oriented approach, focus on the individual and equal treatment. Key notions are freedom, autonomy, impartial rules, justice, and fairness. Just as the Japanese prize loyalty, so too do the Americans; but the Americans prize even more individual freedom and impersonal standards of fairness. 'Rights-oriented' and 'loyalty-oriented' styles of ethics each constitute legitimate, although sharply different, ways for a community to define its concept of 'virtuous'. Embracing absolutism, unfortunately, would compel us to select either the 'rights-oriented' or 'loyalty-oriented' view as the true view, while declaring the other false.

Another problem with absolutism lies in its presumption that the moral language of a single list could capture all moral truth. This is a technical impossibility. As Michael Walzer commented, "There is no Esperanto of global ethics". Even internationally accepted lists of moral principles, such as the United Nations, Universal Declaration of Human Rights, are expressed in languages rich with cultural tradition. The very notion of a 'right', for example, stems from the historical evolution of democratic government in post-Renaissance, Christian Europe and the United States. It does not, however, figure with equal comfort in the Confucian or Buddhist traditions of East Asia.

Even if all underlying values around the world were the same, the particular norms in different industries, nations, and corporations would, and should, vary. It is fitting, for example, that home and host country norms should reflect the realities of a nation's level of economic development. While virtually everyone shares the values of pollution abatement and economic development, trade-offs can rationally be made differently in a struggling Third World country on the one hand, and a highly developed one on the other. At a level of economic development where people remain malnourished or starving, a country may rationally adopt a different principle for regulating water pollution than were it is at a higher level. Such a country may adopt a slightly lower standard of thermal water pollution than that observed in the US or Sweden (resulting in lower fish species, such as carp, and fewer higher fish species, such as trout). Once they reach the higher level of development they too can opt for more trout. But for the time being they prefer chemical fertilizer. Absolutism would have the effect of straight jacketing all nations, regardless of level of economic development, to the same particular norms.

Finally, companies would fail to honor their deeper values if they took absolutism's admonition to insist on "the same ethical behaviour around the world" seriously. If they paid foreign workers exactly the same wages for the same work as domestic ones, the incentive to invest abroad would vanish, with ruinous consequences for both home and host countries. And behaving the same everywhere could even mean loss of life. When 3M Corporation caught an employee stealing in their Chinese subsidiary, it behaved just as they would have anywhere: the company turned him in to the local authorities. To their horror, the local authorities took the man away and shot him. They realized that they would need to behave differently in the future, in order to succeed in behaving ethically.

When it comes to ethics, facts also make a difference. Consider the issue of price gouging in controlled economies. Price gouging is more unethical in a closed market than an open one because free markets automatically restrain arbitrary pricing (If one seller gouges, then another will grab his customers). In more controlled markets, however, sellers can avoid competition and gouging as an ethical problem increases. When polled years ago, Soviet executives ranked price gouging as the worst ethical problem they confronted in business. In contrast, Western executives ranked it (as they do today) near the bottom of their concerns. When the rules of the game are different, so too are the ethics of playing it.

Facts necessitate a 'stricter' approach in some contexts and a 'less strict' approach in others. One of the lessons of Union Carbide's tragic experience is that the way to handle methyl isocyanides may be different in Bhopal, India, than in Boston. A stricter set of safety precautions along with less sophisticated technology may be appropriate in Bhopal, where technological infrastructures are less developed, than in Boston where they are well developed. Sometimes the situation is reversed. Fewer precautions may be appropriate when, say, a chemical responds more safely to local conditions. The chemical EDB, a soil fungicide banned for use in the US, responds differently in Senegal. In Senegal it turns to a harmless state faster because of intense solar radiation and high soil temperatures.

The Global Values Map

From what has been said, it should be obvious that managers unprepared to live with moral tension abroad should pack their bags and return home. Savvy managers will need to steer a path between two extremes. One extreme is an unyielding imperialism that refuses to grant any validity to any values than those of the home culture. The other extreme is a relativism that waters down a company's core beliefs and standards of conduct. The ethical picture abroad, then, is complex. In turn, any manager who has room in her moral imagination for only black and white, for the actions being either 'ethical' or 'unethical', has missed the mark. As Einstein once noted, "Things should be as simple as possible—but no simpler."

A more complex, but also more accurate, framework is the following:

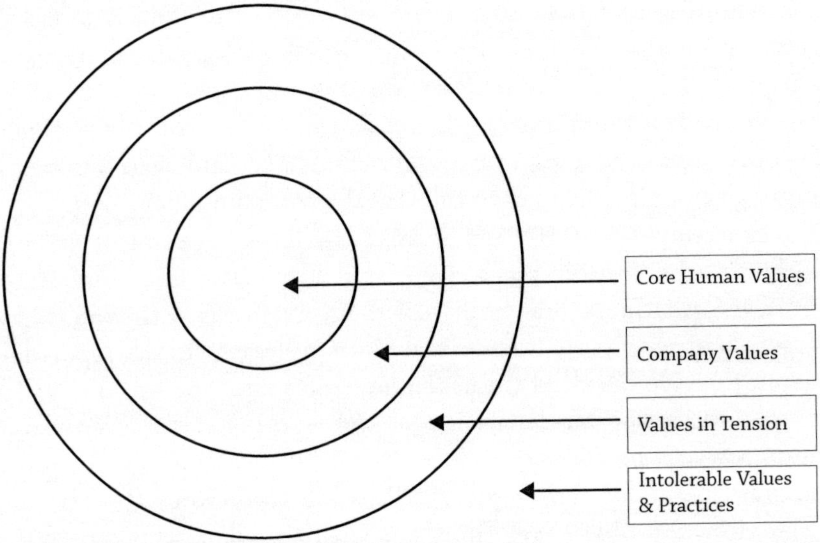

The concentric circles represent types of values held by particular corporations, industries, or cultures. All other values outside the concentric rings are 'intolerable values and practices'. Collection of points on the circles may be used to represent any corporation's values as expressed through its actions and policies.

Core Human Values

In avoiding the extreme of relativism, one of the most important concepts is that of core human values. Core human values are by definition the ones relevant to all cultures and all organizations, and are aids in establishing a minimum moral threshold for companies operating abroad. Many different ethical 'languages' can be used to formulate such a threshold, including the world's great religions and doctrines of human rights. We have already seen that constructing a 'list' of universal values (the claim of the absolutist) is probably impossible. Yet this notwithstanding, there are ways of phrasing at least a rough, overlapping consensus of human morality. Surely, for example, Aristotle, Kant and other moral theorists are correct to assert that all global inhabitants share at a minimum the obligation to treat other humans with respect, and to factor into personal calculations some consideration of broader human welfare. The point of attempting to articulate a minimum moral threshold is to clarify what business must avoid. Once established, such a threshold makes it possible to say to any corporation that falls below the threshold "you've made a moral mistake", and to say this even if the company has not committed a legal or economic mistake, and even if the host country's practices happen to tolerate the company's behaviour.

For example, in 1992 Levi Strauss concluded that one of its large suppliers, the Tan family, had violated international principles of employee treatment and broke off doing business with them. Levi Strauss had repeatedly warned the Tan family, which was reportedly keeping twelve hundred Chinese and Philippine women in guarded compounds in the Mariana Islands, and working them seventy-four hours a week. In making its move, Levi Strauss cited its "Business Partners Terms of Engagement". This is a framework that, among other things, prohibits relationships with suppliers whose practices are so offensive as to violate any reasonable conception of ethics.

Probably the most popular language in the world for establishing a moral, threshold for international behaviour is that of 'rights'. The UN's Universal Declaration of Human Rights is a widely recognized way to attempt to specify absolute minimums of moral conduct. Elsewhere I have identified ten "Fundamental International Rights" including the right to personal freedom, physical security and wellbeing, political participation, informed consent, and the ownership of property (see also Donaldson's Ethics of International Business). Moral philosophers note that whenever there is a right, there is not only a duty to avoid depriving people of the right directly, but sometimes a duty to protect people from its deprivation. Such duties sometimes fall on businesses. For example, surveys of people in Central America show that the average Central American went to work at the age of eleven. If we assume that everyone has a right to a minimum education (although the definition of this right may vary enormously), then hiring young children of seven or eight for ongoing full-time labor almost certainly fails the moral threshold test. Any German, Japanese, or US corporation who did this would have failed to live up to their duty to protect the basic human right to a minimal education from deprivation.

Company Values

Correct ethical behaviour in business contexts must be seen not only in relation to abstract, universal values, but through the concrete understanding of business people. The values in the next ring of the diagram, designated 'company values', are less abstract than the core human values in the center of the diagram, but are wholly consistent with them (indeed, if they are not, they should be either jettisoned or revised). Ethics codes and also vision-value statements, such as Johnson and Johnson's famous "Credo", represent increasingly popular attempts to define company values. Ninety per cent of all Fortune 500 companies have codes of ethics, and 70 per cent have vision-value statements. In Europe and the Orient the numbers are lower, but are increasing rapidly. Nonetheless, what companies say in their formal statements or credos, and what they actually believe, often diverges considerably. A better yardstick for the ethical beliefs of many corporations lies in the concept of "*mokita*". *Mokita* is an expression used in traditional South Sea Island society. We do not have a corresponding term in English. *Mokita* means the truth that everybody knows, but nobody speaks.

Just as core human values define the minimum standards for all persons everywhere, company values define minimum standards for all members of the corporation. Company values are analogous to 'universal' principles, and because of this, companies must treat them as non-negotiable pillars of behaviour. Because they are company 'universals' they cannot be trumped by host country standards. In the 1950s a senior Latin American manager at Motorola approached the legendary Motorola leader, Robert Galvin. "I have good news" the manager reported, "the host country government officials in Latin America want to buy 10 million dollars worth of our new micro-relay product!" He did not need to point out to Galvin that the high margin on the prospective sale meant that it would result in a near doubling of that year's profit. "The bad news", he continued, "is that they want us to invoice them for $11 million, and although the additional one million is supposed to cover handling fees, we are confident that it will be pocketed by politicians". Mindful of Galvin's well-known commitment to ethics, he added, "So I will refuse the offer". After reflection, Robert Galvin responded with emotion "You've done the right thing to refuse the deal. Congratulations! But I want to add two more points. When you return to the host country, please tell the government official that we will not accept even a reformulated $10 million dollar package omitting the bribe. Also, make certain that Motorola never does business with that government ever again". Told and retold over the intervening decades, this story has had a remarkable effect reinforcing Motorola's ethics, and on clarifying Motorola's minimum standards.

Some will assert that Motorola's entire ethical posture is loftier than it should be. But whatever level of corporate ethics one endorses, Motorola's example of sticking to its ethics is worth emulating. Once penned, whether accomplished through formal statements or leaders' example, a company's ethics stance should not waver. This insight is the glaring exception to the dictum mentioned earlier—"Show respect for other cultures". If a company wavers on its own ethics, either at home or abroad, only moral mayhem can result. A code of ethics with a statement that reads "Do not accept gifts from suppliers in excess of $X" is meaningless when it is allowed to be interpreted as "Almost always do not accept gifts from suppliers in excess of $X". For, who is to define the exceptions to the almost always? If for any statement, exceptions are likely to arise, companies are better off to omit the statement, to design a formal process to arbitrate expectations to the statement, or to spell out the statement's exceptions in writing, than to endorse the statement only to later compromise on fulfilling it. In short, companies must be absolutist about one thing—their own ethics.

Values in Tension

The modified corporate absolutism mentioned above should be sharply distinguished from the cultural absolutism discussed earlier. Any community, local, national, or international, has a right, within limits, to define its own standards. If Motorola insists on its own standards, it is not indulging in cultural absolutism. Rather, by insisting upon its own standards, it is merely exercising the same right that it should grant to others in shaping their cultures, companies and communities. This right is a vital instance of what we call 'moral free space'.

As one moves from the center of the values circle towards the periphery, the tension between the core values and a particular value increases. After a certain point, one encounters the ring labeled 'values in tension'. Values in this ring express distinctive and strongly held community beliefs. What is more, they reflect tension between these beliefs and one or more core human values. Most global managers will encounter such tension spots sooner or later, and the question rather obviously is how to manage them. For example, suppose that one of your company's main suppliers is the Tata Steel Company in Jamshedpur. You learn that an important perk offered by Tata to its employees is the right for one of their children to gain a job with the company once the child is old enough to enter the job market. Tata makes good this offer even if the child is less qualified than rival applicants. Not surprisingly, the perk is the one most cherished by Tata employees. As manager of a company using Tata as a supplier, how should you respond to the practice? Should you criticize Tata for its 'nepotism'? Should you refuse to buy from the company until it discard this policy? Clearly such a perk would be branded unacceptable nepotism in St Louis or Amsterdam.

Yet while Western companies are correct to insist on meritocratic hiring practices for their companies in India (again, companies should be absolutist about their own fundamental values), they should hesitate before pointing a finger of blame at Tata. Attempting to 'reform' the Tata Company or refusing to do business with it would verge on being unethical because it would fail to respect the cultural integrity of a foreign community. By placing practices such as this in the ring labelled `values in tension', the Global Values Map acknowledges that the Tata Steel company's policy is in tension with at least one or more core human values but stops short of declaring it fully in conflict with them. It is therefore placed outside the circle in the 'impermissible' sector.

Consider another example of values in tension, gift giving in Japan. Even US and European companies known for strict anti-bribing policies, such as IBM, have different limits on gift giving in Japan than they do for other parts of the world. This is because the tradition of gift giving in Japan is tied to deeply-held, traditional Japanese values. Whereas a $60 value gift would constitute a bribe in many countries, under many circumstances in Japan it would not. Clearly, excessive gifts can constitute bribes in Japan, just as they can elsewhere; but what counts as a "bribe" in Japan may be different than what counts as a bribe elsewhere. Hence, while recognizing that a more lavish gift giving policy in Japan is in tension with prescriptions against economic corruption, a company is not necessarily wrong to adopt the more lavish policy.

Intolerable Values and Practices

Finally, when values or practices transgress permissible limits (as specified by fundamental human rights or corporate values and principles) they fall outside the circle and in the 'intolerable' zone. We have already referenced many such examples, including unreasonable levels of carcinogens (asbestos), child labour, and the dumping of pollutants in Third World countries. Not all behaviour that fall outside the circle has such salient consequences. Sometimes the issue is simple honesty. In one instance, a Russian sales agent for his nation's joint venture with Baird Corporation overstated the product characteristics of the firm's spectrometers. Although the salesman considered this perfectly reasonable behaviour, the American manager took him aside and explained that it was unacceptable business practice, both because it violated Baird's ethics and because it was dishonest. As this example also suggests, Western nations can serve as helpful role models in shaping the new capitalistic ethics of former communist countries.

Navigating on the Global Values Map

By exhibiting the possibility of values in tension, the Values Map suggests that we should revise a common litmus test for ethics, namely, the one that asks, "How would you react if your actions were described on the front page of the Wall Street Journal?" And sometimes ask the additional question: "How would you react if your actions were described on the front page of Bangkok's Daily News, Rome's Corriere Della Serra, or the Buenos Aires Herald?" But even as other cultural attitudes must be respected, it is equally clear that company ethics and core human values must set the limits on recognizing other values. The trick is to respect other cultures while at the same time drawing clear limits.

Consider, for example, differences between American and Japanese work habits. On the one hand, Americans must be able to respect the fact that Japanese culture has a different conception of what constitutes a "fair" work week. As is well known, most Japanese companies define the ethical limits on the amount of work and number of hours per week much differently from, say, US or French companies. Indeed, more Japanese than US companies evaluate negatively the availing of all allowed paid vacations. Yet while being able to respect these differences in the cultural ethics of work, and, in turn, allowing a certain amount of 'moral free space' in which communities can define their ethics, almost everyone would agree, including the Japanese, that there should be limits to such moral free space. So, for example, if it reaches the point that significant numbers of people are killed by "Kiroshi" (death by overwork), then the situation becomes morally unacceptable.

Why Giving into Bribery Does Not Count as "Respecting Another Culture"

Little has been said so far about the most discussed, and arguably most difficult, problem of international business ethics—bribery. Where does bribery fit on the Global Values Map? Despite the fact that no country's laws permit bribery, the practice flourishes around the world. Only the United States prohibits bribery beyond its own borders (the Foreign Corrupt Practices Act) and even this act explicitly tolerates a considerable amount of "petty" bribery, i.e., where the amounts are small and the payment is necessary to receive services that should have been rendered in the first place. Many officials in developing countries only wink at the practice, in effect acknowledging its permanent place in the economy. Some multinationals operating in developing countries finds it impossible to move goods through customs without paying low-level officials a few dollars. The payments are small and often uniformly assessed. Sometimes the salaries of such officials are sufficiently low that they appear to be set with the prevalence of bribery in mind.

Why not, then, regard this 'value in tension' as a minor cultural annoyance, and write corporate ethics codes in a way that recognizes the inevitable? Before passing bribery off as a mere cultural curiosity, however, we should note its appalling economic consequences. A core human value is at stake in the instance of bribery, and it is economic welfare.

The first but least important way in which bribery harms economic welfare is its damage to predictability. In one striking example, a large US company's crates were regularly pilfered by handlers when unloaded on the docks of Rio de Janeiro.

The handlers would typically take about 10 per cent of the contents of the crates. The company not only lost the contents, but never knew which 10 per cent of the contents it would lose. In desperation the company began sending two crates for everyone sent in the past. The first crate contained 90 per cent of the merchandise normally sent; the second contained 10 per cent. The handlers learned to take the second crate and to leave the first untouched. The company viewed this as an improvement. It still suffered a 10 per cent loss—but it now knew which 10 per cent it would lose!

But bribery destroys much more than predictability. By misallocating resources, it also demolishes the underlying efficiency of market mechanisms. When I spoke to CEOs in India I was not surprised to hear that their companies constantly engaged in bribery and payoffs. They argued that the practice began with the Indian government and that they were forced to bribe. What surprised me, however, was their disgust for the practice. They had no illusions about the propriety of bribery, and were aware that its most pernicious aspect was its effect on efficiency. They realized that inefficiency metastasizes, as decisions are made not on the basis of price and quality but on the basis of how much money people were getting under the table. The market is a remarkably efficient tool for allocating resources, but only works if people buy based on price and quality—not clandestine payoffs. A trip later to the streets of Kolkata brought home the bitter fruits of corruption. The current Indian economy is so inefficient that even dramatic redistribution of wealth would leave most of its inhabitants in dire poverty. Most of the Indian executives I interviewed believed that much of India's economic inefficiency is driven by the presence of massive corruption.

At the level confronted by most individual managers, bribery has no satisfactory solution. Refusing to bribe is very often tantamount to losing business. Often sales and profits are lost to more unscrupulous companies with the consequence that both the ethical company and the ethical individual are penalized. Of course, companies help employees caught in the bribery trap, by having clear policies and giving support to employees who follow them. The answer, then lies not at the level where individuals face bribery, but at the level of the host country's background institutions. A solution involves a broad-based combination of business pressure, legal enforcement, and political will. Companies, in turn, should make a point not only of speaking out against bribery, but of doing so in cooperation with other companies.

Moral Imagination

The complexities of international business spawn incredible ethical challenges. Respecting other traditions, not compromising on the parent company's fundamental values, even as we return a profit to investors, can strenuously test our moral imagination. Happily, examples of ethically creative companies are not hard to find. Donating services, tools or machine parts can sometimes prevent the need for private payoffs. British companies have refused to bribe Tanzanian poaching patrols, but have donated tools and machine pads to aid their anti-poaching activities. Not long ago, Coca-Cola paid Egyptians to plant thousands of fruit trees. In both cases, their actions achieved political support, lower local employment, and higher public trust.

When Levi Strauss & Co. learned that two of its contractors in Bangladesh employed children under the age of fourteen, it looked at its "terms of engagement" principles. It found that though the practice appeared not to violate local laws; it violated Strauss's principles that prohibit engaging contractors who use child labour. Still, forcing the contractors to fire the children would cause disastrous hardship for the families who depended on the children's wages. Moreover, the children would probably not return to school, but go to the streets. What was the company to do? Because of a creative arrangement between Levi Strauss and the contractors, the contractors agreed to pay the children's regular wages while the children went to school. The contractors also agreed to offer each child a job at the age of fourteen. Levi Strauss, in turn, agreed to pay for the necessary books, uniforms and tuition. The children are now happily attending school.

Conclusion

As we have seen, it does not follow that just because A's conception of business ethics is different from B's, one of the two is wrong. A certain amount of 'moral free space' exists in which it is appropriate for communities to define their own ethics. This does not, however, mean that companies can resort to a convenient relativism; companies must be absolutist about their own core values and standards. In short, we must eschew mono-moralism in economic affairs while we eschew cultural relativism. When leaving Tokyo or New York and travelling to Rome we should not simply do as the Romans door exactly duplicate what we do at home. We should allow for differences even as we remain true to our own deeper values; doing this well means preparing for our trip to Rome in advance.

8

Human Excellence through Education

Human excellence through education is an effort to stimulate our thinking in the direction of value-building. We study books, hear class lectures, take part in sports, sit for and pass examinations—all these are certainly part and parcel of education; but the most important part of education is the shaping of our mind and character, the training of our mind to be fit to shape ourself and our environment so as to fulfill our life's purposes. This is the most important aspect we ought to have today in our education.

The Missing Element

We are living in a very great civilization, which is the product of modem Western science and technology. It is a wonderful world that modern science has created for us. We are living in the amazing space age of this civilization. What a tremendous change it is now from what it was 100 years ago! We now have vast knowledge of the macrocosmic and microcosmic universe and a command over so many useful gadgets. We have plenty of comfort, and speedy means of travel and communication of ideas. We have gone to the moon; our sputniks have gone to other planets and one is just now racing towards the outskirts of the solar systems and into outer space.

All these, and many other similar achievements in the various fields of science are great human achievements. But something vital is missing in our otherwise great civilization; and that missing item must be identified and we should delve over it with searching minds. That missing item is revealed in its bitter fruit, in the worldwide phenomenon of tension, anxiety, and unhappiness within man, and the psychic and social distortions resulting from them.

Now, anxiety is a form of fear. For example, in the pre-scientific ages, in Europe, the people were primitive; they had no knowledge of nature or her processes, and they lived hard lives. They were in constant fear of nature and her forces—thunder, lightning, the wolf and other wild animals, and various kinds of diseases. But, today, we have science with us, and we have become civilized by controlling nature's forces. So the fears arising from external nature do not assail us. But we cannot claim that science has banished, and left us entirely without, all fear. Science-civilized man is afflicted with other forms of fear from those referred to above. The truth is that physical sciences have destroyed some fears; but, in its wake, other fears now assail man. And these other fears arise from man's inner nature where the arm of our physical sciences does not reach. And these fears create psychic distortions in us, which manifest themselves as anxiety, tension, frustration, boredom, as well as violence, crime, and even inclination to suicide. These are all the evil fruits of psychic distortions within man, even though our physical sciences have brought order and richness in our outer life.

Demolition of Value-Based Education by British Domination

Lord Macaulay, in his speech in the British Parliament, reveals a lot more than intended about the real nature of British colonialism and the damage it has caused the nation:

> *I have travelled across the length and breadth of India and I have not seen one person who is a beggar, who is a thief Such wealth I have seen in the country, such high moral values, people of such high calibre, that I do not think we would ever conquer this country, unless we break the very backbone of this nation, which is her spiritual and cultural heritage, and, therefore, I propose that we replace her old and ancient education system, her culture, for if the Indians think that all that is foreign and English is good and greater than their own, they will loose their self-esteem, their native self-culture and they will become what we want them, a truly dominated nation.*

Preventive Science

How can we prevent these psychic distortions? It is not enough that we discover and apply cures for them. We are already doing that though not with satisfactory results, and often giving rise to undesirable side effects and other maladies. The most vital question is how do we prevent them. Why should man, in this highly amazing space age, with his vast control of nature's forces, experience this tragedy of inner dissatisfactions and distortions? And is there a science, which can save man from these inner maladies and their outer expressions of social distortion? That science is best which prevents ailments and not merely cures them.

I am sure that this question is a challenging one, and the handling of it by modern man will be a rewarding experience. If the mind is fine, everything is fine; if the mind is distorted, everything is distorted. It is like looking into a minor. You distort your face, and you will find the minor distorting your face. If you have a beautiful face, you find the mirror reflecting that beauty. This is an important part of all human education. Namely, how to train the mind in knowledge, strength, steadiness, and fearlessness, so that it can withstand the powerful currents of all difficult and distorting experiences in life. Human life provides plenty of occasions to face the pressures of difficult experiences. Such occasions will be certainly less in young life; but as you grow in your physical and psychic maturity and enter the mainstream of life, you are bound to come across such intractable experiences, which sometimes create psychic breakdowns and social distortions. Modern sciences like psychiatry and psychotherapy deal with such minds and offer some help. Suppose a child does not get parental love and care in its early life; the mind gets badly distorted from childhood. What is the training of the mind, what is the energy that a child must acquire, through its family environment at first and by itself later, by which it can stay steady and prevent psychic distortions arising from such privations? What is the nature of that inner energy resource and how can we acquire it slowly and steadily from childhood onwards? I am sure, that this preventive knowledge should form an essential part of education.

It is obvious that energy, that strength, does not come from external physical nature; nor does it come from our muscles or from our brain, because men and women with plenty of muscle and plenty of brain also suffer from these distortions. Naturally, we have to search for it in the deeper levels of man, in the spiritual dimensions of the human personality.

Vedanta and Scientific Temper

The science and philosophy of *Vedanta* developed in India ages ago, and continued to be cultivated down to our own times is a universal, comprehensive, rational, and practical philosophy of life possessing high intellectual and spiritual prestige. It is no wonder, therefore, that it has attracted the attention and interest, in this scientific age of several of our modem scientists, some of whom quote passages from the literature of Vedanta in their own books.

The word *Vedanta* is composed of two words, *veda* and *anta*. *Veda* means science, or knowledge; and *anta* means the end or the essence. Thus '*Vedanta*' means, in one sense, the *Upanisad*, which form the end as well as the essential portion of the vast and varied Vedic literature and, in other sense, the essence or consummation of all knowledge, namely, wisdom. Wisdom is matured knowledge. Knowledge, so understood, covers, according to one of the oldest books of the literature of *Vedanta*, namely, the *Mundaka Upanishad* (1.5), not only all positivistic knowledge, such as physical sciences, economic, politics, sociology, but also all the world's ethnical religions and their holy scriptures. Wisdom indicates the maturing of all this knowledge through the experience by man, of deeper dimensions of reality than what his sense organs revel.

This philosophy of *Vedanta* allows you, expects you and welcomes you to ask questions about the truths before you. That is what makes it a science, a science of man in depth. The more you question and inquire, the more you get from it. Usually, religions are based on dogmas, which you are forbidden to question; and you have just to accept. When you question, the dogma breaks down, or they who propagate it break the head of the questioner himself or herself! Hence, the ban on questioning and inquiry in all types of ethnical religions. From this arises their opposition to science whose very lifeblood is based on questioning, and rational enquiry. If you want to understand the uniqueness of Vedanta, you should grasp the fundamental difference between science and ethnical religions. One is born into any of these ethnical religions; one has no choice about it. But with respect to science, one seeks it. No one is born into physics or chemistry or other sciences. You choose it or seek it above its more obvious ethnical expression. It comes to you when you seek it in a critical spirit of truth seeking. Says the British mathematician and astronomer, late Arthur Eddingtion:

You can neither understand the spirit of true science nor of true religion, unless you keep seeking in the forefront.

This philosophy of Vedanta breathes that scientific temper and spirit. It is the product of a sustained rational questioning and investigation of experience, of inquiry into the true nature of man and his destiny conducted by brilliant minds of ancient India thousands of years ago, among whom were men, women, children, kings, emperors, and common people. The literature known as the *Upanisad* conveys to us the scientific temper and outlook of these pioneering minds, the methods they adopted and the truths which they discovered and verified and which they placed before us for our own discovery and verification.

The profoundest truth that they discovered about you and me is that we are all potentially divine, and that there is an infinite and immortal dimension behind the finite and mortal body and mind which we think rye an, according to our sensory experience. Suppose I ask any one of you the question; who are you? You will answer: I am so and so, I am so many centimeters tall, so many kilograms in weight. Can we say that these describe everything about you? They leave out many physical and mental possibilities, which will emerge as you grow and mature; they also leave out a very profound dimension—the depth dimension of your personality. Behind the body behind the nervous system, *Vedanta* discovered the divine spark in every being—ever pure, ever free, and ever luminous: and they called it the *Atman*, the infinite Self. But man's sensory apparatus cannot reveal this dimension. The senses reveal only the physical dimensions of man. The American Nobel prize winner, medical scientist, late Alexis Carrel wrote a book many years ago titled Man, the Unknown. The physical dimensions constitute man, the known, behind which is *man, the unknown*. The *Upanisad* discovered this truth about man, the unknown through a penetrating investigation and they proclaimed it as the truth about every human being. This Atman, they declared, is of the nature of pure consciousness which is infinite and non-dual. The same infinite Atman is in you, in me, in all. At the back of our finite limited consciousness, there is this infinite unlimited consciousness in which we are all one. And that is the center says Vedanta, of infinite energy resources and constitutes the true meaning of what religions call God.

Education and Prevention of Psychic Distortions

In modem civilization, this infinite dimension of man remains neglected. Unknown, and unrecognized and therefore, unutilized. Civilized man lives only at his physical and psychic levels. What lies beyond these levels is a terra incognito to modern civilization, to modern thought, and to modern man. Vedanta says that is why, in spite of such beautiful and powerful technological achievements, modern man is still suffering from fear, tension, and other psychic distortions and ailments. That is also the reason for the ever increasing crime and violence in our civilization. The current spiritual malnutrition is at the back of the increasing psyche of psychotherapists and psychiatrists and police.

Modern technical civilization helps you all to prevent physical malnutrition by providing you with enough nutritious food and exercise; it helps you all to prevent intellectual malnutrition by providing you with schools, libraries, and many other avenues of intellectual knowledge. In these two fields, the healthy principle adopted is prevention and not cure. But there is no provision to prevent the malnutrition of man's inner life. In this vital life, alas! there is so little emphasis on prevention, and all emphasis is on cure only. That is the biggest challenge before human knowledge and human wisdom today. Why should men and women and children remain ill-nourished and weak internally while they are well nourished and strong externally? Do you not see highly intellectual people becoming inclined to even commit suicide? All this shows only that modern man lacks spiritual strength. He or she may have physical strength, even intellectual strength; but spiritual strength is lacking. Is it not the role of education primarily to stress and concentrate on prevention of psychic distortions? Is it not the role of modern education to make modern man achieve all-round strength and fearlessness?

In modern life, man is subjected to various pressures, but he or she is not given the spiritual strength to withstand these pressures. Why should science created by man and the energies released by man through his physical sciences destroy the creator himself? It is because man has no grip on these energies and cannot discipline them and guide them to suit his or her own growth and fulfilment. To do so he must have great spiritual strength within, but this is lacking. It is like a youth riding a powerful horse without learning how to discipline the horse and guide it in the direction desired by him or her in a masterly way; and so the horse takes its rider wherever it likes and the horse enjoys the ride and the youth becomes a victim of that ride! If only he or she knew how to grip the horse and discipline and guide it in the proper direction, what a beautiful experience that ride would be to that youth!

Similarly, if modern man learns to discipline the energies of his body and mind, and the other energies released by science and technology outside of him, he or she will command a grip on the outer situation, making it serve his or her own purposes of life's development and fulfilment. Only men and women who develop the spiritual dimension of their personality from childhood achieve this. Today's children must start developing that rich dimension of their personality and achieve a parallel spiritual growth along with their physical and intellectual development. Otherwise, the world will shape them, instead of them shaping the world. That will be the greatest tragedy of man—tragedy which is enacted every day in our contemporary civilization.

'Learning to Be' versus 'Learning to Do'

Our education must provide against this tragedy afflicting man. There are plenty of books and journals coming out regularly, that describe this contemporary tragic human situation. You read about the spurt in many types of social distortions like criminal acts, sexual abuse and drug offence. This is a grave challenge to address through education. It is good to understand these problems and seek not only short-term remedies through psychotherapy and other techniques, but, still more important, from the point of view of education, scientifically authentic permanent preventives. Merely talking and writing about the evils of our society do not help us much; anyone can do it. That may be the role of other disciplines like politics and public administration, but not of education. Lighting a candle is more important than shouting about darkness. The truth is to seek for a science of living which will prevent these maladies from afflicting humanity. That is the role, that ought to be the role, of all education.

It is in this context that one begins to understand the Vedantic emphasis on the truth of the inner world of man, the truth of the within of nature as revealed in nature's finest evolutionary product, namely, man. There is need for an inquiry into this truth to become an essential and integral part of any healthy educational policy and programme. This is the new dimension of education, long neglected, but now compelling recognition, due to the contemporary human and social distortions. This compelling need is reflected, even if only as a glimpse, in the title of a book first published by the UNESCO in 1972, *Learning to Be: The World of Education Today and Tomorrow*. It is the report of a UNESCO Commission enquiring into the problems of education in the post-second World War world, presided over by M. Edgar Faure, then Minister of Education and later Prime Minister of France.

Says the commission in the very opening pages of its report:

Four basic assumptions underlay our work from the start. The first, which was indeed the justification for the task we undertook, is that of the existence of an international community which amidst the variety of nations and cultures of political options and degrees of development is reflected in common aspirations problems and trends and in its movement towards one and the same destiny..

The second is belief in democracy conceived of as implying each man is right to realize his own potential and to share in the building of his own future...

The third assumption is that an aim of development is the complete fulfilment of man in all the richness of his personality, the complexity of his forms of expression, and his various commitments as an individual member of a family and of a community citizen and producer inventor of techniques and creative dreamer.

Our last assumption is that only an overall life long education can produce the kind of complete man the need for whom is increasing with the continually more stringent constraints tearing the individual as under. We should no longer assiduously acquire knowledge once and for all but learn how to build up a continually evolving body of knowledge all through life learning to be.'

And in the chapter headed 'Toward the complete man', the report says

A new man for a new world!...

His knowledge of his own powers spreads to knowledge of his own consciousness. Never until now has he stretched to such limits his attempts to elucidate the mystery of his inner world.

For training purposes, one of man's dimensions—that of intellectual cognition—has been arbitrarily chopped into pieces, while others have been forgotten or overlooked, and have been either reduced to an embryonic state or left to develop in anarchic fashion. For the supposed needs of scientific research or higher level specialization, the full general formation of many young people has been mutilated.

Much of this thought and language is Vedanta, without the authors of the report knowing it, and without the philosophic strength of a conscious insight into the spiritual dimensions of the human personality. In his pre-second World War writings, Bertrand Russell also speaks Vedanta without obviously knowing it.

Man has been disciplined hitherto by his subjection to nature. Having emancipated himself from this subjection, he is, sowing some of the defects of slave-turned master. A new moral outlook is called for, in which submission to the powers of nature is replaced by respect for what is best in man. It is where this respect is lacking that scientific technique is dangerous. So long as it is present, science will deliver man from bondage to nature and proceed to deliver him from bondage to the slavish part of himself.

This respect for what is best in man and the science which will proceed to deliver man from bondage to the slavish part of himself is what *Vedanta* developed ages ago in its *adhyatma-vidya*, in its science of the inner world of man, in its science of human possibilities. The intellect in which the light of the Atman shines becomes enlightened reason which is very different from the intellect which is enslaved to the sense organs and the outer sensory world.

Education must thus comprise learning to be, as much as learning to do. It is when you stress this aspect of learning to be that you are led to the recognition of, and inquiry into the inner world of man and its discipline and development. This is the one source of character energy in man, and all healthy character is centred in a humanely oriented will. Man lives in two worlds—an outer world and an inner world, a without of nature and a within of nature. Teilhard de Chardin in his book *The Phenomenon of Man Learning to Do* refers to our dealing with the outer world. Modem man thinks of the inner world only when he or she is in some psychic trouble. Then he/she hands himself or herself over to a psychiatrist or a psychotherapist, who studies and handles that disturbed inner world with its tensions complexes and self-insufficiencies. In many cases these are not set at least in the short term. But rarely does it restore one to his or her original health, well being and efficiency.

From this current curative approach we have to turn over to the preventive approach, which is the true function of education. You can ask the question: which is better—curative or preventive? I am sure the answer will be that preventing being ill is better than falling ill and getting cured. This preventive aspect of total human health and well being, with which is associated the concept of learning to be, is a profound science which views man in his or her wholeness, physically, mentally, and spiritually. This is a science like any other science—the science of spirituality. We have to get an insight into it in our education, so that the inner man gets nourished and our reason catches a few rays of the light of the Atman behind it and becomes enlightened, and radiates love and peace. Today, as I said, some physicists, biologists, sociologists, and psychologists are trying to understand this science of spirituality of India known as Vedanta and yoga.

Education in the Light of Science of Human Possibilities

Famous biologist and humanist, the late Sir Julian Huxley of England, had referred to the urgent need for modern physical science to develop a new science capable of guiding humanity to the goal of fulfilment. He called it a science of human possibilities. This is what India developed in her Vedanta ages ago, and has continued to nourish ever since. Says he:

> *In the light of our present knowledge man's most comprehensive aim is seen not as mere survival not as numerical increased, not as increase complexity of organization or increased control over his environment, but as greater fulfilment—the fuller realization of more possibilities by human species collectively and more of its component members individually'.*

It is good to ask this question: What are the possibilities hidden in me? When you look at the eyes of a living baby, you find it different from the eyes of a baby doll. There is depth in a living baby's eyes, which you miss in the doll's eyes. What are the hidden possibilities disclosed by those living eyes? What depths of experience do they reveal? Is this not a wonderful subject of scientific investigation? Our modern physical sciences tell us about the possibilities hidden behind physical nature. They disclose the enormous energies hidden in the subatomic technology to bring out these nuclear energies and use them either to enhance human life or to destroy all life. This is certainly a great achievement, though it is not a happy prospect that modern man may use these nuclear energies for destroying all life.

A hundred years ago, knowledge of this technique and the possibility of enormous energies that can enhance life or destroy all life, were not available to man. What was the source of energy for our ancestors over 800 years ago? Only combustion energy. It was limited in scope. When you eat food, it is that same combustion energy that breaks down and digests the food and gives you physical and mental strength. Then, in the late nineteenth century, modern science discovered a deeper and more immense source of energy in matter, namely, electrical energy; and that revolutionized our civilization. Then came the amazing twentieth century. Physics discovered a more immense source of energy in matter in the wake of the splitting of the nucleus of the atom by the famous British scientist Rutherford. Quick developments followed in the investigation into this nuclear field, giving man command of vast nuclear energies; for destructive purposes through the atom bomb, hydrogen bomb, and now the neutron bomb, and for peaceful and constructive purposes in the field of health and agriculture. Now we know Einstein's famous formula for the immense dimensions of this nuclear energy: $E = mc^2$.

Wisdom versus Folly

Today we have nuclear bombs and missiles in the hands of four or five nuclear powers in the world, enough to kill all humanity ten times over. This is not a happy situation because, in spite of man having enormous power in his hands, there is no certainty that he would use that power only to enhance life and not to destroy it. We need a transformation within man himself to be able to make him inclined and capable to use his enormous powers for peaceful constructive purposes.

Bertrand Russell, in one of his post-second World War writings, pointed out the danger of knowledge remaining at the level of knowledge alone, along with the power that the knowledge brings. He stressed the need for knowledge to rise to the level of wisdom.

Broadly speaking, we are in the middle of a race between human skill as to means and human folly as to ends. Given sufficient folly as to ends, increase in the skill required to achieve them is not good. The human race has survived hitherto owing to ignorance and incompetence: but given knowledge and competence, combined with folly, there can be no certainty of survival. Knowledge is power. But it is power for evil just as much as for good. It follows that, unless men increase their wisdom as much as knowledge, increased knowledge will only be increase of sorrow.

It is this energy of wisdom within man to control and guide and use all physical energy resources for constructive and peaceful human purpose that we have to discover and acquire today. Whether it is physical energy resources, or politics, money or other forms of power in the hands of man, whether it is small or immense in quantity, the main question is, and has always been, if he will use it constructively. And that depends entirely upon the nature and state of the development of the inner world of man, the level at which her or his consciousness functions. If one of you has a strong muscular body, you can use that muscular energy either to help people or to harm people. Which way you will use that muscular energy does not depend upon the energy itself, but upon the energy within your mind. Therefore, along with the possession of external energy resources, such as muscular, intellectual, financial, political and military, we need also the energy that can control and direct all such energies for constructive and peaceful purposes. It is in this field that physical sciences become helpless and you seek help from the science of spirituality. That is the role of Vedanta as the science and technique of total human development and fulfilment, both individual and collective. It is the science of depth dimension of man, which reveals the enormous spiritual energy resources lying in store behind those eyes of any living child, and which provides the technique for the manifestation of these energies in life and character. The supreme form of the manifestation of this spiritual energy is love, with its varied expressions in compassion, dedication, and service. This capacity for love is largely missing today because modern humanity knows so little about the spiritual dimensions of personality. That is why there is anxiety and fear everywhere.

Tat Tvam Asi!

Apart from external threats of nuclear war, there is a constant threat from within man himself, in case you are in a state of depression. Is there any energy which you can command from within yourself that can lift you up? Suppose one is about to commit suicide;

is there any energy that can make him or her stop doing it? The positive answer to these questions come from Vedanta—the science of the enormous spiritual energy resources hidden in every human being and the techniques of manifesting them in life and inter-human relationships. Vedanta gives you an equation for the immense spiritual energy resources within man, just like the above-mentioned Einstein's equation for physical nuclear energy. It proclaims the profound truth that in each one of us there is not only our growing muscular energy, there is not only our developing intellectual energy, there is also the infinite energy of what the great world religions call God, hidden in us all.

It is a wonderful truth worth pursuing by all. If religion means going to some heaven after death, there is no harm in waiting till old age to pursue religion; but if it means this science of spirituality, the technique of gaining strength, fearlessness, and love in this very life, it is worth pursuing from early life itself. Vedanta gives us a similar equation for the enormous spiritual, divine, energy resources present in each one of us. It forms the heart of a famous statement from a teacher and father by name Aruni to his student son by name Svetaketu, occurring in the *Chandogya Upanisad*.

Sa eso anima, aitat atmyamidam sarvam,
Tat satyam, sa atma,
Tat team asi, svetaketo
Every thing in the universe has this subtle (reality) for its self. that is the truth. That is the atman, and that thou art, 0 Svetaketu.

'That thou art' a simple three-word equation! We must get over it. The sages of India studied man in depth. Those sages discovered the infinite man behind the finite man, the immortal man behind the mortal man. They discovered the extremely subtle but powerful spiritual energies hidden behind all forms of the gross and subtle energies in the human psychophysical system. The word tat or 'that' stands for that infinite divine dimension with its infinite energy resources behind nature and man. The word *tvam* or 'thou' stands for you and me and all others—the finite individual with his or her limited physical and intellectual energy resources. To a little child who seeks a rock projecting out of the depth of an ocean bed, it is just a small stone, but its elders will explain that it is an immense rock whose tip alone can be seen above water level and is visible to our senses; the rest of the rock is beyond human sight. To your sensory vision, similarly, you see a limited finite being and others too appear the same to you. But this truth of tat *tvam* lies at the deepest level of your personality, beyond the reach of your senses and sense-bound mind. Whenever your limited mind says that 'I am a finite human being with limited energies, I am a person of 50 or 70 kg weight, I am weak, I am afraid, I am helpless', this science of man-in-depth tells you that you should not evaluate a piece of matter in terms of sensory evaluation of it.

Vedanta is happy that, in this modern age, thanks to modern scientific achievements and the bringing of the people of the world close to each other, it can convey this profound hope-inspiring truth about man to millions everywhere. This is the great task that late professor William James, the noted psychologist and philosopher of Harvard University, attributed to Swami Vivekananda. He said:

The paragon of all monistic systems is the Vedanta philosophy of Hindustan, and the paragon of Vedanta Missionaries was the late Swami Vivekananda who visited our land some years ago.

Vedanta, therefore, presents to all this profound truth of *Tat tvam asi* to make you strong, to make you fearless, to make you fulfilled, so that you can enjoy life through having a grip on it.

This is the truth about man; not an opinion, not a utopian thought to console man. *Vedanta* provides the technique to unfold these immense energy resources hidden in man; and the technique covers the whole range of man's life and work, and not just a few religious practices. It is the philosophy of a comprehensive spirituality dealing with man at labour and man at leisure, man interacting with other human beings and man in his aloneness; man at work and man at worship. Sri Krishna, therefore, exhorts one and all in the *Bhagavad Gita*:

Man ansusmara yadhya ca

Meditate on Me (as your own inner Self) and carry on the battle of life.

The whole of modern civilization needs this philosophy of a comprehensive spirituality to unify and stabilize man's outer and inner lives.

The steady unfolding of these inner spiritual energy resources manifests it self, as I have already said, as strength, fearlessness, love, compassion, and work-efficiency. What a beautiful idea it is—the energy of love, the energy of compassion coming from the spiritual dimension of the human personality! Modern man is ignorant of it so far; modern psychology also knows very tittle about this, but it is progressing steadily in that direction. Let us listen again to what our agnostic thinker, the late Bertrand Russell, says with a bit of apology.

> *There are certain things that our age needs, and certain things that it should avoid. It needs compassion and a wish that mankind should be happy... the things that it must avoid and that have brought it to the brink of catastrophe, are cruelty, greed, competitiveness, search for irrational subjective certainty, and what Freudians call the death wish.*
>
> *The root of the matter is a very simple and old-fashioned thing: a thing so simple almost as harried to mention it, for fear of the derisive smile with which wise cynics will greet my words. The thing I mean—please forgive me for mentioning it is love, Christan love, or compassion. If you feel this, you have a motive for existence, a guide in action, a reason for courage. An imperative necessity for honesty.*

Character Built on Rock versus Character Built on Sand

Suppose any one of you understands and appreciates this *Vedantic* teaching which tells you that there is a profound spiritual energy centre hidden within you beyond your muscular and intellectual energy levels. Then suppose one day you felt depressed; your muscular energy is then of no help to you, nor is your intellectual energy of any help to you. Why are you in this depressed state? You are the infinite Atman, you have infinite energy hidden within you, you are a child of immortality—*amrtasya putra*, as the *Upanisad* proclaim, or as Jesus said: 'the Kingdom of Heaven is within you'. When this truth dawns on you even slightly, you wake up from your state of weakness, from the condition of depression. Your weakness slowly vanishes and you feel strong, you feel confident. This is not like the old psychology's prescription of autosuggestion. It is the autosuggestion of waking up to it and makes you also loving and compassionate in your inter-human relationships. This is the perennial message of Vedanta. In Indian literature, this message of Vedanta is compared to the lion's roar. Swami *Vivekananada* says that before it 'the foxes of fear and hatred and pettiness will fly to the holes!'

Men and women in modern civilization need great spiritual strength to be able to live sane, happy, and fulfilled lives. At present this unique strength is not there. Life throws us up and down like shallow-rooted trees getting shaken and uprooted by even mild winds. I like to recall what Jesus says in his famous Sermon on the Mount:

> *A foolish man built his house on sand; and the rains descended, and the floods came, and the winds blew, and beat upon that house; and it fell; and great was its fall. But a wise man built his house on rock: and the rains descended, and the floods came, and the winds blew, and beat upon that house; and it fell not, because it was built on rock.*

What a beautiful example! Let all of us ask this question: On what base shall I build my character, on sand or on rock? If it is sand you will fall down with the slightest touch of a breeze of shock, trauma, or temptation. If it is rock, you will stand strong and steady against all such adverse winds. What stands for this sand, and for this rock, with respect to human life?

Modern biology has something unique to say. It says that, at the human stage, evolution has risen from the organic to a new level. And what is that new level? Evolution at the human stage has become primarily psycho-social evolution. What does biology mean by this psycho-social evolution? The human psyche, till now confined to and limited by genetic or organic system of man, becomes capable of detaching itself from that system and expend itself in understanding, love, sympathy, and compassion, so as to enter into and to be entered into by millions of other psyches in society.

Psycho-Social Evolution as Spiritual Growth

Thus you will realize that what biological science calls psycho-social evolution is what *Vedanta* calls the spiritual growth of the man.

Just as there is a physical growth of man, just as there is an intellectual growth of man, so there is also such a thing as spiritual growth of man. Mere intellectual growth does not continue your psycho-social evolution, since it does not, by itself, take one beyond the pressure and pulls of the organic system. You see so many people around you within the high spiritual growth; but you also see them committing anti-social acts like bribery, crime, violence, and exploitation of others. Therefore, mere intellectual growth is not enough. For, in that growth you are still tied down to your genetic system and view everything, everybody else in terms of the profit and pleasure of your own genetic system. But psycho-social evolution as spiritual growth takes you beyond all such genetic limitations and makes you feel spiritual, and one with millions of other psyches in society. This is the meaning of love and compassion. This is the energy that the world must develop today through science and technique, through taking the first step and marching steadily on the long roads of psycho-social evolution, along with developing nuclear, solar or other forms of physical energy resources through the help of the physical sciences. Technology of physical science gives us only that same muscular energy multiplied a million-fold, such as you find in the modem space rockets. But modern man is realizing slowly but steadily that the supreme energy is the energy of the spirit, manifested as love. And it is located in every one.

In this connection, it is interesting to recall a statement made by Napoleon who was a consummate wielder of the sword and the gun and was a great military genius. When you study European history and study Napoleon's part in it, you are struck by the high efficiency and organizing power of his mind, of his tremendous capacity to win battles with even a small number of soldiers;capable, sometimes, to take more prisoners than the number of his own soldiers. Then he lost everything in 1814 at Waterloo at the hands of the British and, a year later, the British sent him as a prisoner to the isolated island of St Helena in the west of Africa where he died six years later.

He seemed to have become somewhat wiser during that hard life, contemplating his ambitious and wonderful life and career. A bit of that wisdom finds expression in a remark he made to his prison companion:

> *There are in the world two powers—the spirit and the sword. And the spirit has always vanquished the sword. Alexander, Julius Ceasar, Charlemagne, had founded great empires. But upon what did the creation of our genius depend? Upon force? Jesus alone founded his empire upon love, and today this very day millions would die for him.*

This is a unique testament to the power of the love from a man like Napoleon who used the entire resources of the state and church to further his ambition by force. We must realize the truth of that statement today. We have developed enormous physical resources; we have developed enormous intellectual resources and at the same time we have developed and stock-piled highly destructive armaments. All this development will ultimately be a destroyer of all life in the absence of the development of the ever present spiritual energy resources within us. The modern angle demands that the knowledge and technique of unfolding this tremendous spiritual energy in man must become an integral part of all education. Otherwise that education will remain imperfect and inadequate to meet the tremendous challenges thrown by the modern age. That is the significance of what I referred to earlier, as the need for a new stress on learning to be incorporated in all education.

Meditation in Education

When you are outwardly active, working and interacting with other human beings, you are in the field of learning to do. When you sit down and are silently active in an inward penetration through meditation and such other techniques, and cease to be gregarious, you are in the field of the process of learning to be. And Vedanta is the philosophy of such a comprehensive education and unified human life. Meditation gives you insight into your own inner dimension, your own hidden possibilities. When you discipline the sense organs and the sense-bound mind and turn their energies towards the inner man, you come in touch with the profound spiritual dimension of your being. When these same energies, bearing the purifying elevating touch of the divine within, are later turned outward into the field of work and inter human relation, they scatter fearlessness, love and peace all around. They bear the touch of the union of philanthropic efficiency with philosophic calm, in the language of the British sociologist Herbert Spencer.

This is the message of the philosophy of *yoga* of the *Bhagavat Gita*. There are many types of *yoga*. With great relevance, it exhorts every one of you to combine meditation with work, inward penetration with outward action. With the help of this philosophy of yoga as expounded in the *Gita*, we can transform modem civilization into a stable, rich and beautiful human achievement.

Education for both learning to do and learning to be is helped by the practice of meditation; because doing becomes an outflow of an enriched being within. Meistereckhart, the great German mystic of the thirteenth century, expresses this truth beautifully: 'what you take in by contemplation, that you pour out in love.'

Conclusion

Let me conclude by sharing with you a Sanskrit hymn, which breathe the spirit of universality and human unity, the spirit of the modern world that tends towards a mankind of awareness and international peace:

Sarve bhavantu sukhinah
Sarve bhavantu nirmayah;
Sarve bhadrani pasantu
Ma kascit dukkha-bhak bhavet
May all (beings) be happy; may all (beings) be free from ailments. (physical or mental); may all (beings) experience what is good and auspicious; and may none be subject to sorrow and suffering!

9

Motivation/Work-Life Balance

What You'll Learn in this Chapter

- Espresso Culture at Work
- How Motivation/Work-Life Balance is Reflected in Society.
  The Impact of Motivation/Work-Life Balance in Business

Motivation/Work-Life Balance Refers to

- How people identify the ways they accomplish status, whether through professional achievement or personal life; how people define their status in society, whether from personal life or work achievement.
- How one's work influences one's self-image and self-perception
- Motivation for success: Why people work and What it means
- How much work-life balance is valued
- Which is more motivating: Time off or Promotion
- The presence or absence of laws and policies promoting family benefits. What constitutes status

Espresso Culture at Work

Joshua Sturtevant, Director of Technology for RW^3 LLC, tells a story about when he was at the university in Genoa, Italy. He was completing a Master's degree in Music Technology for New York University. The program divided students into three groups on the basis of their primary interests: dancers, musicians, and technicians. The first two groups were made up of students from various countries, but the tech team consisted of only Italians except Joshua. The team members communicated well because they all spoke "technology," whether in English or in Italian.

From the outset, there had been differences in the way the three teams approached their assignments. The dancers worked all the time. The musicians loved music, sat and played together, and built a strong camaraderie in an attempt to support one another and make one another sound great. The Italian technical team was extremely competent but felt that work was only one part of life and should be integrated with one's social life, not dominate it. They took long lunches and many coffee breaks, and since all of them except Josh were Italian, they couldn't understand why he was always focused on his work and trying to exceed the director's expectations at the expense of having a good time.

At the end of the semester, the class was preparing for its culmination performance, which was to be held at a prestigious venue for a student performance, and the entire class was excited and nervous in anticipation. The agreement was that tech team would set up the equipment two hours before the dress rehearsal to be sure that everything was there and worked flawlessly. At the time the dress rehearsal was scheduled to begin, all the equipment was set up, but none of the members of the tech team except Joshua was there. The achievement-oriented dancers were in costume, and musicians were at their instruments. The Italians on the tech team, who were much more focused on being with their friends, were nowhere to be found.

"The director, who was a teacher at New York University and a perfectionist who was focused on getting work done before anything else, was livid," Joshua said.

Joshua was beside himself. Thinking that perhaps his fellow team members had been held up at the university, he took off at a run across the town and up a huge hill to the university. About halfway up the steep cobblestone hill, Joshua paused to catch his breath and caught sight of his tech team classmates having espressos after a long lunch in a sidewalk cafe!

Breathless and drenched in sweat, he approached them, astounded that they were still there, only to discover that he was unable to speed them up. He was surprised that they couldn't understand why he was so stressed.

In spite of his cajoling, they finished their espressos. It was painfully clear to Joshua, an American from the Midwest, that to the Italians work-life balance meant that a social lunch followed by a coffee was as important as promptness in arriving at the dress rehearsal. To Joshua, commitment and accomplishment were primary motivators, whereas to his Italian colleagues, who wouldn't have wanted to disappoint their fellow students and also had high standards, the primary purpose of life was to balance enjoyment of everyday pleasures with their work.

The performance went well, and at its conclusion Joshua's Italian teammates pointed out to that everything had gone well. They made a point of emphasizing how unnecessary his anxiety was. So what if they were a bit late?

It's obvious that culture determines people's priorities. Clearly, Joshua's top priority was to succeed and excel at work, and he couldn't have enjoyed leisure time when he knew that the tasks needed for a successful performance were outstanding.

What is Motivation/Work-Life Balance?

Motivation/work-life balance describes the emphasis that people in a society place on achievement and status by hard work versus the focus on personal time and activities.

How Motivation/Work-Life Balance is Reflected in Society

Motivation/work-life balance refers to how much work-life balance is valued in a society. Which is more motivating: personal time or a pro-motion at work? What do you consider personal sacrifices, and what do you consider reasonable requests for work? Is it reasonable to be asked to work on a weekend or to reschedule a vacation? What's the separation between your work and personal life? Do you live to work or work to live?

Although we'd all like to think we strive for balance in our professional and personal lives, cultures differ in the values they hold regarding the importance of work versus personal time. Those differing values are reinforced by organizational and government policies regarding vacation time, flexible work arrangements, child care provisions, and other family benefits. The dimension of motivation/work-life balance covers this tug-of-war.

Generally speaking, more individualistic societies tend to produce people who are driven by the ideals of personal achievement, self-fulfilment, and possibly economic gain and material rewards. To achieve their goals, those individuals are willing to sacrifice personal time, work into the night and on weekends, take their laptops with them on vacation, and hop onto a plane at a moment's notice. Although the outward signs are obvious, under the surface what motivates people may not be financial security as much as status and personal satisfaction. This isn't just a matter of individual choice. Countries with a work-oriented culture tend not to have state mandated vacations or welfare benefits for those who are out of work.

In cultures at the other end of the continuum—strong motivation/work-life countries—there's a feeling that one's personal life always takes precedence over work. People work to live, not live to work. People are not likely to socialize with colleagues outside of work and rarely, if ever, discuss business at a social function. Personal achievement and economic gain take second place to the quality of one's life. When you're asked, "What do you do?" it is just as likely to be a question about your hobbies as about your career.

In France, for example, it's against the law for employees to work more than 35 hours in a week. Let us see what Dimitra Manis of AXA Corporation, an Australian who got a transfer to France in 2005, has to say in this regard. Dimitra told several stories about her adjustment in terms of her work ethic and commitment to the job to being a manager in a French workplace in which the 35-hour workweek is mandatory and month-long vacations are common.

"During my first year, I would come to work on public holidays and almost every weekend," she said. "Of course, the office was a ghost town. When members of my team learned that I had been working on holidays and weekends, they assumed that I didn't have a happy home life."

"I didn't take much leave the first year while I mastered the job and accomplished the significant challenges I had taken on for myself, but I decided to take a month off during the summer after that first year."

"My colleagues said to me, 'It has taken you a long time, but now you are French!'"

Dimitra also talked about how her Australian work ethic had her carrying an extremely heavy workload—working from 8 a.m. to 10 p.m. almost daily—and how the local human relations department had to warn her that she was pushing her team too hard and might encounter problems with the French labor "secret police."

In many countries that are high in work-life balance, government or corporate policies enforce long vacations and limit work hours. There are programs, such as lengthy maternity leave, to help parents. Failure to take one's full quota of paid leave is considered foolish. The people who are always last to leave the office are considered not dedicated but inefficient—they can't complete their work within the allotted time.

Typically, countries that are high in motivation/work-life balance are also cultures that are somewhat hierarchical; status may be bestowed at birth and derives from attendance at preferred schools and universities. In those cultures, family connections and school ties are important and valued. Many arrangements are made on the basis of whom you know rather than what you've accomplished. For example, there you end up speaking about someone not in terms of what he or she does but in terms of who his or her family is and how important that family is in the society. Such societies view work as what needs to be done to survive and enjoy life. Since people in those societies don't gain power and status by dint of hard work, they typically limit their time at work and concentrate their energies on family, friends, and vacations.

On the other end of the spectrum are cultures in which people work hard and sacrifice personal time and family because work-related achievements are a key means of gaining power and status. Organizations rooted in cultures that value achievement over work-life balance think nothing of asking employees to give up family time or sacrifice vacations for work responsibilities. Self-fulfilment comes from economic gain and recognition at work.

Another differentiator of societies is how much people identify themselves by their personal lives or their work titles and achievements. For example, is it appropriate to discuss business during social interactions?

The Impact of Motivation/Work-Life Balance in Business

Attitudes toward motivation affect the hours you work, your willingness to have organizations interfere during your personal time, and the relationship between how you think about yourself and what you do for a living. In high-status countries, people feel that you should accomplish many things and that what you achieve is determined by hard work. Work and accomplishment should be rewarded and recognized.

What you achieve defines your importance and status in the world, leading to a sense of well-being. People are valued for their measurable contributions, and these high-motivation cultures are goal-oriented, often measuring people's values against their abilities to achieve those goals.

In those cultures, objectives are clearly defined and on-the-job performance is measured against those objectives for bonuses, promotions, retention, and recruitment for participation in special projects. People are always available on their Blackberries and reply their e-mails even when on the move. They don't resent receiving phone calls during off-work hours. People in the other types of cultures think it is rude to interrupt their evening and think you'd be crazy to give up family time or postpone a vacation.

In cultures in which the primary motivation is for work-life balance, great value is placed on relationships and personal characteristics. For example, job satisfaction is often more important than setting and reaching arbitrary goals. Since status isn't determined by individual accomplishments, people more often seek harmony in the work environment.

In high-balance cultures, people work to live rather than live to work. The organization cannot interfere in the private lives of individuals easily. Since expectations directly affect motivation, status is tied closely to reward structures. People aren't as likely to be motivated by compensation because money isn't a source of status. As a result, finding common ground for rewarding and motivating workers is a significant challenge in dealing with employees.

Although people in these societies are reluctant to talk about their personal accomplishments, that doesn't mean they don't have such accomplishments. This is a big error high-status-attainment individuals make when interviewing potential job candidates from low-status-attainment societies. In high-status-attainment cultures, people are more comfortable talking about what they've accomplished. When going on job interviews, they are coached to emphasize the amount of money they've earned for the company and the number of people they've managed. The objective is to show that they were an integral component in the company's success. In low-status-attainment cultures, individuals may consider it inappropriate to flaunt personal achievement. Instead, resumes are expected to be more comprehensive and outline the jobs and skills individuals have mastered. Recommendations from prominent individuals have great value. Additionally, information related to age, schools attended, and other affiliations may be more significant to an interviewer in a low-status-attainment culture.

In high-status cultures in which achievement is coveted, people are willing to work on weekends when necessary to get the job done. In most of the low-status attainment countries in Europe people will never surrender their six-week vacations and are unlikely to work on weekends to earn more money. Contrast that to the United States where executives rarely take their allotted vacations and regularly take work home on weekends after putting in a 60-hour week.

The motivation/work-life balance dimension is very subtle and sometimes difficult to recognize. For example, the fact that an English person may find it intrusive to work on a holiday doesn't mean that she or he is unmotivated. It means that achievement—and working hard—is not part of that person's way to achieve status. Living to work is not part of the culture, and long hours at the office do not constitute status attainment to an English person. Contrast the English afternoon high tea break with an American coffee break that consists of standing and gulping coffee from a Styrofoam cup. The British society makes sure that it allocates time to pursue other interests on Saturday and Sunday.

In high-status-attainment cultures, families readily allow work demands to interfere with a person's private life because working hard and showing that one is very busy is a way of attaining status. It may mean carrying a pager or a cell phone or simply handing out one's home phone number to important clients. If a crisis occurs over the weekend, it means dropping everything to head for the office. In low-status-attainment cultures, you have or don't have status because of who you are. Moreover, work hours are shorter and weekends are spent relaxing with friends and family. A call from a manager may evoke feelings of anger and intrusion, since leisure time is considered sacred.

Furthermore, in high-status-attainment cultures, people are comfortable with informal introductions at social events. Parties consist of eclectic groups of people that cross social strata. Attendees often discuss business, even at social events. In low-status-attainment cultures, formal introductions take place at social events, and parties tend to be more homogeneous. It's likely that everyone will know everyone else or have the same sorts of backgrounds or connections. Since achievement is a secondary concern compared with family and background, discussing business would be in poor taste at a social occasion.

Table 9.1 illustrates the challenges you'll face when crossing cultures. Use the table to help tailor your expectations and business behaviour.

Table 9.1

Crossing Cultures: Motivation/Work-Life Balance

Status to Balance	*Balance to Status*
• Don't expect work to interfere with people's personal lives. People are less likely to relocate for a promotion.	• Expect work to be of primary importance to your employees and colleagues. People will relocate readily if it means a promotion.
• Don't expect people to work on weekends or late into the evenings. The organization cannot interfere in the private lives of individuals easily.	• People are willing to work on weekends or late in the evenings. It is expected that business demands sometimes overlap with personal lives.
• Don't expect people who come for interviews to discuss everything they have achieved. It is immodest to brag overestimate their abilities.	• People will provide details about their work successes enthusiastically. Don't consider them immodest or about personal achievement.
• Don't expect people to define success only in terms of task performance or accomplishments. They focus more on quality of life and job satisfaction.	• Don't expect broad definitions of success. Achievement, performance, and profits often define the success of an operation.
• Think beyond individual achievement in structuring jobs. Integration of personal and family life and a positive working environment are related to satisfactory job structures.	• Individual achievement is the key to structuring jobs. Motivation for high performance relates to increased earnings, promotion, recognition, or intellectual stimulation.
• Focus on win-win negotiations.	• Focus more on aggressive negotiations that provide you with the optimal market position.
• Organizational goals may not be articulated clearly. Your effectiveness is evaluated relative to your organizational compatibility and affiliations.	• Respect for organizational goals is highly valued. Success is evaluated against your ability to meet these goals.
• Being a "fast-tracker" is not as important as having influential connections.	• Having proper connections is not as important as working hard and setting and reaching goals.

Definition for this Chapter

Work-life balance: The degree to which people negotiate the competing demands of job and personal lives.

Lessons Learned to Develop Your Cultural Skills

- How motivation/work-life balance is reflected in society

- The impact of motivation/work-life balance in business
- Why some people are motivated by achievement and others are motivated by personal time

Questions to Ponder

1. You're an American expatriate who has just moved to Spain. You work late into the night, long after everyone else has left. You can't understand why people don't comment on your strong work ethic. What do you think is happening? Directions: Go to *http://book-culturewizard.com* and join the discussion.
2. Your American boss is not all that amenable to allowing long vacations for employees. You want to take a three-week vacation in several months. How will you approach the situation?

Directions: Go to *http://book.culturewizard.com* and join the discussion.

What Do You Think?

You have had your own experiences. Share them.

Go to *http://book.culturewizard.com* and join the discussion.

10

Doing Business with a Global Mindset

What you'll Learn in this Chapter

- Integreon: The Global Mindset in Knowledge Outsourcing
- What is a Global Mindset?
- What do you Need to Know to have a Global Mindset?

Integreon: The Global Mindset in Knowledge Outsourcing

Liam Brown strides into the conference room in Los Angeles, eager to activate his executive management team's "weekly tactical" conference call. Already on the projected computer screen are the faces of the members of his executive team, who hail from: Mumbai; New York; Manila; Delhi; Fargo, North Dakota; Washington, D.C.; and London, ready for the call. Despite the early hour, his British-accented "Let's get started" is delivered enthusiastically. This is a high-energy, take-charge guy who is comfortable anywhere in the world. In fact, Liam was born and educated in the United Kingdom, was trained as a physician, lived and worked in major cities around the world, studied culture, and is the embodiment of a person with a global mindset.

These meetings are part of the regular management structure that Liam has established for Integreon. The weekly meetings last 90 minutes and involve each executive at his or her desk with a webcam enabled computer. They are fast-paced, information-rich meetings in which everyone updates the other members and responds to them with active forthright suggestions and constructive candid questioning. It's obvious that the team has built a strong bond and a trusting relationship, sharing information readily. Liam feels that the webcam video and shared desktops enhance the quality of the communication in these virtual global meetings. This meeting is an illustration of the global mindset with which Liam manages Integreon.

Integreon is a knowledge and legal process outsourcing (KPO and LPO) company serving lawyers, bankers, management consultants, and accounting professionals. Its customers include U.S. and U.K. law firms, investment banks, hedge funds, and many Fortune 100 and FTSE 100 corporations. The company has about 2,000 employees, including MBAs and lawyers educated at leading universities. Liam is the president and CEO of the company, having taken it from a start-up in 2001 to its current position as one of the leaders in its field in 2008.

What gives Liam a global mindset? He has an unusual ability to grasp the gestalt of a global organization—the business strategy and tactics as well as the entire employee life cycle (hiring, training, and retaining)—and translate it into a unique corporate culture that embraces national cultural differences as a marketplace advantage. As if he were playing three-dimensional chess, Liam saw that he would need to create a company that integrated global best practices in its operations from the inception. With extremely assertive clients who expect high quality and major cost efficiencies, he knew that Integreon would have to: hire the best talent around the world; train those skilled people in intercultural communications and cross-cultural understanding so that they could interact effectively with one another as well as with the clients; offer them development opportunities so that they would remain with Integreon as long as possible, since their knowledge and domain expertise is extremely valuable; and create a robust virtual environment that would support the weight of a rapidly growing organization in a burgeoning industry.

Headquartered in Los Angeles with offices in New York City, Mumbai, Delhi, London, Manila, and Fargo, North Dakota, Integreon's mission is to provide high-quality research, legal publishing, and accounting support services to the top firms in the world at dramatically lower costs than they could get elsewhere. Integreon's talent comes from the United States, the United Kingdom, India, and the Philippines. This posed enormous challenges from the outset that required all of Liam's skills as a business leader with a global mindset. He realized that the company would have to overcome the distances between people—both physical and cultural—if it was to succeed. If the firm was to capitalize on the intellectual talent of people from around the world, it was obvious to him that cultural differences would be a positive part of the equation because Integreon's "product" is the brainpower of its culturally diverse employees.

Liam read everything he could get his hands on about how successful multinational corporations created culture and managed and sustained their corporate success. He grappled with the issue of where to hire from and where to locate the executive team. He pondered what kind of framework to build so that his global executive management team could manage locally and at the same time function globally. Team members would be virtual but would need to develop close working relationships. Should they be located in one place so that they could daily interact face to face, or should they be dispersed so that Integreon could get the best people from around the world? He opted for the best talent in the world operating from various locations.

Liam knew that to make that strategy work, the team members required to develop rapport and trust with one another. If the vision was to succeed, especially within the virtual constraints of a global company, people needed to develop strong ongoing relationships with one another. In fact, Liam was infusing the corporate culture with his global mindset. It followed that the company invested heavily early on in trust-building face-to-face meetings among members of the team, supported by more frequent, brief virtual meetings so that everyone could keep abreast of what the others were thinking and doing. Thus, the huge investment of time and money in the face-to-face meetings would yield a considerable return on investment over time. The team has these in-person meetings twice annually.

These gatherings aren't blue-sky, what-if exercises; instead they are a matter of rolling up one's sleeves, getting passionate, and trying to solve business problems. "You really have to dig in and debate and argue. We did that together—in person," Liam said. "The only way we could build trust with each other was to argue and say, 'I don't agree with you,' and get past that to where we could trust the other person. We focused on trying to get it right instead of being right."

Meetings are a key discipline in the organization. In addition to the weekly tactical meetings, the executive management team has daily 5-minute "water cooler" conference calls to check in with one another. They adhere strictly to those time lines and agendas. They use technology—video, telephony, instant messaging, e-mail and intranet—as easily as if they were opening the door to the office next door. Liam refers to "rhythm" a lot, and the meetings have a kind of rhythmic regularity. He admits that it took the team some time to embrace a strict rhythm, and new executives initially find it intrusive until they realize the efficiency benefits.

Liam used his global mindset intuitively when building the team. He knew that for the cultures on the team, trust was going to be critical. He knew that he would have to create a direct, open communication culture in which people weren't afraid of conflict because the organization's success depended on that trust. He would have to overcome specific cultural barriers to do that. He also brought in technology to enable a relationship culture.

He instituted wide-ranging professional development training programs to create a strong corporate culture and prepare employees throughout the organization to be effective members of global teams. Liam understood that cultural training affects the bottom line, especially in this field. If Integreon's employees didn't understand culture, they couldn't deal with clients—or with one another. Joyce Thorne, Integreon's director of training and professional development, said, "Training is critical for a global knowledge and legal process organization because it enables our associates to work effectively with our clients and each other." She went on to say, "We approach training with a global vision, but with a local touch, recognizing that the professional development required for associates in Fargo, North Dakota, is different from that needed in Mumbai, India." Not only does the firm teach culture, but it also teaches important interpersonal skills such as assertiveness training and conflict resolution.

For example, the company has off-site workshops where employees learn interpersonal skills, human behavior, general communication, conflict resolution and assertiveness, and build professional leadership skills.

Liam was intent on building relationships with and among the management team that would create the underlying trust that was necessary for a global organization. He was building a corporate culture that mirrored his global mindset and in that process creating the relationships that Integreon would require to succeed.

Integreon's professional development training supports the corporate culture and teaches employees how to work with one another and with demanding corporate clients. The training teaches culturally based expectations in regard to the clients and attempts to acknowledge but temper the individual's cultural preferences so that the employees can respond to a customer's demands and one another's needs with fewer barriers that might prevent the mission from being accomplished.

Through working in a company with a global mindset, Integreon employees around the world have come to realize that the demands of their U.S. and U.K. clients are not an assault on their personal values, that harmony isn't always going to be maintained, and that candor, however difficult, is critical for the success of the business outcome. All of this is part of Integreon's global mindset. It's not only reflective of its CEO but is embedded in its corporate culture and is an inextricable component of its success.

What is a Global Mindset?

A global mindset is the ability to integrate everything you've learned about culture into your attitude and behaviors reflexively. It's about having the ability to read the visible clues of behaviour so that you understand what maybe going on under the surface and make use of those cues in your actions and thoughts. You're able to interpret behaviour and know what it means. Thus, when your French colleague gives a shrug of the shoulders to a statement you make or your Jordanian host takes you by the hand, you know what it means without having to think or at least know enough to put it into cultural context and move on regardless of how foreign it may seem.

In other words, it is like learning a new language. For a while you need to translate sentence by sentence, and then you start to think in the language in which you're speaking instead of consciously translating your thoughts. Having a global mindset is not necessarily new, but it has become increasingly important.

Most of us know people who seem to have a knack for working effectively across cultures and managing efficiently in multicultural settings. They seem to be able to address colleagues and situations appropriately, retaining cultural sensitivity without sacrificing their personal values and styles. In spite of being multicultural, they're congruent with their own belief systems and are consistent with others' expectations of the way they will behave.

In a globally connected world, this kind of skill is one to which all global managers aspire. Throughout this book, we've talked about the cultural dimensions: the values they represent and how important they are. We've described the seven cultural dimensions as keys for understanding the behaviors you'll encounter. To gain a global mindset, you need to meld your understanding of these seven dimensions with an ongoing process of learning about the history, mythology, and heroes of the specific countries you're working with, because, like dialects in a language, each country is unique and has its own way of expressing the seven dimensions.

Although the seven dimensions will give you a guide, to have a global mindset, you need to understand the individual country because that will affect those values and behaviours profoundly. For example, the cultural dimensions won't tell you why you can make jokes about the queen in England and why it is very bad manners to joke about the monarch in Thailand. It won't explain why you can make a self-deprecating joke with your colleague in Japan but should not do that in China. It won't explain why cows are in the streets in India or why it's difficult to find a cheeseburger in Israel. Thus, specific information about a country is very important to learn to develop a truly global mindset.

Having a global mindset means that you:

- Have the ability to be effective in interpersonal relations
- Understand local markets and take advantage of business opportunities
- Recognize talent regardless of the "package" in which it comes
- Adjust your personal strategies and plans in a foreign culture

Effective managers develop a strategy and a plan, know what the objectives are and move toward those objectives, and continually fine tune tactics to match the realities that are encountered. That's tough in a domestic setting, but a manager with a global mindset is able to do it with the enormous added complexity of different cultures.

Another example of developing a global mindset is the story of Microsoft in China.[1] Bill Gates's first trip to China took place when he was CEO of Microsoft in 1980, when the company was already a $60 billion enterprise. The story goes that Gates got off the airplane in blue jeans and a sweater, carrying only a backpack, and made a perfunctory visit without paying his respects to the political and governmental hierarchy. For the visiting head of a corporation, that was seen as a significant affront to the Chinese.

It took Gates and Microsoft Corporation many more visits to create the very successful relationship they now have with China. In the meantime, Microsoft suffered mightily in that country. Without question, the software was being used in huge numbers, but not much of the money was going to Microsoft. The software was pirated, and Microsoft and China developed a contentious relationship as the company tried to protect its intellectual property and get the Chinese government to support a crackdown on the counterfeiting.

In spite of huge efforts and huge legal costs, the company got minimal satisfaction until it recognized that its true potential in China would be achieved by partnering with that country. It began building significant local research and development labs, hiring Chinese research engineers in large numbers for its global (as well

---

1. Robert Buderi and Gregory T. Huang, *Guanxi (The Art of Relationships): Microsoft, China, and Bill Gates's Plan to Win the Road Ahead*, Simon and Schuster, 2006.

as Chinese) operations, and promoting China as a research and development (R&D) partner. At that point, the equation changed and the Chinese government, seeing this as a partnership, began to support a crackdown on piracy. For China, the relationship had to be a win-win situation with mutual respect and trust. It wasn't until Gates and the Microsoft Corporation developed a global mindset that they realized the opportunity China presented and began to build a hugely profitable, mutually beneficial relationship.

As a manager with a global mindset, you see cultural differences for what they are and are able to develop strategies that take on-the-ground realities into account without losing effectiveness and momentum. In effect, having a global mindset means that the tools in your kit have universal fittings and can work everywhere in the world.

Finally, you realize that it doesn't matter how it's done "at home". People with a global mindset see the potential cultural impact on endeavors, recognize cultural influences, and integrate them into the plan.

What do you Need to Know to have a Global Mindset?

The requirements for achieving a global mindset are illustrated in Figure 10.1.

How do you gain and maintain this critical asset? You already know that culture is learnable and know the seven keys to learning culture and the importance of integrating them with country knowledge. To gain a global mindset you need to do the following:

- Recognize your cultural values and biases.
- Understand that others are a product of their cultures.
- See the manifestations of the seven keys and learn about the specific cultures of the countries in which you work.
- Develop personal strategies to adjust to signals in other cultures.
- Be a continuous learner.

Figure 10.1

Gaining A Global Mindset

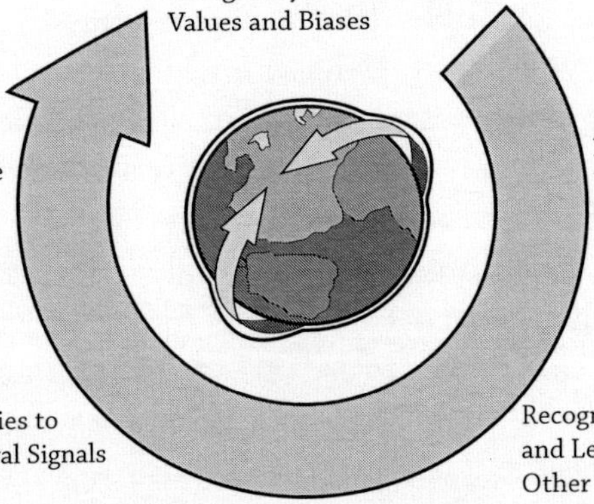

Recognize Your Cultural Values and Biases

Until you know how profoundly your personal values are defined by your culture, you may think that everyone thinks the same way you do. However, your personal values are not universal. Until you viscerally realize that your values are a product of your upbringing, you can't appreciate the depth of others' experiences.

To gain a global mindset, you begin with an appreciation that we're all a product of our own cultures. Our values and behaviours are a result of our backgrounds and what we've been exposed to since earliest childhood. These things are reinforced throughout our lives, starting with children's stories and the heroes of our youth.

American children are told heroic tales of George Washington, the father of the United States, the leader in the Revolutionary War, and the first president. They are also told the fable of George Washington and the cherry tree, in which young George chops down the tree and is confronted by his angry father. George says, "I cannot tell a lie," and confesses.

"I cannot tell a lie" has worked its way into American culture. It is seen in the legal system when people are convicted of perjury rather than the crime itself and in the way the notion of not lying is a deeply held national value. People become outraged when someone lies to them. It also speaks to the sense of individual responsibility and accountability. However, you would be in error if you assumed that all societies have the same sense of personal accountability. In some cultures, for example, this is a non-issue because the group determines how you are to behave and imposes restrictions that would make lying unnecessary or inconsequential. In other words, a profound aversion to lying is not necessarily a universal value.

American optimism is another example. The United States is an enormous landmass with generous natural resources; the egalitarian nature of the political structure allows for social mobility and the notion that one can move up in status through achievement and hard work. It follows, then, that as a generalization, Americans are supremely optimistic and believe that "tomorrow will be a better day." That's not a universal truth either.

British children recite "Humpty Dumpty;[2]" they're schooled in the knowledge of the shrinking empire. They went from "the sun never sets on the British Empire" to today's reality. Thus, although the British and American cultures are extremely close, they don't have the same degree of optimism. Again, optimism is not a universal value.

You are making a mistake if you believe that because your world-view appears to be universal, it is shared by other nations. In addition, as we've mentioned all along, your personal background (your location, ethnicity, age, level of education, and experiences) affects the way you filter your country's values. It follows that you need to understand where your preferences lie.

Setting Aside Prejudices and Assumptions but Remaining Genuine

Managing people and projects and meeting business objectives require a clear sense of mission and purpose and a passion for accomplishment without imposing one's cultural values on others. This is accomplished by learning from the environment and managing

2. Humpty Dumpty sat on a wall / Humpty Dumpty had a great fall / All the king's horses and all the king's men / couldn't put Humpty together again.

with its constructs, as opposed to against them. However, it does not require compromising one's inner values.

Fred Hassan, chairman and CEO of Schering-Plough, who was born in Pakistan, says, "Having a global attitude is not the same as being able to imitate local styles. It's just as important for managers to be themselves.... Being yourself while also showing interest and openness is at the heart of a global attitude.[3]"

Your attitudes are a combination of the influences of your society and your personal experiences.

Figure 10.2 has spaces for you to fill out your Personal Cultural Profile scores.

Figure 10.2

Personal Cultural Profile

Your Personal Cultural Profile

Low					High
	5-9	10-13	14-17	18-21	25-25

Seven Key Dimensions	Total Scores
1. Egalitarian/Hierarchical	
2. Group Focus	
3. Relationships	
4. Communication Styles	
5. Time Orientation	
6. Change Tolerance	
7. Motivation/Work-Life Balance	

Take a good look at your Personal Cultural Profile and try to commit it to memory. That shouldn't be difficult to do because it's a reflection of your personal style with which you're already very familiar. Now that you can see your cultural preferences in black and white, you can use it as a personal compass. When you encounter different values, whether subtle or strongly visible, knowing who you are helps you refrain from making value judgments and enables

3. Fred Hassan (chairman and CEO, Schering-Plough), "In Search of Global Leaders," *Harvard Business Review*, Perspectives: A Changed World issue, August 2003, p.41.

you to more effectively manage perplexing situations to achieve your desired outcomes.

Once you fully grasp how your own culture has programmed your value system, it is easier to take the next step in gaining a global mindset. It should make one appreciate the fact that people in other parts of the world have had similar exposure to another set of values and hold their beliefs as dearly as you hold yours.

Understand that Others are a Product of their Cultures

To have a global mindset, you now need to apply the same recognition that you did about yourself when you learned that your values are programmed by your culture. These values, though different, are neither good nor bad in and of themselves. They are the result of the "the collective programming of the mind."[4] The important point here is that others hold their beliefs as unquestioningly as you hold yours and also tend to assume that their values are universal.

In some cases the values others have been exposed to are similar; in others they're dramatically different.

There was an Austrian manager who was put in charge of a French business unit in Paris. When he called his first general staff meeting for 9 a.m., he was astounded to see people strolling in casually for the first 15 minutes of the meeting. He advised the team that this behavior was not going to be tolerated; from that day forward, the door to the conference room would be locked at one minute past nine, and those who weren't there by that time would be barred from the meeting.

He was satisfied because at the next meeting no one was late. In fact, no one ever came late to any of his meetings. However, his tenure as manager of the business unit was short-lived because his accomplishments were few, and he was never able to engage the loyalty and enthusiasm of the workers.

This episode illustrates the fact that the first task of an effective global manager is to learn how things get done in a culture and find a way to achieve the business objectives that is culturally consistent.

4. Geert Hofstede and Gert Jan Hofstede, *Cultures and Organizations: Software of the Mind*, McGraw-Hill, 2005.

In this case, the manager was so intent on his own value system that he compromised the business mission.

Recognize the Manifestations of the Seven Keys and Learn about the Specific Cultures of the Countries with which you're Dealing

You've already spent a lot of time learning about the seven dimensions of culture and how those dimensions are the reflections of deeply held beliefs. Nevertheless, this is a good time to think back to those seven keys and focus on the importance of learning and appreciating the unique histories, religious ideals, mythologies, and other influences that have created the national cultures with which you are dealing. Learning about holidays, traditions, and everyday behaviors will be different in every society, and although the seven cultural dimensions reflect those values, you need to know the unique stories if you're going to be effective with people from a specific country.

Develop Personal Strategies to Adjust to Signals in Other Cultures

Fundamentally, you need to be real—to be yourself—so that you can adjust to different cultural challenges while remaining authentic. Developing cultural dexterity does not mean compromising your personal values. It does mean that you recognize the signals and adapt your behavior to them. In order to achieve this you have to suspend your prejudices and adjust your tactics while keeping the goal clearly in mind. You don't compromise the objective; you try alternative, culturally adaptive methods to meet it.

How do you do that? It's not easy, but it's well worth the effort. For instance, if you're finding that a decision is taking too long to be made and instinctively want to impose an end to the discussion, be mindful that the culture you're with has its own decision-making process. It may make you feel uncomfortable because the process isn't what you're accustomed to, yet you know it's unwise to short-circuit the effort. Your challenge is to look at the reality of the situation and assess how the outcome of the local process is likely to affect your objectives. Then you must figure out how to accomplish the business task.

By all means, remember that under pressure we all tend to revert to our traditional styles. Keep in mind that forcing people to do things your way would lead to the least productive outcome.

Ed Hannibal, a senior vice president of ORC Worldwide, was working to design and implement human resources policies to apply to a newly merged organization. The companies were American and northern European. The teams from both organizations met for three days, wrote the policies, and decided on an implementation scheme.

Ed was not quite comfortable that the plan had been bought into fully, but the head of the American team had to return to the United States and was convinced that they had drafted a fully actionable program. The Americans proceeded to implement the new plan, but as it turned out, the Swedes did not.

A few months later the group reconvened to examine some snafus that had occurred because the Swedes had never implemented the plan. Ed asked the Swedes why they hadn't gone forward.

"They explained that they really had never finished discussing the plan and understanding how it would work with their employees," Ed said, "So rather than implement a policy they weren't comfortable with, they stayed with the old one." It's clear that neither the Americans nor the Swedes had adapted to the other's culturally based decision-making process.

Be in a Continuous Learning State

Throughout this book, we've been encouraging you to be mindful of your own culturally based behavioural style and preferences. As you were reading about each of the seven key cultural dimensions, we hope you were thinking about how you would respond in those situations. That is an introduction to the continuous learning state, which is critical to developing a global mindset. Continuous learners use the flood of information and experiences they're surrounded by to enhance and refine their understanding of the world.

Peter Senge, whose work is renowned in this field and whose 1990 book *The Fifth Discipline* coined the phrase "the learning organization", explains that continual learning is interwoven with personal mastery. Continuous learners:

1. Recognize priorities or overall values about themselves and how they want to live and work—they have a personal vision.
2. Take an active role in the world and work.
3. Continue to reflect on their experiences in the world and work.
4. Seek ongoing feedback about the world (including work) and their activities in it.
5. Remain as open as possible to feedback.
6. Make ongoing adjustments, based on ongoing feedback, to the way they live their lives and conduct their work to meet their priorities and values.[5]

There is no greater application of continuous learning than building a global mindset. You get it by training yourself to recognize culturally based behaviors so that you adjust to the signals you're getting. You learn enough about the history, religion, customs, and values of the country you're dealing with so that you have the context and background to understand what motivates people. The global mindset requires the ability to translate your penchant for accomplishment and achievement into a viable model.

Integreon's Liam Brown is a good example of how continuous learning leads to a global mindset and why it is so valuable in building a successful enterprise in the twenty-first century. Integreon managers participate in continuous training that involves the following:

- Building the trust required by his high-relationship managers so that they are effective when working virtually.
- Using the brevity of communication required by his American colleagues so that they get concise feedback reports from far-flung operations.

5. Carter McNamara, Authenticity Consulting, Copyright 1997-2008. *http:// www.managementhelp.org/trng—dev/design/cont-Im.htm#anchor440098*; Peter M. Senge, *The Fifth Discipline: The Art and Practice of the Learning Organization*, Doubleday/Currency, 2006.

- Creating an atmosphere in which direct and blunt dialogue is acceptable
- Developing the ability to deal with demanding global clients who have little regard for saving face and avoiding conflict by providing assertiveness and other training

Nobody gave Liam a road map for this structure. It came as a result of his background, his personal style, and the continuous integration of the feedback his global experiences had given him.

Having a global mindset doesn't mean changing your core values. On the contrary, the stronger and clearer you are about your core values, the easier it is for you to integrate a continuous stream of new information, some of which will not be congruent with your assumptions and beliefs. No doubt, being able to do that requires a great deal of self-confidence, and that self-confidence needs to be rooted in wisdom and understanding. Even with the best intentions and a flexible disposition, the wisdom of a global mindset can come only from a continuous effort of building on learning experiences and the continuous integration of those experiences into a personal knowledge base.

Definitions for this Chapter

Global mindset: The ability to recognize and adapt to cultural signals so that you intuitively see global opportunities and are effective in dealing with people from different backgrounds around the world. A global mind-set is the ability to integrate the seven cultural dimensions into personal behavior and management styles without compromising your authenticity.

Continuous learning state: Simply put, the ability to learn from the information and signals you receive. This is somewhat more complex than it appears since it requires continuing openness to acquiring new information and using newly learned techniques.

Outsourcing: "At its most basic, outsourcing is simply the farming out of services to a third party. With regard to information technology, outsourcing can include anything from outsourcing all management of IT ... to outsourcing a very small and easily defined service, such as disaster recovery or data storage, and everything in between.[6]"

KPO (knowledge process outsourcing): This involves processes that demand advanced research and analytical, technical, and decision-making skills. Less mature than the business process outsourcing industry, KPO work includes pharmaceutical R&D, legal work, data mining, and patent research. The KPO industry is just beginning to gain acceptance in corporate America.[7]

Lessons Learned to Develop your Cultural Skills

- The elements of a global mindset and how you acquire one.
- The importance of continuously learning about culture and the behaviours and values of the countries in which you're working.

Questions to Ponder

1. You're going on a business trip to five different countries to make a presentation, visiting one country a day. How do you make sure your presentation will be appropriate in each country?

Directions: Go to *http://book.culturewizard.com* and join the discussion.

2. You have spent three days in meetings and it's time to return home, yet you can't seem to get the meeting participants to agree on the plan you've been discussing. You decide to return home and reconvene the group virtually.

Was that the right decision? What other options did you have? Directions: Go to *http://book.culturewizard.com* and join the discussion. What Do You Think?

You have had your own experiences. Share them.

Go to *http://book.culturewizard.com* and join the discussion.

---

6. Stephanie Over by, "ABC: An Introduction to Outsourcing," *CIO*, March 9, 2007, available at *http://www.cio.com/article/40380/ ABC—An-Introduction—to—Outsourcing#1*.

7. Ibid.

Bibliography

Ajaya, Swami. (1983) *Psychotherapy East and West: A Unifying Paradigm*. Honesdale, PA: Himalayan Publishers.

Amir, Y. and Sharon, I. (1987) 'Are social-psychological laws cross-culturally valid?' *Journal of Cross-cultural Psychology*, 18, pp. 383-420.

Balodhi, J.P. (1986) 'Perspectives of Rajayoga in its application to mental health'. *NIMHANS Journal*, 4(2), pp. 133-138.

Balodhi, J.P. and Mishra, H. (1983) 'Patanjali Yoga and Behaviour Therapy'. *Behaviour Therapist*, 6(10), pp. 196-197.

Berry, J.W. (1974) 'Canadian psychology: Some social and applied emphases'. *Canadian Psychologist*, Vol. 15. pp. 132-139.

Bhagawat Gita with Adi Shankara's Commentary by Swami Gambhirananda, (2006) Calcutta: Advaita Ashrama Publication.

Bhagawat Gita: The Scripture of Humankind by Swami Tapasayananda (2003), Madras: Math Publication.

Bhatnagar, Deepti, and Dixit, U.K. (1996), 'Deep Valley Solutions Limited: Managing Expectation from and Relationship with Customers'. The Alacrity Foundation. Mimeo Case, IIMA, 1994.

Bharati, D. (1990). *Manav Mulya Aur Sahitya* (in Hindi; transl.: "Human Values and Literature") Delhi,:Bhartiya Jnanpith.

Brihadaranyak Upanishad with Adi Shankara's Commentary by Swami Gambhirananda. (1998) Calcutta: Advaita Ashrama Publication.

Chakraborty, S.K. (1988) 'Guna Dynamics Can Enrich Transactional Analysis'. *Vikalpa*, 13(3), pp. 39-50.

Chakraborty, S.K. (1991). *Management by Values*. Delhi: Oxford University Press.

Complete Works of Swami Vivekananda, Vol. 1/2/3/4/5/6/7/9, (1996) Calcutta: Advaita Ashrama Publication.

Copp, D.R., and Copp, A.M. (1991) India's Silent Revolution: The Swadhyaya Phenomenon'. *New Realities*, XI (4), pp. 9-15.

Coward, Harold. (1989) 'Jung's Conception of the Role of Religion in Psychological Transformation'. *Humanistic Psychologist*, 17(3), pp. 265-273.

Dayananda Saraswati, Swami. *The Value of Values*, (1993), Arsha Vidya Pitham Publication. Edition 1985, Reprint 2001.

Devaraj, N.K. (1988) *Humanism in Indian Thought*. Delhi: Indus Publishing Co. Florsheim, Paul. (1990) 'Cross-Cultural Views of Self in the Treatment of Mental Illness. *Psychiatry*, 53(3), pp. 304-315.

Fromm, E. (1981) *To Have or To Be*. New York: Bantam Books.

Grof, S. (1983) 'East and West: Ancient wisdom and modern science' pp. 3-23 in S. Grof (Ed.) *Ancient Wisdom and Modern Science*. Albany, NY: State University of New York Press.

Gupta, R.K. (1991) 'Employees and Organizations in India: Need to Move beyond American and Japanese Models', Economic and Political Weekly, 26 (2), pp. 68-76.

Gupta, R.K. (1994) 'Challenges in Developing Indigenous Theories of Organization and Management: An Indian Perspective'. Indian Journal of Social Work 54, pp. 220-236.

Gupta, R.K. (1995) 'The Truly Familial Work Organization: Extending the Organizational Boundary to Include the Employees' Families in Indian Context'. Paper presented at the IAAP Symposium, Asia-Pacific Regional Conference of Psychology, Guangzu, China, August 27-30, 1995.

Gustaysson, B. (1992) 'The Transcendent Organization'. Doctoral Dissertation, Department of Business Administration, University of Stockholm.

Harung, H., Haton, D.P., and Alexander, C.N. (1995) 'Unified Theory of Leadership: Experiences of Higher States of Consciousness in World Class Leaders'. *Leadership and Organization Development Journal*, 16(7), pp. 44-59.

Hofstede, G. (1992) 'Cultural Dimensions in People Management: The Socialization Perspective' pp.139-158 in V. Pucik, N.M. Tichy and C.K. Barnett (Eds.) *Globalizing Management*. New York: Wiley.

Isha Upnishad with Adi Shankara's Commentary by Swami Gambhiranda. (1998). Calcutta: Advaita Ashrama Publication.

Jhunjhanwala, L.N., Iyer, R.J., and Srivastava, P.K. (1987) 'Indian Psycho-philosophy and Human Response in Organizations'. *Vikalpa*, 12(1), pp. 33-42.

Kabir, S.A. (1996) Value based Management – The case on Alarcity Foundation Innovations in Asian Management (ed.), Dharni P. Sinha, Hyderabad: Delta Publishing House. pp 154-69.

Katha Upanishad with Adi Shankara's Commentary by Swami Gambhirananda. (1999). Calcutta: Advaita Ashrama Publication.

Kena Upanishad with Adi Shankara's Commentary by Swami Gambhirnanda. (1999). Calcutta: Advaita Ashrama Publication, Kolkata.

Lala, R.M. (1992) *The Creation of Wealth*, Bombay: IBH Publishers.

Manishapanchakam by Adi Shankara's, (2005). 'Explanation by Swami Viditatmananda'. Arsha Vidya Publication, Chennai.

Mesaroric, M.D. and Pestel, E. (1974). *Mankind at the Turning Point*. New York: E.P. Dutton.

Mukherjee, R. (1965) *The Social Structure of Values*. Delhi: S. Chand.

Mundaka Upanishad with Adi Shankara's Commentary by Swami Gambhirnanda. (2001). Calcutta: Advaita Ashrama Publication.

Mandukya Upanishad with Adi Shankara's Commentary by Swami Gambhirnanda. (2001). Calcutta: Advaita Ashrama Publication.

Nadkarni, R.P. (1992) 'Transformation of Work Culture and Improvement in Work Productivity and Quality through Industrial Kirtan'. *Industrial Engineering Journal*. American Institute of Industrial Engineers (AIIE). Bombay.

Nadkarni, R.P. (1992) 'Experience of 600 Training Programs for Industrial Workers: Lessons to Learn'. Industrial Engineering Journal, pp. 22-24.

Perry, Chad. (1993) 'Requirements and Methods for Management Development Programs in the Least Developed Countries in Africa'. *Management Education and Development*, 24 (3), pp. 225-245.

Rahnema, Majid. (1991) 'Swadhyaya: The Silent Singing Revolution of India'. pp. 114-134 in Mark Macy (Ed.) *Healing the World ... and me*. Knowledge Systems. Indianapolis, MN.

Rama, Swami, Ballentine, Rudolf, and Ajaya, Swami. (1976) *Yoga and Psychotherapy*, Honesdale, PA: Himalayan International Institute.

Ranganathananda, Swami. (1992) *Eternal Values for Changing Society*, Vol. VI, Bharatia Vidya Bhawan Publication.

Rokeach, M. (1973) *The Nature of Human Values*. New York: Free Press.

Roy, Ramashray. (1993) 'Swadhyaya: Values and Message', in Ponna Wighnaraja (Ed.) *Social Movements in the South*. London; Zed Books Ltd.

Schmidt-Wilk, J., Alexander, C.N., and Swanson, G.C., (1996) 'Developing Consciousness in Organizations: The Transcendental Meditation Program' in *Journal of Business and Psychology*, 10(4), pp. 429-444.

Schwartz, S.H. (1994) 'Are there universal aspects in the structure and conduct of human values?' *Journal of Social Issues*, 50, No. 4, pp. 19-45.

Shaw, J., and Patel, B. (1998) 'Vipassana and Business Management', *Chinmaya Management Review*, 2(2), pp. 81-88.

Shaw, V.P., Sheth, N.R., and Visaria, P. (1998) 'Swadhyaya: Social Change through Spirituality' in M.L. Dantwala, Harsh Sethi and Pravin Visaria (Eds.) *Social Change through Voluntary Action*. New Delhi: Sage.

Sheth, N.R. (1994) 'Children of the Same God: A Spiritual Approach to Social Transformation'. Working Paper #59, Ahmedabad: Gujarat Institute of Development Research.

Sinha, J.B.P. (1994) 'Indigenization of OB Reserch in India: A Subjective View' *Indian Journal of Social Work*, 54, pp. 238-242.

Srinivas, Kalburgi M. (1994a) 'Cosmologies of Man and the Models of Organization Development', Paper presented at the international Association of Applied Psychology, Madrid.

Srinivas, Kalburgi M. (1994b) 'Organization Development: Maya or Moksha'. in R.N. Kanungo and M. Mendonca (Eds.) *Work Motivation: Models for Developing Countries*. New Delhi: Sage.

Srinivas, Kalburgi M. (1995a) 'Achieving Excellence in Indian Organizations: New Opportunities for Psychologists'. *Psychology and Developing Societies*, 7 (2), pp. 185-216.

Srinivas, Kalburgi M. (1999) 'Organizational Development for National Development: A Review of Evidence'. pp. 197-224 in David Saunders and R.N. Kanungo (Ed.) *New Approaches to Employee Management – Employee Management in Developing Countries*. Greenwitch: CN JAI Press.

Srinivas, Kalburgi M. (1998) 'Spirituality-at-Work in the Land of Dollar God', *Journal of Human Values*, 4(1), pp. 45-64.

Srivastava, R.J. (Ed.) (1998) *Vital Connections: Self Society and God*. New York: Weatherhill.

Tripathi, A.N. *Human Values*. New Delhi: New Age Publishers.

Westwood, R.I. and Chan, A. (1995) 'The Transferability of Leadership Training in the East Asian Context'. *Asia Pacific Review*, 2(1), pp. 68-92.

Wilson, Stephen R. (1985) 'Therapeutic Processes in a Yoga Ashram'. *American Journal of Psychotherapy*, 39(2), pp. 253-262.

Wilson, Stephen R. (1991) 'Self-Actualization and Selflessness: A Social-Psychological Analysis. *Journal of Social and Behavioural Personality*, 6(5), pp. 97-108.